TURKISH BERLIN

GLOBALIZATION AND COMMUNITY

Susan E. Clarke, Series Editor
Dennis R. Judd, Founding Editor

21 *Turkish Berlin: Integration Policy and Urban Space*
ANNIKA MARLEN HINZE

20 *Struggling Giants: City-Region Governance in London, New York, Paris, and Tokyo*
PAUL KANTOR, CHRISTIAN LEFÈVRE, ASATO SAITO, H.V. SAVITCH, AND
ANDY THORNLEY

19 *Does Local Government Matter? How Urban Policies Shape Civic Engagement*
ELAINE B. SHARP

18 *Justice and the American Metropolis*
CLARISSA RILE HAYWARD AND TODD SWANSTROM, EDITORS

17 *Mobile Urbanism: Cities and Policymaking in the Global Age*
EUGENE MCCANN AND KEVIN WARD, EDITORS

16 *Seeking Spatial Justice*
EDWARD W. SOJA

15 *Shanghai Rising: State Power and Local Transformations in a Global Megacity*
XIANGMING CHEN, EDITOR

14 *A World of Gangs: Armed Young Men and Gangsta Culture*
JOHN M. HAGEDORN

13 *El Paso: Local Frontiers at a Global Crossroads*
VICTOR M. ORTÍZ-GONZÁLEZ

12 *Remaking New York: Primitive Globalization and the Politics of Urban Community*
WILLIAM SITES

11 *A Political Space: Reading the Global through Clayoquot Sound*
WARREN MAGNUSSON AND KARENA SHAW, EDITORS

10 *City Requiem, Calcutta: Gender and the Politics of Poverty*
ANANYA ROY

9 *Landscapes of Urban Memory: The Sacred and the Civic in India's High-Tech City*
SMRITI SRINIVAS

8 *Fin de Millénaire Budapest: Metamorphoses of Urban Life*
JUDIT BODNÁR

7 *Latino Metropolis*
VICTOR M. VALLE AND RODOLFO D. TORRES

6 *Regions That Work: How Cities and Suburbs Can Grow Together*
MANUEL PASTOR JR., PETER DREIER, J. EUGENE GRIGSBY III, AND MARTA
LÓPEZ-GARZA

(continued on page 203)

TURKISH BERLIN

Integration Policy and
Urban Space

ANNIKA MARLEN HINZE

Globalization and Community, Volume 21

University of Minnesota Press
Minneapolis
London

Maps drawn by Leah Patgorski

Published by the University of Minnesota Press
111 Third Avenue South, Suite 290
Minneapolis, MN 55401-2520
http://www.upress.umn.edu

Library of Congress Cataloging-in-Publication Data
Hinze, Annika.
    Turkish Berlin : integration policy and urban space / Annika Marlen Hinze.
        pages cm. — (Globalization and community ; volume 21)
    Includes bibliographical references and index.
    ISBN 978-0-8166-7814-3 (hc : alk. paper) — ISBN 978-0-8166-7815-0 (pb : alk. paper)
1. Assimilation (Sociology)—Germany—Berlin. 2. Turks—Cultural assimilation.
3. Turks—Germany—Berlin. 4. Group identity—Germany—Berlin 5. Emigration and immigration—Turkey. 6. Emigration and immigration—Germany. I. Title.
    HM843.H56 2013
    303.48'2563043—dc23
                                            2013010389

Printed in the United States of America on acid-free paper

The University of Minnesota is an equal-opportunity educator and employer.

20 19 18 17 16 15 14 13   10 9 8 7 6 5 4 3 2 1

This book is dedicated to my mentors,
Sultan Tepe, Dennis Judd, and David Perry.
They are an inspiration for me to always be
the best scholar I can be.

CONTENTS

ACKNOWLEDGMENTS ix

INTRODUCTION Babel Berlin, German Immigrant
Capital xiii

1. Integration or Exclusion? Understanding Turkish
Immigration in Germany 1

2. Talk of the Town: Space, Visibility, and the
Contestation of German Identity 33

3. *Mein Block:* The Neighborhood as a Site of Identity 75

4. Location as Destiny: Integrating Kreuzberg and
Neukölln 111

CONCLUSION Learning from Immigrant Neighborhoods 145

APPENDIXES

A. Zeynep's and Bilge's Kreuzkölln 163

B. Berlin Senate 167

C. The Buschkowsky Administration's Ten-Point
Integration Agenda for the District of Neukölln 171

NOTES 175

BIBLIOGRAPHY 187

INDEX 197

ACKNOWLEDGMENTS

A book is never the work of a single person. From the first ideas to the final product, many, many people are involved in its development. This book grew out of what started as a dissertation project in 2006 at the University of Illinois at Chicago, but has since evolved into so much more. Therefore, I want to start by thanking my incredible teachers at UIC, who helped me become the scholar that I am today. The spark that inspired everything was David Perry's Ph.D. seminar on Contested Cities at the College of Urban Planning and Public Administration at UIC, one of the most stimulating and interesting seminars I have taken in my life, and I will forever remember all his excellent intellectual advice. But I was also inspired by the social context of Chicago. Had I not moved there on that sweltering day in early August 2004, this book would have never been written. Dennis Judd, then graduate director for the Department of Political Science at UIC, was the first professor in Chicago I ever communicated with. His advice and intellectual feedback during my first year of graduate studies laid the foundation for a way of thinking. My dissertation chair, Sultan Tepe, an incredible role model, has always pushed me to take my mind one step further, to bend it around one more corner. Her amazing intellect and strength were and continue to be both foundation and inspiration for my work. Her genuine interest in her students' intellectual growth makes her one of the best teachers I have ever known!

Anthony Orum at the Department of Sociology at UIC and Garbi Schmidt, now at Roskilde University, Denmark, were also irreplaceable intellectual advisors on my dissertation, and their feedback was indispensable in moving this project along.

During my field research in Berlin, I found a home at the Research Unit for Migration, Integration, and Transnationalization at the Wissenschaftszentrum Berlin für Sozialforschung; I would like to thank Marc Helbling and Zuhal Kavacik for their unwavering support and feedback. But most of all, I am indebted to all my interviewees for the time they were willing to spend with me and all the questions they were willing to answer. This book relies on their stories, and it could not exist without them. A special thank you goes to Mümüne Gücük for getting me in touch with the *Stadtteilmütter* Neukölln, Arnold Mengelkoch for providing me with incredible amounts of information on immigration in Neukölln, and Safter Çınar at the Turkish Union Berlin-Brandenburg (TBB) for answering all my questions about Turkish community leadership and getting me in touch with other leading figures from the TBB. I also thank Regina Reinke for the long hours she spent answering my questions about integration policy in Kreuzberg, and Dr. Erhart Körting, senator at the Berliner Senatsverwaltung für Inneres und Sport, for agreeing to a personal interview.

The bulk of the first version of this book was written during my time as a visiting professor at Washington and Lee University in Lexington, Virginia. Therefore, I would like to thank the Department of Politics and Dean Peppers for giving me the great opportunity of teaching as a visiting professor. In a bleak job market, this opportunity provided me with the serenity and security to work on this book. I would also like to thank Ayşe Zarakol for her friendship and good advice about writing, publishing, and the profession as such. Her amazing success continues to be an inspiration for me to keep on going. I would also like to thank Becky Davies and Valentina Dimitrova for their friendship and support during my time in Lexington. A big thank-you also goes to Debra Prager and Dan Kramer, not only for their advice and support, but also for their genuine friendship. Thank you, Lexington friends—I could not have done this without you.

At Fordham University, where most of this book in its current form was written and an additional chapter was added, I am grateful for all the help and support I have received from my new colleagues in completing this book. I am especially grateful to Bruce Berg, Jeffrey Cohen, John Entelis, Chrissy Greer, Bob Hume, Paul Kantor, and Rosemary Wakeman for their support and valuable advice.

Back at UIC, I would like to thank all my nerdy friends, who kept me going through all the long hours of writing in the windowless computer lab, and whose friendship was the best support during my years in graduate school and beyond. Among them, Nawojka Lesinski, John French, and Abe Singer deserve special mention.

I would like to extend a special thank-you to my friend and colleague Elisabeth Muhlenberg in Chicago, who spent many hours editing the text and providing feedback. Without her brilliance and incredible eye for detail, the book's preparation would have taken a lot longer, and without her friendship in our little German immigrant enclave in Chicago, I would not have been as at home so far away from home.

My friend Leah Patgorski is the other reason why Chicago became a home to me. Besides being a friend for life, she is also the one who produced all the beautiful maps for this book.

I would like to thank John Mollenkopf, whose support, insights, and feedback were incredibly helpful. At the University of Minnesota Press, I would like to thank Susan Clarke for her friendly encouragement and her touching support for young, inexperienced scholars like myself. I would also like to thank my editor, Pieter Martin, and the editorial assistant, Kristian Tvedten, whose friendly openness, encouragement, and responsiveness made the whole process fun and easy.

Being creative is much easier with a genuine support system of friends and family. This book would have never been written without all the people who kept me grounded and loved and supported me for who I am. I would like to thank Andrew Becker, Monika Bauer, Alan Collard-Wexler, Seiya Fukuda, and Vilas Menon for their awesome friendship and all our wonderful, inspiring conversations around the campfire and elsewhere. I am also grateful for the friendship of all the strong women in my life who continue to amaze and inspire me—Dimitra Katsikidis, Jenny McCord, and Natalia Fitzgerald, this one goes out to you!

Back in Germany, I would like to thank my three best friends, Saskia Christ, Nicole Ciesinski, and Simone Reuss, for remaining my friends all these years, keeping me grounded, and making me feel loved. Ihr seid mein Fels in der Brandung, Mädels!

I am grateful for my grandmother, Maria Meinhardt, whose life story in between countries, worlds, wars, languages, identities, and families was the first I ever wrote down. Her heartbreaking life story, which accompanied my childhood, was like an exciting novel to me when I was little. I was her biggest fan and best listener. Only as an adult did I realize the pain, heartbreak, displacement, and tragic loss inherent in the story. She was, years after her death, the inspiration for me to listen to and write down the stories of the women in this book.

I would like to thank my incredible parents, Dr. Joachim Hinze and Sabine Meinhardt-Hinze, for bringing me up with all the exceptional opportunities I've had in my life, and for tolerating and supporting (despite the pain it causes them) my decision to cross the Atlantic more permanently.

They both continue to inspire me—they are the best of me, and therefore the best of this book. In my life with one foot on each side of the Atlantic, I will, like the women whose stories are told in this book, always be a bit "neither here nor there."

Finally, I would like to thank my wonderful husband, Gregory Holyk, who is the kindest and most loving person I know. He is also the strong man behind my strong woman. Without his incredible support and patience, I would have never been able to, time and time again, chase after and catch my dreams.

INTRODUCTION

Babel Berlin, German Immigrant Capital

Gewiß, zwei Völker und zwei Sprachen werden einander nie sich
so verständlich und so intim mitteilen können wie zwei einzelne, die
derselben Nation und Sprache angehören. Aber das ist kein Grund,
auf Verständigung und Mitteilung zu verzichten. Auch zwischen
Volks-und Sprachgenossen stehen Schranken, die eine volle Mitteilung und ein volles gegenseitiges Vertrauen verhindern, Schranken
der Bildung, der Erziehung, der Begabung, der Individualität.
Man kann behaupten, jeder Mensch auf Erden könne grundsätzlich
mit jedem andern sich aussprechen, und man kann behaupten, es
gäbe überhaupt keine zwei Menschen in der Welt, zwischen denen
eine echte, lückenlose, intime Mitteilung und Verständigung möglich
sei-eins ist so wahr wie das andre.

Clearly, two peoples and two languages will never be able to
communicate as intimately as two individuals who belong to the same
nation and language. But this is no reason to forgo communication
and understanding. Even countrymen sharing the same language face
barriers which hamper complete communication and trust between
them, barriers of education, upbringing, talent, and individuality.
One could claim that on principle every human being on earth could
communicate with every other human being, and one could also
claim that no two people exist in the world whose communication
and understanding of each other is complete-one claim is as true as
the other.

—Hermann Hesse (1943)

BEFORE I BECAME AN IMMIGRANT MYSELF, I had never given
much thought to immigration, immigrant identity, and the meaning of it
all. When I moved to Chicago in 2004, I found that immigration was an
ever-present topic of debate, highly visible, highly salient, on top of the

political agenda. Furthermore, as I walked the city, I discovered not only the incredible cultural and ethnic diversity of this Midwestern metropolis, but also how the different (immigrant) identities were deeply embedded in the urban fabric itself—how much the marriage of place and identity creates the city itself. In this way, all cities truly resemble living organisms that develop and change and reinvent themselves constantly through the interaction of their individual cells with outside forces. It is this very dynamic between identity and place that provides the theoretical foundation for this book.

My experiences in Chicago brought my mind back to Berlin and became the basic engine for this research: the comparison of one social and spatial context to another sheds light on systemic aspects that are hidden from view precisely because they are all too familiar. Immigration has shaped Berlin's identity in the last fifty years almost as much as Chicago's. Growing up in Berlin, I experienced its impact mostly with respect to food: Berlin features superb (high-end and low-end) Italian restaurants and ice cream, a huge number of Croatian and Greek restaurants, and some hip and authentic tapas places. However, despite this wonderful variety, it is the Turkish *Döner Kebap*, a sandwich filled with rotisserie meat, salad, and sauce, that is omnipresent in Berlin and has become *the* local specialty. Restaurants, of course, are a superficial way of measuring the presence of diversity. But the symbolic meaning of the presence of "ethnic food" can at least reveal some clues about the presence of ethnic groups in that city. There is a reason why Vancouver is famous for its sushi, Chicago for the authenticity of its Mexican food, and New York City for—well—everything. Thus, the omnipresence of the Turkish *Döner Kebap* and the general insertion of Turkish food into what would be defined as Berlin's local cuisine underline Berlin's identity as a Turkish immigrant capital. In fact, there are now more *Döner Kebap* stands in Berlin than in Istanbul! (Angelos 2012).

In any city, the label of foreigner or immigrant invariably points to the stereotypes about the largest ethnic minority group. In Chicago, a Mexican represents the popular, rather negative stereotype of the typical immigrant who is possibly undocumented. In Berlin, the stereotypical image of the immigrant is of a Turk and a Muslim. These obviously prejudice-laden characterizations of immigrants resemble each other in the sense that they stigmatize the largest immigrant group in each city as foreign or different. However, there is also a difference. In Chicago, a Mexican could eventually become an American not only in the legal sense, but in terms of a general acceptance into American society. In American society, Americans are those who are citizens and native speakers of English.

Embracing a civic ideal of being American without shedding one's cultural differences provides an avenue for foreigners to become Americans. This does not mean that the American experience of immigration has been or is devoid of racism or exclusion. In fact, the current immigration debate in the United States seems to indicate quite the opposite. Across history, the American immigrant experience includes its fair share of racial and ethnic conflict. The definition of who is an American has been in flux over the last hundred years; along with racial and ethnic conflict, segregation, and discrimination, it has also created room for change. However incremental, this potential for change has kept the concept of American identity flexible over time.

Living in Chicago led me to question the German antipathy to cultural difference. In Chicago, immigrant groups and established residents have been able to create the space for negotiating cultural difference. The presence of a variety of visibly different groups has more or less been perceived to be an implicit feature of the American urban context. What are the reasons for such a different debate in Germany? Is it simply a difference in how each country perceives itself? After all, the United States has been a country of immigration for over a century, and Germany—reluctantly[1]—for only forty years. My hometown of Berlin is Germany's hippest, largest, and especially its most diverse city. What role does it play in the German immigration debate?

In Germany, as in any nation, national and local approaches to immigrant integration are historically inextricably connected to Germany's self-understanding as a nation. A particular definition of national identity characterizes the immigration discourse, the debate on integration, and the visibility of difference. In other words, the question of who can be German hinges on the underlying question of what is acceptable as a mainstream German identity.

In this book, I engage in a theoretical and political examination of these questions. I focus on the integration discourse in Germany, and specifically in Berlin, to identify the factors that affect the process of immigrant integration. Understanding the term *integration* leads back into the history of German national identity, which makes possible the identification of the social and historical premises that have shaped its meaning. As a political and theoretical term, *integration* in the German context is not only undefined but is also the subject of scholarly contestation. The absence of a universally accepted definition of integration in the literature is regrettable but also opportune: it allows scholars to apply a broader lens to integration than has been the case so far. This broader lens includes the immigrants' experiences in the city. In this view, the city is perceived as an organism that makes visible the dynamic process between immigrants, identity, and space. By examining the microcosm of two Berlin neighborhoods densely populated by Turkish immigrants, I explore how a broad spectrum of local Berlin policy makers on one hand and German Turkish residents on the other hand interpret integration, refer to it, and apply it to daily life and urban policy making. The analysis contrasts the views of German authorities with those of Turkish immigrants who practice integration in their daily lives.

The book's micro-level perspective reveals unique aspects of immigrant life practices that may be overlooked by national or even individual level analyses that tend to focus on the perspectives of authorities, such as policy makers and government officials. This comparison of micro-level immigrant practices with the way immigrant integration is framed within the city-level policy debate explores in-depth the spatial practices of immigrants, their self-perceptions, and their own way of integrating themselves into their neighborhood and the urban framework at large. Thus, I stress a dual approach to integration. In comparing immigrant and policy perspectives on integration, I provide a broader look at integration as a political and social concept. At the same time, the research identifies potential gaps between the way elites understand integration, and the way immigrants perceive and practice it. Overall, I present a comparative sociopolitical analysis of integration policy and practice, embedded in the city and in the immigrant neighborhood. The analysis of integration at different levels of policy and immigrant practice thus integrates space as a key variable: different conceptions of integration become visible when the immigrant identity is contested through the lens of urban space: the neighborhood itself.

A History without Integration

The tension between Germany's assimilationist history and its increasing diversity is historically contingent. It has become a key issue in Germany's integration discourse. In 1999, Germany's political leadership finally revised the traditional political stance of *Deutschland ist kein Einwanderungsland*— "Germany is not a country of immigration"—to acknowledge the permanent presence of large numbers of former guest worker immigrants in the country. A large majority of those immigrants and their descendants originate from Turkey. The changed self-perception of Germany as a country of immigration mirrored the inevitable recognition of many other European countries that their demographics had permanently changed. Until the late

1990s, the denial of being a receiving country of immigration had dominated Germany's post–World War II immigration policy. The attitudinal change forced a change in the formal legal and political approach to the immigrants themselves:

> Before, the fact that immigration and integration of millions of people were increasingly essential in shaping the society of the Federal Republic of Germany had been politically ignored. Because of this, an integration- and migration policy that would shape and accompany these processes had long been missing—because what is being ignored cannot be organized. (Reissland 2005, 128)[2]

Why the change, and why at so late a date? A brief foray into history explains the reasons. The first guest workers arrived in Germany from the Mediterranean in the early 1960s. Initially, the German government dealt with the influx of immigrants mostly by spatially isolating immigrant minorities from the German population. Upon their arrival in Germany, guest workers[3] were originally housed in temporary barracks. Many of these original restrictions fell away as the number of guest workers grew. Guest workers began to move into the decrepit neighborhoods of former West Germany's urban centers, occupying especially those neighborhoods that had been designated as blighted and were scheduled to be torn down as part of 1960s urban renewal projects. The children of guest worker immigrants often attended *Ausländerklassen* (foreigner classes), where they were intentionally isolated from German children to prevent socializing between them (Stomporowski 2004).[4] By the 1980s, the federal government started providing financial incentives and even legal support for the guest workers' journey home via the *Rückkehrförderungsgesetz*[5] (return-promoting law) passed by the conservative Kohl government in 1983. The Kohl administration, with the support of general public opinion in Germany, acted on the assumption that (Muslim) guest worker immigrants from Turkey would be unable to integrate into a Western society steeped in mainly Christian values (*Bundeszentrale für Politische Bildung* 2007).

The political discourse on integrating guest workers expanded in the late 1980s and early 1990s when the government began to offer legal and financial support to immigrant guest workers willing to return to their countries of origin. Guest workers choosing to remain in Germany became subject to the federal government's official policy of assimilation, which was established to promote the incorporation of immigrants into German mainstream society (Ehrkamp 2006; Ehrkamp and Leitner 2003). Most of the immigrants affected by this new strategy had lived in Germany for more than two decades.

German policy makers had imported the term *assimilation* from the American context. It implies that "over time, immigrants will adapt to the host society and become indistinguishable from the majority population in terms of norms, values, and behaviors" (Ehrkamp 2006, 1675). These types of expectations are based on the assumption that immigrants in Germany would not retain aspects of their own culture important to them. Most immigrants found the assimilationalist expectation of adaptation to be a challenge, particularly because they perceived themselves to be unwanted and outsiders in German society, a perception underlined by the implications of the *Rückkehrförderungsgesetz*. As the twentieth century came to a close, German society viewed the "Turkish problem" as increasingly urgent, both politically and culturally. A window of opportunity opened for the development of a new political strategy for immigrant incorporation when, after sixteen years of conservative governance, a center-left governing coalition took office in 1998 and sought to address the increasing evidence of "parallel societies" and social divisions (Weiss and Thränhardt 2005).

After the 1998 federal election, the political discourse shifted away from assimilation to integration. Assimilation had gradually acquired too many negative connotations and reminded Germans painfully of previous forceful efforts to Germanize different ethnic groups (Brubaker 2001; Ehrkamp 2006). Integration, on the other hand, had more neutral connotations, while still underlining the need to incorporate immigrant minorities into the mainstream population. Ehrkamp (2006) argues that integration policy, as heir to assimilation policy, mostly continues the ideas of assimilation under a different term. The handling of ethnic diversity in Germany appears to be still one of identifying ways to make immigrants fit into German society instead of simply acknowledging their ethnocultural differences as part of German culture. Understanding the history of recent immigration in Germany illuminates the important meaning of the term *integration* for the German public and its policy makers, and provides important clues about the term's value and usage in Germany's political debate on immigration.

Both historically and conceptually, the German discourse on immigrant incorporation is quite different from the discourses in other European countries, notably France. Through school and army, France has historically attempted to reeducate (and thus assimilate) immigrants from its former colonies into Frenchmen (see Brubaker 1992). The United Kingdom also chose a different approach than Germany. It followed the Canadian path and instituted an official policy of multiculturalism after World War II, until that approach became controversial in the late 1990s (Malik 2010). The term *multiculturalism* is as controversial and contested as the term *integration.* Policy makers,[6] the media, and scholars in different national settings (such as the United Kingdom, Canada, the Netherlands, and the United States) have questioned the political and social effectiveness of multiculturalism as a strategy for successfully and fairly incorporating minorities into diverse societies. For example, Bissoondath (2002) notes in reference to the Canadian case that multiculturalism, which is an official state policy in Canada, is inherently controversial because it tries to maintain diversity even as it simultaneously aims to assimilate minorities into political institutions, which have formed in accordance to a particular cultural tradition.

The integration approaches practiced in other countries have influenced the political discourse in Germany. It is possible that, over the long run, European Union policy may cause convergence in integration policies between E.U. countries. Almost ten years ago, in 2003, Heckmann reported that Germany's leaders had reached a political consensus on integration: Germany must find its own integration strategy. The current German discourse on immigrants and their incorporation is unique given almost a century of a strictly ethnic definition of German citizenship and nationhood (Brubaker 1992), as well as Germany's ongoing political confrontations with its own painful history of violence and genocide against ethnic minorities. Within this unique discourse, the new German integration debate builds the foundation of my analysis.

The Importance of the Urban Context

In this book, I aim specifically to examine how German Turks experience integration in the local context. The urban environment can function as a microcosm of social reality and represents an important lens for the investigation of social processes (Isin 2000; Orum 1998; Sandercock 1998). Whereas social processes are talked about and framed within the national context, social interaction takes place on the local level, on street corners, in neighborhoods, communities, and cities. Human relations and social processes are shaped in those places where people live closely together and interact with each other on a daily basis. At a time when people increasingly live in large urban agglomerations, the city becomes an important focal point for investigating social processes (Roy 2005, 2009; Sassen 1996).

Berlin is a special case in its own right. It is the city with the largest Turkish immigrant population in Germany in absolute numbers, and Germany's biggest and most culturally diverse city. Of Berlin's 3.38 million inhabitants, approximately 448,200 do not have German citizenship (Ohlinger and Raiser 2005). However, the city's population of people with an immigrant background (the original German term, *Migrationshintergrund*, refers to individuals with at least one parent of non-German descent) is estimated to be around 25 percent of all residents (Bömermann, Rehkämper, and Rockmann 2008). Berlin has also played a special role as the center of the Cold War, which imprinted itself spatially on the city's urban fabric. This is also true in regard to the distribution of immigrants across the city.

Map 1 illustrates the spatial distribution of immigrants across the city of Berlin. It shows that Berlin's inner-city neighborhoods exhibit a much higher density of people of immigrant background than the districts on the periphery. It also demonstrates the remarkable differences between the former eastern and western parts of the city. While immigrants cluster in the former western downtown districts, their distribution across the former eastern inner-city districts is comparatively thin. Berlin's immigrant settlement patterns mirror the overall differences between the eastern and western parts of Germany. While the former East Germany has few to no

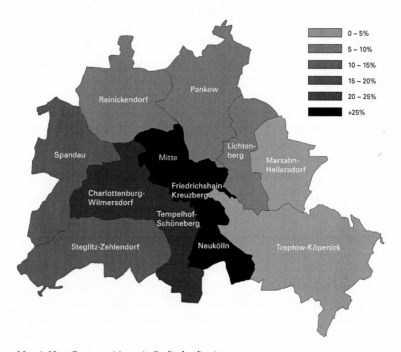

Map 1. Non-German citizens in Berlin by district.

immigrant residents, the formerly western part shows significant clusters of immigrants. In Berlin, these clusters reside close to the city center and the notorious Berlin Wall that once separated East and West.

A Spatial Approach to Integration

The city is a fascinating site for trying to understand two critical questions: (1) how are immigrants framed and conceived of politically—as opposed to (2) how do immigrants perceive themselves and the way in which they practice their daily lives? I begin by exploring the first question, namely how local policy makers frame the challenge of urban immigrant neighborhoods and how they formulate urban concepts for integration. The answers provide insights into the local dynamics between immigrants and the majority population. The way in which local policy makers portray the immigrants' visual and cultural influences on the urban environment offers clues about their approaches to and acceptance (or lack thereof) of integration, the immigrants themselves, and the changes they bring to urban life.

The relevant data used to explore this question come from two primary sources: an analysis of integration policy statements in the party programs issued by the main political parties in the Berlin parliament, and from interviews with the policy makers involved in local immigration and integration policy approaches. Statements and policy platforms of the Turkish Union Berlin-Brandenburg (Türkischer Bund Berlin-Brandenburg/Berlin-Brandenburg Türkiye Toplumu) are also included. The Türkischer Bund Berlin-Brandenburg is Berlin's largest Turkish community organization, which seeks to politically represent the interests of the entire Turkish immigrant community. The statements of its representatives provide important insights into how the influential German Turks in Berlin perceive the Turkish community at large, and whether the divisions within the community are stronger than the common immigrant experience.

The second question, how immigrants perceive themselves, is equally important for the discourse on integration, if not more so.[7] The urban environment represents a particularly important site for understanding the micro processes of the immigration debate on the local level, and how the debate at that level may differ from or converge with the debates in the political and national realms. The research focuses on two inner-city communities with a high density of immigrants: Kreuzberg and Neukölln. The locality and former district of Kreuzberg is seen as a traditional area of Turkish immigrant settlement and alternative lifestyles. Formerly the center of

Germany's leftist scene, Kreuzberg is often portrayed as the prime example for successful multicultural coexistence. The district of Neukölln, the traditional home of working-class and low-income families, has experienced an increasing influx of lower-class German Turks after the partial postreunification gentrification of Kreuzberg. The districts have many similar characteristics. They have an exceptionally high percentage of Turkish immigrant residents who have a working-class background, low per capita income,[8] an overall left-wing political orientation, and are entrenched in their *Kiez*.[9]

They also differ in important ways. From the perspective of framing the political discourse, their most salient distinguishing characteristic is the way outsiders perceive them: Kreuzberg is seen as a hip, young multicultural neighborhood that attracts students and artists. Neukölln frequently makes headlines as a neighborhood of drug dealing and violence in its schools, particularly among the children of Turkish and Arabic immigrants. In some Neukölln areas, immigrant children are said to outnumber "German" children eight to one (*Neue Zürcher Zeitung,* September 19, 2010). The public discourse presents Kreuzberg as a model for successful multiculturalism in Germany, while Neukölln is framed as the opposite: a failure of integration due to the high residential concentration of low-income immigrants (Gesemann 2006).

Kreuzberg and Neukölln serve as excellent models for understanding the common and different self-perceptions of Turkish immigrants in their daily lives. The two districts, their history, and their residents also help to answer the question why their self-perceptions are important, how and why they differ from their public image, and why such differences need to be included in the political debate. The analysis of the life stories of Berlin's Turkish immigrants and their accounts of the personal challenges they face provide insight into how immigrants practice their own ways of integration, and how much or how little they coincide with the integration approaches of policy makers (Bertaux and Kohli 1984). Furthermore, the question whether place makes a difference to integration (Orum 1998) can be answered by comparing the challenges, experiences, and self-perceptions of immigrants in Kreuzberg and Neukölln. These two districts seem to have so much in common yet are quite different—in terms of current policy discourse as well as their local history. The densely populated urban environment provides an important context for this investigation: immigrants and host population live here side by side; differences become visible and controversial as cultural–visual differences stand in direct and continuous confrontation with one another (Roy 2005; Sassen 1996). Thus, immigrants' life practices within their urban neighborhoods serve as insights into their lives and their individual ways of integrating themselves into the receiving society.

Urban Space as a Lens for Understanding Social Processes and Power Relations

Urban space in itself represents a crucial variable for the contestation of national identity and integration (Isin 2000). Many scholars of urban space point out that territory and space are not external to social relations and politics but inherently socially constructed (Lefebvre 1984; Soja 2000). Thus, the city is not merely a container of social processes; the urban environment itself also influences and shapes these processes. Henri Lefebvre, one of the most recognized contributors to this debate, argues that "space is becoming the principal stake of goal-directed actions and struggles" (1984, 410). Inspired by Lefebvre, other scholars, such as the social geographer Edward Soja (1996, 46), note that an "unspatialized" social reality does not exist. Thus, space is not a marginal component of social reality, but social relations are inherently spatial in nature.

In its role as an active component in the formation and alteration of social relations, space can serve as a lens for explaining and analyzing specific aspects of these social relations, such as marginality or power differentials. Liggett and Perry (1995) state that space can serve as a means of understanding how power in politics and social reality is constituted and how it operates. For example, the planning of urban space or the contestation of certain areas of the city can exhibit how power struggles in the city manifest themselves over the very meaning, usage, and presentation of the space itself.

Perhaps one of the best examples of how space and politics are intertwined can be seen in divided and contested cities. Scott Bollens (1999) illustrates the relationship between the governance structures in metropolitan areas and the inequality of opportunity across individuals and localities, using the divided cities of Belfast and Johannesburg as cases. He refers to the geographical and ethnic division of urban areas, where "ethnic and nationalist claims combine and impinge significantly and consistently" on the urban environment (3). In other words, visual claims to ethnic, national, or even religious identities can play out spatially in the city. Different groups make their claims to urban areas, competing with other groups, as well as the government over the meaning and content of urban space.

Even in urban spaces like Berlin, which is not violently contested like neighborhoods in more segregated cities, claims of identity materialize. Historically, Berlin has not only borne witness to the separation of Germany into east and west, but has participated actively in this separation. The wall that ran straight through the city did not merely separate east and west; the city space was, in fact, divided into four different allied zones, which were occupied by the United States, Great Britain, France, and the Soviet Union, respectively, the four victorious allies of World War II that laid claim to the city. Berlin, the central site of the Cold War until German reunification, was not even official German territory but rather an allied occupation zone, dominated by the four Allied powers.

Berlin today is the primary site of the contestation of the meaning and content of German identity. The city boasts the largest Turkish community outside of Turkey, a fact that supports its role as a primary location for the debate and observation of Turkish immigration processes. As such, it has also become the focal point for debates on German identity and immigrant integration, as immigrants occupy and become visible in particular neighborhoods of the city. Indeed, the city of Berlin and its neighborhoods have gained increasing importance vis-à-vis the national level for debating the visibility of immigrant identity. Manuel Castells argues that in an increasingly globalizing world, the locality gains primary importance as a "source of self-recognition and autonomous organization" (1997, 64).

Berlin presents a particularly appropriate setting for exposing and exploring the spatialization of identity formation processes of immigrants. Rather than a sui generis case for identity contestation, the city can be seen as a microcosm of national spatial identity–related debates. The two different Berlin neighborhoods examined in this research represent vantage points for observing the ways in which immigrants negotiate their identity through certain geographical places. Local and national integration policies, coupled with a feeling of exclusion from the majority population, complicate the process. Immigrants' ways of negotiating their identities are spatialized in the immigrant neighborhoods; as these neighborhoods become spaces of self-identification for the immigrants, they become, at the same time, visible targets of integration policies from above.

Visibility is a key concept within the German debate on immigrant incorporation, as well as within the local debate in Berlin. The high visibility of immigrant culture and ethnicity in certain neighborhoods of the city continues to shape Berlin's image in the German national discourse on integration. The city is known throughout Germany for its multicultural

Figure 1. Berlin, the secret Swedish capital.

character and its large and quite visible Turkish immigrant community. Figure 1 shows how Berlin's identity as a city of immigrants has made inroads into the Germany's popular culture and is even used for marketing purposes.

The visibility of difference (in culture and ethnicity) through the presence of immigrants in certain areas of the city—their signage, their communication with one another in a different language or in accented German—does not merely create hybrid expressions of culture. In fact, such visibilities also serve as a vital part of the discourse on integration and national identity in local politics. The spatial representations of the urban environment itself become a lens for the reality of the immigration and integration discourse, nationally and locally. Modan (2007, 331) notes:

> Public discourse is closely linked to public space; they are both elements in the public sphere. It is in public space and in public discourse that disparate people can come across each other and interact, where members of communities can debate and negotiate values, behaviors, and impending changes.

The abstract spatial contestation of identity in the policy discourse manifests itself most prominently in specific places in the urban environment: the immigrant neighborhood. In these neighborhoods, the ethnocultural differences of immigrants become visible, presenting a challenge to the national mainstream. Thus, the neighborhood becomes the place of tension between the policy discourse and immigrants' everyday practices, which escape the images and ideas of such discourses (Modan 2007; Orum 1998; Roy 2005, 2009; Sassen 1996). The immigrants' everyday experiences, however, do not exist in a vacuum: "Spaces of representation themselves are also shaped by representations of space, and both are shaped—and in turn shape—spatial practices" (Modan 2007, 311). The importance of space, spatial practice and the political framing of sociospatial reality are all inherently correlated. Therefore, space can be an excellent tool for understanding the social processes that are embedded in it.

The social reality of the immigrants' lived space is not easily accessible to outsiders and is impossible to capture through integration indicators or other quantitative measures. Therefore, the methodological approach used here is qualitative, based on findings from fieldwork in Berlin over the course of a year (2008 to 2009). Semistructured and open-ended interviews captured critical information about top-down framing and conceptions of integration policy regarding Turkish immigrants from Berlin's executive and legislative policy makers responsible for the immigration and integration policies. Policy makers and career bureaucrats from various administrative departments within Berlin's local government were interviewed about immigrant integration, legal matters, and women's issues. In addition, representatives of the largest and most strongly politically involved Turkish community organization in Berlin voiced their opinions about integration policies and the situation of Turkish immigrants in the city.

Finally, and most central to the research, the book captures the life stories and experiences of second-generation immigrant women living in Berlin in two immigrant neighborhoods, Kreuzberg and Neukölln. Their stories, as well as their lives as women in an immigrant community, exhibit their own personal ways of integration, which are strongly rooted in the space of the neighborhood itself. The second generation of immigrants must directly bridge the gap between the culture of their parents' country of origin and the (new) country they were raised in. Their stories therefore provide the strongest clues about how integration—the life between and across two cultures—is actually experienced by the immigrants.

Women as symbolic figures—and embodiments of national and ethnic identity (Yuval-Davis and Anthias 1989)—are central to the integration discourse. Women's bodies and their social roles are often targeted by policy makers from outside the community and by leaders from inside the community. In this way, women's bodies and social roles serve both as indicators for the community's integration (as perceived from the outside), and symbols for the community's distinct identity (as perceived from the inside). Women's life stories and integration experiences therefore provide insights into the potential gap between lived integration and the policy discourse on integration.

The in-depth interviews and life stories with second-generation Turkish immigrant women that I feature in this book provide unique insights into the real lives of those who are often overlooked: the women beyond the public discourse.

> If the truly disadvantaged are to be given a voice—if they are to be heard—it must be through the careful collection of case material by social scientists who take the worldview of the economically disadvantaged and set the latter's voices (and their pain) in relationship to the powerful organizational structures that influence their lives and over which they have so little control. (Sjoberg et al. 1991, 60)

My dual approach compares the life stories of women as the physical symbols of both the German and the Turkish nations to the way their stories are framed in the public arena by local policy makers and Turkish community representatives.

Outlining the Study

The introduction has established the purpose of the research and set it briefly against the historical and conceptual background. Chapter 1 develops the full conceptual framework that guides this project and delves deeper into the historical intricacies of the German immigration debate. The concept of space is applied as a specific conceptual lens in order to understand social reality and discourse by grounding and contextualizing social processes. By using a two-level approach to space, this section introduces a framework for understanding the issues brought about by policy prescriptions that are divorced from local practices. This conceptual approach builds on aspects from Soja's (1996, 1999) concept of Thirdspace by using it to analyze the lived realities of Turkish immigrant minorities in Berlin.

Chapters 2 and 3 elaborate on and question the policy level and the lived reality, respectively, in the Berlin context based on empirical findings. Chapter 2 focuses on the policy discourse and on how integration and the situation of Turkish immigrant minorities are framed at the city level.

Conceived space, an abstract and imagined perspective by those in power positions (Lefebvre 1984; Soja 1996), provides a lens for teasing out the power differential between immigrants and the policy discourse. From this conceptual perspective, the policy discourse is seen as a hegemonic discourse, which frames public opinion and affects media reporting. As a result of their power position, policy makers can frame their imaginations of urban space and immigrant integration as realistic policy recommendations without taking immigrants' social reality into consideration.

Chapter 3 explores the antidote to conceived space. It provides a glimpse into immigrants' life stories and their lived ways of integration, which are likely to stand apart from what policy makers conceive as viable avenues to integration. Lived space, or what Lefebvre (1984) has called *l'espace veçu,* provides a lens for reading the immigrants' life stories and self-perceptions as alternative ways of integration. Chapter 3 also illustrates that immigrants are conscious of and react to the way they are perceived and framed within the dominant discourse. They react to the policy discourse by way of their own integration strategies inside the neighborhood. The empirical findings indicate the possibility of a bridge between the hegemonic policy discourse on integration, and the immigrants' alternative ways of lived integration: Policy makers are increasingly interculturally competent, the result of their personal or professional experiences and encounters with immigrants. Whether this neighborhood-level development will significantly alter the city-level discourse over the long run remains to be seen.

Chapter 4 grounds the empirical findings in the sociohistorical fabric of the two neighborhoods, Kreuzberg and Neukölln. The experiences and life stories of the immigrants interviewed are contextualized against the sociohistorical background as well as the current integration debates of each specific place. By exploring the historical context of the place itself, this chapter underlines the intricate connection between immigrant identity and lived integration and the social context of the neighborhood itself. Immigrant identity formation and political empowerment on the one hand and the sociohistorical context of the neighborhood on the other hand have a strong mutual impact on the other.

The conclusion summarizes the empirical findings and points to the conceptual and policy implications of this research. The concept of lived space as a conceptual lens for the neighborhood context can lead to a better understanding of the problems inherent in the creation of integration approaches and open new avenues for understanding the lives of immigrants. From a theoretical perspective, the conclusion emphasizes the importance of a two-level analysis to a specific issue (integration) in an underresearched empirical context (the urban neighborhood). This approach can lead to improvements in the scope and depth of integration research in general. The conclusion also suggests some avenues for further research.

1 INTEGRATION OR EXCLUSION?

Understanding Turkish Immigration in Germany

Fällt von ungefähr ein fremdes Wort
In den Brunnen einer Sprache,
So wird es solange darin umgetrieben,
Bis es ihre Farbe annimmt und seiner fremden
Art zum Trotze wie ein heimisches aussieht.

If out of nowhere a strange word falls
Into the fountain of a language
It will be floating in it until
It will adopt its color
And despite its strange ways will look like a native.

—Jacob Grimm (1890)

INTEGRATION POLICY is inextricably tied to a nation's attempt to preserve its national identity. This chapter delves deeper into the history of national identity and immigrant integration in Germany and outlines the key conceptual tools for following the central arguments of this book. National identity and integration are the major topics that structure how the information in this chapter unfolds. A more detailed historical background on German national identity than provided in the introduction is followed by an outline of the history of Turkish guest worker immigration to Germany.

Integration policy in the German context appears as a strategy of German society to preserve the properties of the national mainstream by making immigrants fit. On the basis of Dumper's (1997) concept of the central paradox, according to which state policies tend to often exacerbate the social conditions they seek to ameliorate, this chapter retraces the link between integration and exclusion that some scholars have drawn. Instead of incorporating newcomers, integration policies can often act as the gatekeepers to society. Thus, they often define the basis of exclusion for many immigrants instead of providing an entry point for newcomers into a society.

The current public debate on integration in Germany is discussed next, followed by the introduction of the conceptual and theoretical arguments, which scholars have brought to the political integration debate. Because immigrants require places to live and work, their incorporation into daily life generates a spatial dimension that expands the theoretical and conceptual debates. This chapter introduces the idea that immigrants' struggle to fit into the new society can manifest itself spatially in the sociocultural and economic fabric of the city. Introducing a spatial lens for understanding the consequences of integration policies as well as identity formation processes of immigrants in the city changes the commonly accepted concept of the ethnic enclave from a zone of exclusion to a transnational or hybrid space. Spatial conceptions of identity, integration, and home as exhibited in the debates on integration policy as well as among immigrants can provide specific insights into both the political framing of the integration debate and the immigrants' reactions to it. Therefore, besides being a geographic or planning tool, space can be of explicit political and sociological importance in the analysis of social processes. The chapter ends with an introduction into the methods used, which illuminate the benefits of utilizing Soja's (1996) concept of Thirdspace as a tool for understanding the policy issues and social processes regarding integration in Berlin.

Who Is Germany? History and Current Status of German Citizenship Law

The history of Germany's citizenship law and the dominant definitions of national identity in Germany are closely linked to the current political debate on integration with respect to incorporating immigrants and handling ethnic diversity, as well as the issues that Turkish immigrants face in the country today. The complexity of the immigrants' citizenship status has been heightened by the addition of a transnational layer of identity, for which the policies of the European Union are responsible. The implementation of the European Union has overlaid national identities, loosening real and imagined borderlines between Germany and other European countries, but solidifying notions about and boundaries toward non-European "outsiders," such as Turkish immigrants. Matters of identity and citizenship were complicated further when the liberalization of German citizenship law in 2000 produced a significant shift away from the previously purely ethnic conception of German identity to one including components of both *ius soli* and *ius sanguinis*.[1] The change in law allows the children of immigrant citizens and permanent residents to acquire German citizenship at birth for the first time in German history, instead of restricting German citizenship to those with German ancestry. Because citizenship was until this point based on ethnicity only, ethnic identity implicitly represented a way to limit entry into the German national community. With the loss of this gatekeeping function, new barriers to becoming German, such as the concept of integration, evolved. The book develops the argument that Germany's integration debate symbolizes an etymological shift from a Germanness based on ethnicity to a Germanness based on integration. Integration, therefore, has replaced ethnicity as a way of defining who is German.

The History of German Citizenship Law

Scholarly works on nationalism and citizenship present the German case as an ideal type of the descent-based model of citizenship (Brubaker 1992; Castles 1995; Soysal 2001). Germany's citizenship law, which dates to 1913, required that citizenship (and thus membership in the German national community) was only granted to individuals who were of German descent and who could prove their German heritage through their father's and mother's bloodlines. A brief excursion into the evolution of German citizenship law sheds light on the immigration debates—past and present— outlined in this chapter.

The conception of German citizenship and identity was first codified in the *Reichs- und Staatsangehörigkeitsgesetz* (Empire- and citizenship law) of 1913, which remained the legal basis for the determination of German citizenship until the year 2000. According to this document, German citizenship could be awarded solely based on descent *(ius sanguinis)*. The rule greatly limited the opportunities to obtain German citizenship for any immigrants of non-German ethnic descent. The *Völkische*[2] *Bewegung* (people's movement) in the years between World War I and World War II reinforced the descent-based notion of German citizenship. The movement lobbied for the creation of a German *Volksgemeinschaft* (*Volk* community) made up of *Volksdeutsche* (*Volk* Germans). The idea of the *Volksgemeinschaft*, in this view, conceptually replaces the idea of citizenship. In other words, the legal category of membership inside a national territory, which defined who was and who was not a citizen, was superseded by the ethnic category of the *Volk*, with *Volk* referring solely to a common blood-based descent.

The National Socialists returned to this idea in their 1935 *Rassengesetzen* (racial laws), which provided the legal grounds for the expatriation and exclusion of Jews and others considered to be outside of the *Volksgemeinschaft*. The term *Volksdeutscher* was largely abandoned after 1945, although the German *Grundgesetz* (basic law) mentions Germans who are "not to be considered *Ausländer* (foreigners) despite their lack of citizenship" (Article 16) as having *deutsche Volkszugehörigkeit*—literally, "belonging to the German *Volk*." Article 16 refers specifically to the former *Volksdeutsche*, now called *Aussiedler*.[3]

A Democratic Deficit? Democratic Challenges to Ethnic Citizenship in Germany

Between the arrival of the first guest workers and the 2000 revision of German citizenship law, the ethnic conception of German identity and citizenship rights saw some minor revisions and challenges.[4] In the wake of the Third Wave feminist movement in Germany, German family law underwent minor changes as well—for instance, the father ceased to be considered the legal head of household.[5] This had important consequences for German citizenship law. As of January 1, 1975, German citizenship could be inherited through both parents, whereas before 1975, it could only be passed on by an ethnic German father.

The increasingly visible presence of Turkish immigrants in the German public sphere spurred the political debate regarding citizenship for the largest ethnic minority in the Germany of the 1980s: the Turkish guest worker families. Turkish groups started to organize and lobby for their interests, which helped to move the question of naturalization of and voting rights specifically for guest workers to the top of the political agenda of all major political parties in Germany, mainly the Social Democrats (SPD) and the Christian Democrats (CDU).[6] The SPD organized a few local political initiatives to support the agenda of noncitizen immigrants, while the CDU was largely opposed to expanding the avenues for citizenship or any voting rights to noncitizens. In the early 1990s, the vast majority of German politicians on both ends of the political spectrum agreed to neither encourage immigrants to acquire German citizenship nor to grant them any voting rights without citizenship (Thränhardt 2008).

In the conservative-dominated German political landscape of the late 1980s and early 1990s, political attempts to change and improve the status of immigrants stand out. In 1990 and 1989, respectively, the SPD-led coalition governments of the German states of Hamburg and Schleswig-Holstein offered increased inclusion to their immigrant population by trying to introduce local voting rights for foreign residents. The SPD initiated these proposals in its role as the primary political party representing Turks in Germany. The German constitutional court determined that the proposals were unconstitutional because only German citizens constitute the German state and are the only "carriers of German state power"—that is, to be able to vote (German Constitutional Court decision BVerfG, October 30, 1990). Surprisingly, the significance of the Hamburg and Schleswig-Holstein cases for Germany's history of immigrant incorporation has been largely ignored by scholars, except for Thränhardt (2008).

The decision of the German constitutional court in fact conflicted directly with the Maastricht treaty, which allowed for local voting rights for E.U. citizens in other E.U. countries. When the German parliament ratified the Maastricht treaty in 1993, it in effect reintroduced the Hamburg and Schleswig-Holstein notion of local voting rights for noncitizens (in this case E.U. citizens) in Germany. More significantly, the German constitution had to be amended in order to implement this specific aspect of the treaty (Thränhardt 2008). The amendment specifically included only non-German citizens of E.U. member states and excluded all citizens of non-E.U. member states living in Germany. This two-class system of local voting rights favors non-German E.U. citizens over other foreign residents, and thereby leads to a democratic deficit in Germany, according to Thränhardt, because a considerable number of foreign residents are excluded from the political process. Thränhardt (2008) notes:

> This development is not based on unchangeable cultural German traditions but on political decisions and problematic ideological divisions throughout the 1980s and '90s, which have lead to the political estrangement from German politics of large parts of the migrant population, even though the immigrants mostly feel at home in their social environment and their contacts to the host population are increasing year by year. (4)

Strohmeier (2006) followed up on Thränhardt's study in a subsequent investigation of the consequences of the two-tier system. He argues that the lack of political participation and representation of immigrants at the local level can be directly tied to the two-class local voting rights following the Maastricht treaty. He notes further that this development has especially grave consequences in localities with high concentrations of non-E.U. immigrant residents who are not German citizens. Strohmeier (2006) found that only a third of the adult population participates in local elections in those localities.

Overall, the key revisions of the the German citizenship law in 2000 pertained to the addition of an *ius soli* aspect to German citizenship law. First, children born in Germany can now acquire German citizenship at birth if at least one parent was born in Germany or has resided legally in the country for at least eight years. Second, adult immigrants can naturalize after eight years of legal residence in the country, versus fifteen years under the old law. Third, underage immigrants can acquire German citizenship after legally residing in Germany for at least five years (instead of eight years) if one parent has unlimited residence rights. Fourth, foreign citizens married to a German citizen can acquire German citizenship after three years of legal residence in Germany, if the marriage has been in effect for at least two years (*Bundeszentrale für politische Bildung* 1999).

The amended citizenship law of 2000 failed to provide a general legal acceptance of dual citizenship in Germany, adopting only the four central provisions listed above.[7] Nonetheless, the amendments fundamentally altered the origin of German citizenship from a blood-based *(ius sanguinis)* concept to a more open concept, allowing longtime residents without German descent to acquire German citizenship *(ius soli)*.

This change significantly influenced the political discourse on immigrant incorporation. The verbal shift in discourse from *Ausländerpolitik* (foreigner policy) to *Integrationspolitik* (integration policy) represented the new stage of immigrant citizenship, a new way of perceiving and approaching immigrants. This new stage in immigration policy sparked renewed interest by German policy makers in how other industrialized immigrant countries with more open, soil-based conceptions of citizenship and nationhood approach questions of immigrant incorporation. The terms of the political debates initiated by the government proposal of the center-left "Red–Green" governing coalition between the Social Democrats and the Green Party in 1999 to include dual citizenship among the 2000 reforms of German citizenship and immigration law continued to shape the public discourse. The dual citizenship proposal sparked strong criticism from the political opposition parties, especially the CDU. The CDU began a country-wide campaign for a popular referendum against the dual citizenship proposal. The party argued that dual citizenship would prevent the sustainable and permanent integration of immigrants because only a conscious decision for German citizenship and against their previous citizenship could ensure the immigrants' active willingness to integrate. Not surprisingly, the CDU's argument underlines the important role of integration in replacing decent-based citizenship as the gatekeeper of the national community after the introduction of Germany's new citizenship law. The debate about dual citizenship in Germany has been tabled for the time being, but it is sure to arise again in the future.

The evolution of German citizenship law since the end of World War II, as outlined above, is closely related to the story of guest worker immigration. Guest worker immigration, German attempts at isolation and assimilation of immigrants, and the eventual change in citizenship law have laid the foundation for the new centrality of the term *integration* in German discourse. In the following section, I outline the history of guest worker immigration to Germany as the factor that underpins today's debates.

Setting the Stage: Turkish Immigrants in Germany in Historical Perspective

The German ethnic citizenship model faced a fundamental challenge with the arrival of the first guest workers from countries in the Mediterranean, which included Greece, Italy, Spain, Turkey, and the former Yugoslavia (Brubaker 1992). The bilateral guest worker agreements that the German government struck with the countries sending workers outlined that guest workers were to remain in Germany only for as long as Germany found itself short of manual workers; they would be literally working guests in the country. However, not all guest workers from all countries returned to their home countries. In fact, Constant and Massey (2003) find that different groups of guest workers had different rates of return migration. Migrants from sending countries that joined the European Union returned home in much higher numbers than migrants from non-E.U. countries. Seven in ten Greeks, eight in ten Spaniards, and nine in ten Italians (Italy was a founding member of the European Union) returned to their home countries eventually (Constant and Massey 2003). Guest workers from non-E.U. countries, on the other hand, tended to remain in Germany: only five in ten guest workers from the former Yugoslavia and three in ten guest workers from Turkey ever returned home. Thus, the guest worker agreement with Turkey brought a large number of permanent immigrants to Germany (Kaya and Kentel 2005).

Turkish guest worker immigration in particular commenced after the signing of the guest worker agreement between Turkey and Germany in October 1961. Turkey soon became the most important sending country for Germany's guest workers, passing Italy in 1973 with a total contribution of 23 percent to Germany's foreign workforce (Özcan 2004). The former

Yugoslavia was the second largest contributor with 17 percent, followed by Italy (16 percent), Greece (10 percent), and Spain (7 percent). Overall, roughly 70,000 guest workers arrived in Germany between 1961 and 1971.

Because Germany's immigration policy was based on labor market demand and was strongly affected by global changes, Germany closed its border to further labor immigration when the 1973 oil shock slowed the demand for unskilled labor (Kaya and Kentel 2005; Özcan 2004). Yet the personal needs of immigrants and political developments in Turkey superseded the German government's attempts at controlling immigration. Turkish immigration to Germany after 1973 was granted mainly for reasons of family reunification[8] rather than for work permits or for political asylum after the 1971 military coup.

The government's official termination of the guest worker program failed to halt the increase in Turkish immigration to Germany. The visas of immigrants already trained and working in Germany were often extended, and workers already residing in Germany sought family visas to bring their relatives to Germany as well. As can be seen in Figure 2, the end of the formal guest worker program in 1973 had no influence on the influx of Turkish immigrants to Germany. Because the government still issued family reunification visas after the end of the guest worker program, Turkish immigration actually increased despite the German government's efforts to limit it.

Since 1961, Germany's perception and reception of its Turkish immigrants have gone through different stages of development that parallel the country's changing reality: those once perceived to be temporary guest workers have become a permanent presence. Kartal (2009) has grouped

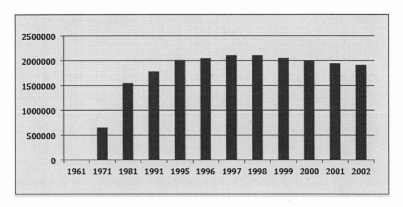

Figure 2. Number of Turkish citizens in Germany.

these changes in German integration and citizenship policy into five phases. Initially, Germans framed Turkish immigrants simply as foreigners in the public discourse on immigration. Over the course of these five phases, Turkish immigrants moved toward a completely new status, defined in this research as immigrant citizens status (Kartal 2009). Immigrant citizens refers to the group of Turkish immigrants in Germany who are legally German citizens but who are not completely accepted as Germans into German society, even though many of them are of the second and third generation and were born in Germany. Thus the immigrant or foreigner stigma remains with them.

The first phase of Turkish migration spans the beginning of guest worker recruitment in 1961 until the termination of the contract in 1973. It is characterized by temporary labor contracts that the German government implemented in order to meet the country's need for unskilled workers. The second phase lasted from 1973 to 1980 and focused on family reunification after the termination of the official guest worker recruitment efforts. German authorities agreed to allow guest workers already in Germany to bring their families into the country despite the official halt in labor recruitment.

The third phase of Turkish immigration to Germany saw a small return wave of Turkish immigrants from Germany to Turkey as a consequence of the *Rückkehrförderungsgesetz* (return-promoting law), which went into effect on January 1, 1984. This law authorized the German government to provide Turkish immigrants willing to return to Turkey with a severance package of 10,500 deutsche marks (approximately $7,500) (Faas 2007, 46), tax breaks, and counseling for reentering the Turkish job market. These measures were intended to give Turkish immigrants an incentive for returning to Turkey, and indeed proved somewhat successful for the first half of the decade, as approximately 250,000 immigrants left Germany (Faas 2007, 46). After the initial success, return migration actually dropped to lower numbers than before the law. The *Rückkehrförderungsgesetz* illustrates the strength and rigorousness of Germany's self-definition as not being a country of immigration. Until the late 1980s, Turkish immigrants in Germany were still categorically defined as foreigners; they were not considered members of German society and were expected to return to their country of origin.

The fourth phase of Turkish immigration to Germany spanned the late 1980s and marked the immigrants' final settlement in Germany. The decision of many Turkish immigrants to remain in Germany came as a result of the difficult political and economic circumstances in Turkey at that time, despite the difficulties they faced in becoming an accepted part of German society. The evidence is unclear as to whether the returning Turks made their decision on the basis of economic and political preference or on personal preference. For many Turkish guest workers, the main impetus behind the decision to remain in Germany seems to have been the desire for a politically and economically stable future (Kartal 2009). However, accepting a final decision to remain in Germany did not eliminate a yearning for the past among the first generation of immigrants or diminish their mourning for the loss of the homeland.

The settlement phase led directly to the fifth phase of Turkish immigration to Germany, which began in the early 1990s and resulted in the formation of permanent immigrant minorities in Germany. This phase moved the question of how to incorporate the immigrants into German society to the top of the national political agenda. The concept of assimilation became a commonly used synonym for immigrant incorporation. If Turkish immigrants decided to stay, then they were expected to meet an impossible requirement: shed all traces of cultural and ethnic difference and become indistinguishable from Germans.

The 1998 election of the first center-left (Red–Green) coalition in Germany in seventeen years opened a window of opportunity for making permanent political and legal changes in the country with respect to immigration. Indeed, in 2000 the center-left coalition passed a liberalized revision of the 1913 citizenship law, which ushered in the sixth and to date final phase of Turkish migration: the establishment of the immigrant citizen. As noted above, the immigrant citizen holds German citizenship, but is neither quite accepted as a German culturally nor considered a foreigner and an outsider to the national community. The remedy to this immigrant citizen status, in the eyes of the German government, is for the immigrant citizen to be encouraged to embrace a German identity through the implementation of integration policies and in this way reach full acceptance.

Figure 3 illustrates that as new avenues opened up for Turks to acquire German citizenship, the number of naturalizations of Turkish immigrants not only peaked but in fact almost doubled. The trend toward naturalization can be interpreted as an indicator of the Turks' willingness to incorporate into German society, as naturalization is not a necessity for acquiring permanent residency status or accessing social benefits. The numbers also demonstrate that, in contrast to the arguments of several policy makers, many Turkish immigrants in Germany did in fact desire to naturalize and embrace Germany as their home country.

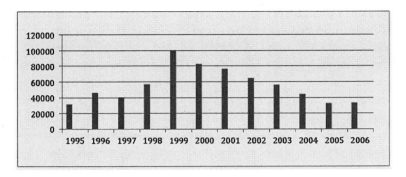

Figure 3. Number of naturalizations of Turks in Germany.

Increases in the numbers of immigrant citizens were not the only consequence of the implementation of a more inclusive citizenship law. Germany's national political debate began to shift from one about foreigners and guest workers to one about immigrants. Suddenly the question about entry into the national community was not purely a legal one, because inclusion in the national community was no longer limited to those of German ethnicity. Instead, under certain circumstances, individuals of different ethnic and cultural backgrounds were now able to become members of the German national community. As a result, the very definition of who is a German—the properties of German national identity—is now in flux. Integration policy (instead of citizenship law) now functions as the new gatekeeper to the national community. The following section outlines the connection between national identity and integration.

Integration and Its Role in Constructing the National Mainstream

In any country, the definition of who is a member of the national community, or the national "mainstream" (Alba and Nee 2005, 11), can evolve over time with changing requirements for legal membership and the influx of new immigrant citizens.[9] Specifically in countries where immigration is considered a permanent social feature, national identity is constantly reconfigured with the arrival of new immigrant groups and their participation in the polity, which is based on newly acquired legal membership. Although new groups of immigrants can become legal members of a new country from one day to the other on the basis of legal changes in their status, changes in the definition of the national mainstream—that is, subjective majority perceptions of who is a member of the national community—tend to be incremental; they rarely come about without tension, resistance, or both.

Traditional countries of immigration such as the United States and Canada provide compelling examples for these incremental changes in the character of national identity. What it means to be an American today is different from what it meant fifty years ago (Huntington 2004; French and Hinze 2010). The continuous absorption of new immigrants into the mainstream (Alba and Nee 2005) affects national identity. Therefore, the content of the national mainstream in countries of immigration is ever-changing thanks to the arrival of new immigrants. The American settler culture started out as white Anglo-Saxon Protestant and incrementally came to include Catholicism and Judaism, as well as non-European ethnicities, such as African American and Latino. Even though American society is by no means free of prejudice against ethnic, racial, and religious minorities, the mainstream content of what is considered American identity has fundamentally changed over the second half of the twentieth century.

In Germany, the emergence of a supranational European identity has created a multilayered perception of the mainstream. The European project has led to the acceptance of most E.U. immigrants. Although Italians and Spaniards carried the stigma of being guest workers throughout the 1970s, 1980s, and early 1990s, the ascendance of a common European identity among younger generations, as well as unlimited residence rights for E.U. citizens across the union, have fundamentally changed the outlook of younger generations on their European neighbors. An understanding of the German mainstream may not include elements of Italian or Spanish identity, but these identities have been absorbed by the European mainstream, where they coexist on an equal basis with German identity. Turkish identity, however, remains excluded from European identity on a supranational level, rendering its acceptance as part of the national German mainstream controversial.

The inclusion of minorities into the national mainstream has historically been the subject of fierce civic and political contestation and debate. In the United States, the importance of the election of John F. Kennedy as the first Irish Catholic president in 1961, the civil rights movement, and the often violent conflicts surrounding it, as well as the ongoing Latino immigration rallies and the quest for bilingual education in English and Spanish, bear witness to the conflict potential of this debate. In Europe, the resistance to changes in the national mainstream is evident in the resurgence of nationalist and anti-European parties. European Union member states are also experiencing an upsurge in the rejection of dual citizenship among their populations in the face of growing numbers of immigrants and increased European integration. Citizens across Europe will continue to defend what is considered traditional mainstream national identity until gradually this definition of identity comes to include what was previously considered the Other—the foreigner. The difference of the Other from the national mainstream is highly subjective and socially constructed; it is a "cognitive mechanism embedded in social interactions, not biological difference" (Alba and Nee 2005, 31).

A glimpse into this historical development of the content of national mainstream illustrates that national culture and identity itself is a hybrid and is malleable over time. Kraidy (1999) argues that all contemporary cultures are hybrid to a certain extent, as they are shaped by local or global interactions. The constant reconfiguration of the mainstream as a result of immigration molds national identity into an ever-changing and inherently hybrid construct, enhanced by the globalization of popular culture, and, in the German case, the influence of supranational governmental organizations, such as the European Union. In the public discourse, however, national mainstream or identity is consistently framed as homogeneous and static.

The discursive power of the assumed homogeneity of the mainstream is particularly strong in a country like Germany, where citizenship was historically based on descent and bloodlines. In immigration countries like the United States or Canada, the national mainstream's hybridity can be traced much more easily through those countries' long immigration histories. Accordingly, we know that American identity not only has roots in Eastern, Western, Northern Europe, and Southern Europe, but also in Asia, Africa, and Latin America. Nevertheless, even in the United States, Samuel Huntington (2004) has made strong efforts to tie American identity to a tradition of Anglo-Protestant nativism, despite the obvious historical evidence for Catholic, Jewish, African American, Latino, and Eastern European influences. This example illustrates that the frame of an ethnically, racially and culturally coherent mainstream has proven a powerful political tool for exclusion of those who represent a challenge to commonly held perceptions of the mainstream.

Reactions to the religious, cultural, and ethnic differences of newcomers to what is considered the national mainstream become institutionalized through the implementation of integration (or assimilation) policies

(Triandafyllidou 2001). Generally, these policies are designed to make the Other fit the mainstream—to somehow eliminate the difference between them. This perceived difference is always tied to specific markers of difference that may be ethnic or racial, cultural or religious, denoting newcomers' obvious difference from majority conceptions of the national mainstream. The general underlying assumption of the integration or assimilation process is that the socially constructed differences, which are tied to visible markers of difference, will be eliminated through assimilation (Alba and Nee 2005)—as long as the individual Other is willing to assimilate.

The Current State of the Integration Debate in Germany

After four decades of incremental immigrant influx to Germany, the question of how to integrate this new ethnic population into the German national mainstream has generated heated public debates in Germany. These debates regarding the definition of German and immigrant identity began only in the late 1990s, after three decades of enforced inner-German separation.

The meaning of the term *integration* is contested in the scholarly literature yet is rarely questioned or investigated. Scholars (Brubaker 2001; Ehrkamp 2006) bemoan the ambiguity of the term, yet they do not offer a thorough exploration of its meaning and effect. Other analysts (Dörr and Faist 1997; Joppke 2007) simply take the term for granted as a new, nonassimilationist strategy of acknowledging ethnic diversity. They do not question its diverse usage and multiple meanings in the political discourse. More than anything, *integration* appears to have become a contemporary, politically correct, but ambiguous term, which has replaced the harsher assimilation approach:

> Integration became a comfortable, "sensible" position for the centre trying to distinguish itself from xenophobic nationalism on the one hand, and radical anti-system discourses on the other. On one level, the success of a term like this can be said to be superficial: it is just jargon that gets picked up as a kind of default language, when other types of argument become unfashionable or distorted by political usage. However, integration has thus far appeared quite impervious to these same problems: even among academics it is rarely problematized or examined, when it is used as a conceptual shorthand. (Favell 2001, 352)

Integration, apart from its warm, welcoming connotations, can be seen as a mode of gatekeeping for membership in the national community. In that regard, it represents a sink-or-swim approach to incorporating immigrants, implying the choice of either becoming like "us" or remaining an outsider forever. Through this process, the national community discharges its responsibility for including the immigrants—matters are in the new-comers' hands. Whatever they choose to do, they will have to deal with (and be responsible for) the consequences. Fundamental questions arise from this approach: Do immigrants have a choice? Is the popular perception correct that their cultural difference keeps them from being integrated into the national community? Or is perhaps their ethnic difference—something they cannot change even if they wanted to—the reason for their perpetual exclusion? These questions define the examination of integration that follows.

Has Multiculturalism Failed? or, Can Turks Be Germans?

The debate about who is German resurfaced in fall 2010 in the aftermath of the publication of Thilo Sarrazin's highly controversial book, alarming titled *Deutschland Schafft Sich Ab: Wie wir unser Land aufs Spiel setzen* (Germany does away with itself: how we put our country at risk). Sarrazin, a member of the executive board of the German federal bank, advanced arguments against the popular but contested political concept of integration. The debate that ensued crossed political party boundaries and rendered the traditional ideological left–right divisions along the political spectrum largely irrelevant.

Sarrazin claims that Muslim immigrants are conquering Germany. He accuses his fellow countrymen of denying this reality and failing to intervene. Sarrazin is a long-term member of the (center-left) SPD. He has a reputation for frequently making controversial statements about the perceived damage inflicted on German culture and the social welfare state society by welfare queens and head scarf girls. His book represents yet another polemic on the same issues with specific mention of the supposed shortcomings of Turkish immigrants, such as their supposed lack of linguistic integration. He suggests that Turks are merely parasites on the social welfare system, and that Germans are in danger of becoming a minority in their own country.

The publication of Sarrazin's book sparked a widespread public debate in Germany about the definition and content of integration policies and the situation of immigrants in the country. On September 10, 2010, Sarrazin was forced to resign from the executive board of the German federal bank. At the same time, the German SPD started the process to expel Sarrazin on the basis of the content of his book. The fact remains, however, that while 70 percent of the German public was outraged by Sarrazin's comments, about 30 percent strongly support them. These 30 percent represent a significant part of the German public that endorse Sarrazin's arguments for a wide variety of reasons: that a citizen has the right to free speech, that it is time to state the "inconvenient facts," that "integration has failed," and that Turkish immigrants are largely relying on the German welfare state (*Frankfurter Allgemeine Zeitung* 2010).

About a month after Sarrazin's resignation, Christian Wulff, then the German president and the country's highest-ranking government official, returned to the topic of integration. His speech commemorating the twentieth anniversary of German reunification touched on the importance of reuniting East and West Germany. He remembered the difficulties experienced on both sides during the preceding twenty years. Finally, he framed the notion of the unification of Germany in a different context: the context of immigration. Without directly referring to Sarrazin, he noted that a public debate in Germany on the topic of integration was important and necessary:

> In 1989 the East Germans called out: "We are the people, we are one people."
>
> We are Germany. Yes: We are one people. Because I care about our fellow citizens who have come from other countries, I do not want them to feel hurt by the debates we need to have. Let us not permit legends to form and prejudice and exclusion to solidify. That course would not be in our national interest. . . .
>
> But before we can do anything else, we must agree on a clear stance. We need an understanding of Germany, of "belonging," that is much broader than a passport, a family history, or one's faith. Without a doubt, Christianity is a part of Germany. Without a doubt, Judaism is a part of Germany as well. This is simply our Judeo-Christian history. By now Islam is also a part of Germany. Nearly 200 years ago, Johann Wolfgang von Goethe expressed this very sentiment in the "West–Eastern Divan": "He who knows himself and others will recognize it here: Orient and Occident are inseparable." (Wulff 2010)

Wulff's statement that "Islam is also a part of Germany" moved the integration debate in Germany to a whole new level. The statement was met with strong criticism from both sides of the political spectrum as well as from the public. The conservative wing of Wulff's own (center-right) CDU was especially outraged by the idea that Islam might be considered in any way as a part of German culture and society. The comment from a fellow CDU politician, Volker Bouffier, president of the state of Hessen, that "Shariah [law] cannot be the basis for successful integration in Germany" (*Deutsche Welle* 2010), exemplifies the kind of criticism against Wulff. Most notably, Islam, in this statement, is heavily conflated with Islamic fundamentalism. Support for Wulff, on the other hand, came from German chancellor Angela Merkel, who attempted to calm the public crossfire in which her (center-right) party found itself after the president's controversial speech. Merkel noted in a speech in Potsdam on October 17, 2010, that Islam was clearly a part of German culture: "The soccer player Özil is not the only indication for that."[10] In the same speech, she stated that multiculturalism in Germany had failed. Merkel framed the issue of integration as one of reciprocity. Immigrants, she said, clearly needed the support of the host country. In return, the host country expected the cultural commitment of the immigrants. "In the past, we have often neglected that," Merkel said.

The two lines of argument advanced in Wulff's and Merkel's speeches bear witness to the political and public controversy regarding the meaning of integration in Germany. Wulff attempted to reconcile cultural differences by framing German culture as inclusive and open to cultural and ethnic differences, while Merkel's rather bleak statement acknowledged that multiculturalism in Germany has failed. Germany has never had an official policy of multiculturalism, so mentioning its failure represents a rhetorical attempt by Merkel to tone down the multicultural implications of Wulff's inclusive statement, which indicates the possibility of a peaceful coexistence between Christianity, Judaism, and Islam in German culture. Merkel and Wulff frame integration in different ways: Wulff emphasizes the importance of a transformation of German culture, while Merkel emphasizes as a central issue the immigrants' willingness to adapt to German culture.

The heated debates about Sarrazin's theses show that integration is one of the most polarizing notions in German politics on the topic of immigration. Contesting definitions and reactions cross party lines and political ideologies. In fact, the participants in this debate defy clear political associations— Sarrazin is SPD (center left), and Wulff and Merkel are CDU (center right).

The recent debate on the meaning and content of integration policy is not necessarily new. It moved to the top of the public agenda only on the basis of the recent controversies regarding Sarrazin's book and former president Wulff's public speech. The integration debate crosses all political and ideological boundaries and is opening up a new formal discourse that questions not only the status of immigrants, but also the very terms of the debate, such as the meaning of integration. This ongoing debate represents an important touchstone for understanding the status of immigrants in Germany, as well as the terms, actors, and neglected and unresolved aspects of such debates. The integration debate has deep roots in German national history, institutions, and identity. The evolution of Germany's citizenship law under the influence of the guest worker program moved integration (as a term and as a policy) to the center of the political debate.

Integration policies are often created to bridge the gap between a growing immigrant population and the popular definitions of the national mainstream (Cole 2000; Joppke 2005). As a leading Turkish minority politician, Cem Özdemir,[11] head of the German Green Party, says in an interview:

> Germany has little experience with diversity, only with assimilation. The question is, what do we do now that we are no longer able to reach everyone with classic assimilation techniques, and there are many who are not even interested in pursuing that path to begin with? The best way to describe the situation is through the concept of "hyphenated identity." Today it is possible to be a German citizen, a committed democrat, and still maintain a close connection with one's country of origin or that of one's parents. (*taz* 2009)

Özdemir's statement captures the paradoxical characteristics of Germany's politics of immigration since the beginning of the country's guest worker immigration policy: there is an inherent tension between increasing ethnic diversity[12] on the one hand, and a historically and politically assimilationist approach to immigrants on the other hand. Germany has failed to develop a political avenue or concept for the successful incorporation of immigrants.[13]

So far, the critical question of what integration really means for Germany and the German people has not been answered. Is integration a new way of acknowledging (and addressing) the presence of increased ethnic diversity in Germany and creating a political and social space for it, or is it merely a new form of assimilationism? Furthermore, does Germany's immigrant population—those who are to be integrated—participate in the political debate on integration and its meaning?

Özdemir's statement captures the positions of the German Turks within the German political discourse. As the son of Turkish immigrants, Özdemir has played a critical role in defining the boundaries of the debates on immigrant incorporation. His statement draws our attention to the lack of flexibility that characterizes current integration policies. Therefore, it is important to establish different conceptual frameworks that can accommodate more hybrid approaches to integration and reconcile diverse cultural practices with rather homogeneous perceptions of German identity and basic German values.

Integration is central to the political and academic debates on immigrant incorporation, and it also embodies the changing meaning of citizenship and of membership in the national community. Policy makers on the left and right of the political spectrum use integration in reference to developing a political strategy for dealing with Germany's increasing diversity. However, the implicit meaning they attach to the term *integration* can differ tremendously.

Integration, Exclusion, and Space

Integration or Exclusion?

While claiming openness toward immigrant minorities, policy approaches often turn into tools of exclusion when the criteria they use for integration set boundaries that define the insiders and outsiders of society. Top-down, government- and majority-prescribed approaches to integration allow immigrants a narrow choice. They can abide by the dominant definitions of integration, which are based on theoretical criteria for integration established by the ethnocultural majority group, or they face exclusion in certain areas of socioeconomic life. Moreover, even if they do abide by the rules of integration, general prejudices against certain minority groups may still exclude them from the national mainstream.

A country's integration policies are typically meant to delineate the path for immigrants to become accepted members of the society they have emigrated to. These policies, perhaps unintentionally, also provide insight into the perceptions of national identity held by policy makers and political parties (Cole 2000; Joppke 2005; Koopmans 2003). Through integration policy, host countries attempt to bridge the gap between the immigrants and the majority population and seek to measure the success of proposed integration.

Since the reforms of Germany's citizenship law between 2000 and 2005, government officials have established indicators to measure the success of integration policies. Integration indicators vary across German cities and communities, but they converge on approximately the same areas, such as socioeconomic achievements, education level, and reliance on social benefits (Worbs 2010). The indicators are intended to provide a direct comparison in these specific areas between immigrants and the host population. Worbs (2010) provides a unique perspective on indicators as measures of integration outcomes. She deconstructs the meaning of these indicators, and as a result of her analysis, she questions the general approach to integration policy, which is often taken for granted by policy makers and the public. Her findings show that measuring integration is not as easily done as it seems. Worbs sees the connection between government policy and successful integration that is made in measuring integration as particularly problematic. She notes that integration may be more individual than is assumed. For instance, immigrants could be integrating well because or in spite of integration policy.

According to Worbs (2010), two central elements generally define integration strategies: the achievement of equal opportunity in socioeconomic

upward mobility, and the adjustment of general standards of living between
the host population and immigrants which refers to an approximation of
socioeconomic and educational status between immigrants and host population. In a different study, Damelang and Steinhardt (2008) synthesize
different approaches to integration along the lines of the following broad
criteria:

1. Culturation: a process of cultural adaptation, such as language and cultural standards in order to ensure societal participation.
2. Placement: immigrants take over certain key positions in society, in the education
   and economic system, as well as citizens: it is the adoption of certain rights, and
   with them the possibility of gaining capital.
3. Interaction: the formation of interethnic networks and relationships, including
   friendships, marriages, community membership, and generally the inclusion into
   social groups and the possibility to gain social and cultural capital.
4. Identification: the individual identification with society, where the [individual
   person] sees him-/herself as a part of the whole. Identification takes place on a
   cognitive as well as an emotional level. (2)

Several communities and urban areas in Germany, among them Berlin, have established (theoretically) measurable demographic, cultural, and
economic integration indicators as a way to clarify and systematize their
attempts to understand the ambivalent and loaded term *integration*. These
indicators feed into a system of what has been called *Integrationsmonitoring*—literally "integration monitoring," a way of measuring the success of
local integration approaches. *Integrationsmonitoring* has become an official
strategy for understanding and informing immigration and immigration
policy across Germany and especially in large and diverse urban centers,
such as Berlin. Data for the official integration indicators are collected from
ten different areas, or indicators of integration, which are grouped along the
lines of cultural integration, socioeconomic attainment and upward mobility, representation, and interaction with dominant population groups.

The first and most important area covers labor, training, employment,
and economy. It encompasses indicators that measure the immigrants' ability to secure professional training and employment, and that measure the
immigrants' rate of unemployment. The second area, education, sheds light
on a number of factors, such as the attendance of immigrant children in
German preschools and kindergartens, their command of the German
language before and after entering school, and their ability to successfully
graduate and participate in higher education. The presence of immigrant
teachers in the German K through 13 education system is also measured.[14]

These first two areas are based on individual-level indicators. In the third area, sociospatial interconnectedness, the state government seeks to capture the success of integration at the community level.[15] It does so by tracking the percentages of residents with immigrant backgrounds in the districts and community councils and by collecting unemployment data for comparison with the city as a whole. Intercultural openness, the fourth area, captures the percentage of immigrants among recent hires, in civil service positions, and the number of interculturally competent employees of private businesses.[16] This area measures the openness of the host population in the city toward their immigrant neighbors. Area five, participation and strengthening of civil society, denotes the general participation of immigrants in political life with respect to voting and representation in the Berlin parliament. It also reports on racist violence against immigrants, crimes committed by immigrants, and the number of binational marriages in the city. Area six covers the city's openness toward refugees. The indicators associated with area six measure how many refugees are admitted as residents in the city and how long they are allowed to stay, as well as how many refugees are able to acquire permanent resident status. Area seven, culture, seeks to measure the immigrants' participation in local culture. Legal integration measures the number of immigrants that acquire permanent resident status, their average length of residence in Berlin, and yearly naturalization quotas on the city and district levels. Area nine, health, captures the participation of immigrant children in general health measures, such as vaccinations and basic examinations. Finally, area ten, social status, captures the percentage of immigrants among recipients of state-sponsored social services.

Although these criteria offer a broad and detailed understanding of the process of integration, only the number of bicultural marriages and number of racist, xenophobic, or anti-Semitic acts of violence draw attention to the general openness of the host population to immigrants. Once again, the criteria remain focused mainly on the immigrant population. Additionally, the indicators of general openness of the host population provide no information about how easily a person of immigrant background can find employment, or whether children of immigrants are evaluated fairly in school in comparison to German children. Thus, while they measure the socioeconomic achievements of immigrants in comparison to the host population, the integration indicators fail to measure their socioeconomic opportunity in the same context.

The integration indicators in all ten areas are largely cultural, demographic, and socioeconomic in nature. Yet scholars of immigration have noted that they inform integration policies that are aimed at mitigating certain features of difference, such as language, and are often framed as an attempt to foster the immigrants' fundamental understanding of and identification with basic liberal democratic values (Joppke 2007).

Subjective perceptions and measures of integration, such as those harbored by the majority population, are often not in alignment with general integration indicators (Triandafyllidou 2001). Triandafyllidou (2001) argues that in fact markers such as hair or skin color, cultural practice, or accents often dominate individuals' subjective perceptions of integration.[17] None of these markers can be overcome merely by the immigrants' effort and willingness to integrate. Thus, integration policies that target socioeconomic markers, language, or historical understanding of the nation, as do the integration indicators listed above, fail to capture the reasons why immigrants often remain excluded from the mainstream despite their efforts to fit in. The immigrant can only become an integrated member of society if the general perception of the national mainstream is expanded to include the immigrant's unchangeable features of difference, such as an accent, a "different sounding name," or a different skin color. Otherwise, the immigrant will permanently remain excluded.

As demonstrated above, integration is a contested term, and policy approaches have been linked to a perpetual state of lingering exclusion insofar as they reinforce the idea of a homogeneous national community (Wimmer 2002). Dumper (1997) refers to this type of problem as the central paradox: state policies exacerbate the very problems of minority groups that they are meant to ameliorate. Integration policies similarly tend to highlight the markers that differentiate immigrants from the majority population and frame these markers as signs of a lack of integration or indicators for immigrants' unwillingness to integrate.

Stolcke (1995) draws a compelling connection between approaches to integration in twentieth-century Britain and assimilation in twentieth-century France. Though the French approach was much more culturally restrictive in terms of difference, neither the British nor the French approach led to a complete incorporation of immigrant or colonial minorities. Both, integration and assimilation policies, merely produced a second class of citizens, as immigrants were stigmatized on the basis of their visible markers of difference. The premises in France and Britain were the same as in twenty-first-century Germany: a call "for the cultural assimilation of immigrant communities 'in our midst' to safeguard the . . . 'nation' with its shared values and lifestyle" (Stolcke 1995, 11). Some scholars have implicitly justified exclusion from citizenship or group rights by arguing that only culturally homogeneous communities can provide the basis for liberal democracy (Offe 1998; Walzer 1983). Cole (2000) addresses the inherent paradox of the exclusiveness of liberal democracy:

> Practices of exclusion cannot be coherently justified within the terms of a recognizable liberal political theory, and yet the practical realization of the liberal project depends upon those practices: the achievability of a liberal political polity made up of free and equal citizens rests upon the exclusion of others. And, finally, the exclusion of outsiders necessary to establish free and equal citizenship for insiders will, in practice make free and equal citizenship for all an impossibility. (11)

Governments in liberal democracies often justify integration policies as means of preserving cultural homogeneity. In this argument, homogeneity is portrayed as a basis for the very existence of liberal democracy. Wimmer (2002) argues that these homogenizing attempts often target newcomers and immigrants.

Integration represents an important issue for the receiving country of immigration, but a frequently overlooked perspective is the influence a sending country can exert on the immigrant citizens. The sending country may use the immigrants as an important tool to influence politics and integration policy in the receiving country when its representatives exhort their emigrants to adhere to the obvious markers of difference discussed above. For example, in 2008, Turkish prime minister Recep Tayyip Erdoğan addressed Germany's Turkish immigrants in a speech in the city of Cologne. Parts of Erdoğan's speech sparked controversy among the German public as well as policy makers when he called assimilation a crime against humanity:

> One the one hand, you have worked here, but on the other hand you have tried to preserve your identity, your culture, your traditions. Your eyes and ears were always aimed at Turkey. The fact that you were able to preserve your language, your faith, your values, your culture for forty-seven years, but more importantly, that you supported one another, this fact lies beyond recognition. I understand the sensitivity very well that you feel toward assimilation. Nobody can expect you to tolerate assimilation. Nobody can expect you to succumb to assimilation. Because assimilation is a crime against humanity. (Erdoğan 2008)

Erdoğan frames Turkish identity in Germany as based on language, faith, values, and culture that are closely connected to Turkey, and he explicitly encourages the Turkish immigrant community to influence German politics in the interest of Turkey. The Turkish immigrant community in Germany finds itself under unique dual political pressures from two sides. Although the Germans expect them to integrate themselves into German society and overcome their markers of difference, Turkey's Erdoğan calls on their loyalty toward Turkey. He praises them for preserving precisely those markers of difference that they are expected to shed in Germany. The two-sided pressure leaves Turkish immigrants with a permanent identity question: Are they Turks resisting rigid assimilation, or are they poorly integrated Germans?

Spatial Exclusion?

This book approaches in spatial terms the dilemma that Turkish immigrants in Germany face between integration and exclusion, between their loyalty to Turkey and their new home in Germany. Other scholars have also explored minority politics and exclusion by adding a spatial dimension to Dumper's (1997) concept of the central paradox. Urban scholars Gaffikin, Perry, and Kundu (2010) suggest that the state itself implicitly produces the territorial contestation of identity, especially in urban areas where minority groups concentrate in ethnic enclaves or ghettos. In essence, the state creates urban territories of sociocultural exclusion by excluding those who do not belong to the dominant sociocultural narrative of the state (Agamben 2005; Roy 2009). This can happen in different ways, such as outright social or implicit legal discrimination against so-called denizens—those whose rights within the (national) community are limited because they do not fit into popular conceptions of collective identity. In the urban context, this process of exclusion brings about the formation of ethnic and cultural enclaves, where minorities flock together in their common isolation from the national mainstream.

Manuel Castells (1997, 9) called the phenomenon of ethnic enclaves "the exclusion of the excluders by the excluded." Those excluded from the mainstream isolate themselves territorially in what is referred to as an immigrant neighborhood, ethnic enclave, or even a ghetto. Bauman (1995) takes a similar approach. He notes that in the enclave, the individual's visible difference from the mainstream through ethnic and cultural markers disappears because everybody inside the enclave is visibly different from the mainstream. Although the individual's visual difference is reduced, the visual difference of the neighborhood space as a minority enclave is heightened.[18] This heightened visibility of the neighborhood space in turn challenges sociocultural and ethnocultural urban cohesion; city planners and policy makers express concern and attempt to create strategies for returning the neighborhood back to the national mainstream. In the process, the neighborhood or enclave becomes the site of contestation of identity and integration in that it visually challenges prevailing notions of collective identity. However, while the enclave may turn into a no-go zone for the majority population (Bauman 1995) and remain outside formal definitions of collective identity, it can at the same time become an informal zone of collective empowerment for those at the margins (Roy 2005; Soja 1999). This argument is reinforced by the fact that ethnic enclaves often provide an extraordinary multiplicity of socioeconomic networks for their inhabitants.

What Goes On in the Enclave?
Space, Transnationalism, and Hybridity

The discussion so far has addressed the scholarly debates on exclusion from above and debates on the outside factors that cause immigrant minorities to cluster in certain spaces in the city. The spaces themselves, however, have dynamics of their own. They can be sites of identity formation and the creation of social networks. An important conceptual foundation for exploring immigrant minority identity and urban neighborhood space comes from the literature on transnationalism. This perspective defines the urban immigrant enclave as a transnational space, where immigrants transfer their language, cultural identity, and practice from their country of origin to a specific space in the urban environment within the new country of immigration (Sassen 1996).

However, this literature offers no clear explanation of the independent effect of the immigrant neighborhood or ethnic enclave space for the identity formation process of those living in it, as most scholars of transnationalism see localized ethnic or racial identity as a mere transplant of national identity from the country of origin to the country of residence (Ehrkamp 2005, 2006; Voigt-Graf 2004).

Transnationalism scholars have defined enclave identity as a hybrid space, in which static definitions of identity from the country or origin and the country of settlement melt into a new hybrid form of identity (Argun 2003; Çağlar 2001; Hall 1991; White 1997). This conception of transnational space as a hybrid space opens up the possibility of identity transcending the nation-state. A hybrid space presumes the formation of new identities that are detached from homogeneous conceptions of territorially defined identities: they form a spatial identity beyond territory—an identity of belonging neither here (in the country of residence) nor there (in the country of origin) (Çağlar 2001).

Scholars have described this kind of identity as hybridity (Kraidy 1999), as creolization (Hannerz 1987), or as a space of *mestizaje* (Martín-Barbero 1993). Plaza (2006, 214) defines hybrid identity "as a fluid, situational, volitional and dynamic phenomenon, one in which ethnic boundaries, identities, and cultures are negotiated, defined and produced through social interaction inside and outside ethnic communities." Scholars note that hybrid identity is a way of reconciling different cultures (Martín-Barbero 1993), and hybrid spaces are characterized by being "spaces of oblique signification where power relations are dialogically reinscribed" (Kraidy 1999, 456). This is especially true for the immigrant neighborhood, where the top-down implementation of integration policies by policy makers is challenged by the immigrants' own ways of accommodating themselves in the new country: their hybrid lifestyle.

The contributions to Kasinitz, Mollenkopf, Waters, and Holdaway's (2008) compelling study of second-generation immigrants in New York City illustrate how the second generation identifies with the city itself as a middle ground between the identity of their country of ethnic origin and the country they grew up in. The city in that sense becomes a hybrid category, which is more inclusive toward ethnic diversity than the national mainstream. A diverse group of second-generation immigrants in New York City defines itself as New Yorkers, a term that incorporates their belonging to as well as their difference from what is conceived of as American identity.

Abu-Lughod (1991, 137) notes that the life practice of *"halfies*—people whose national or cultural identity is mixed up by virtue of migration, overseas education, or parentage"—upsets the "anthropological boundary between self and other." In ethnic enclaves, a hybrid identity is often generated where immigrants attempt to negotiate both push (toward assimilating to the new culture) and pull (toward the identity and culture of their country of origin) factors inside and outside the immigrant neighborhood. The term *hybridity* in this book is defined as a creolized identity between German national mainstream identity and a multiplicity of Turkish immigrant identities. The new hybrid identity can be usefully captured conceptually by what has been called Thirdspace (Soja 1996), *l'espace vecu* (Lefebvre 1984), or the borderlands (Anzaldúa 1999).

Space and Spatial Practice

This book addresses specifically the difference between the way policy makers frame immigrant identities and the way immigrants perceive themselves within the larger society and national community. Immigrants are often burdened and misunderstood due to the great variety of overgeneralizing assumptions that characterize the political discourse on immigrant integration. The result is a disconnect between immigrant identity and self-perception on the one the hand, and the political debate on immigrant integration on the other. In pointing to this disconnect, this book carves out a spatial dimension examining the alternative ways in which immigrants attempt to integrate themselves into society via the spatial fabric of the city. A conceptual framework that emphasizes a spatialized hybridity, a "neither here nor there" that manifests itself within a spatial dimension as proposed by scholars like Anzaldúa (1999), Lefebvre (1984), and Soja (1996) is useful for exploring the central questions that guide this book. It conceptualizes the transnational hybridity of minority groups in certain areas of the city against a policy discourse from above.

Soja's (1996) concept of Thirdspace builds on Lefebvre's (1984) emphasis on the importance of lived space along with time and historicality for understanding social processes. Lefebvre criticized the perception of space as dead and lifeless, as opposed to the vivid substance that had been attributed to time and historical context by philosophers. This approach attends to the critical role of space specifically for understanding the "cultural politics of identity and difference" (Soja 1996, 52). A "spatialized social reality" (46) proposes a new tool for understanding dominant symbolic representations of spatial reality.

Opposite this spatialized social reality lies the political discourse. The relationship between lived social reality and the political discourse can be seen as a power relationship because power is an inherent constituent in how and why the political discourse is framed a certain way. The concept does not denote power per se but can be understood as the dominant way of framing social reality and capturing the prevailing political discourse. Lefebvre's spatialized social reality creates a third dimension of what scholars call the Other, which transcends the political discourse and succeeds in capturing elements of resistance and empowerment in the hybrid dimension, the space of the Others. The conceptualization of this third dimension is influenced by Anzaldúa's (1999) conceptualization of hybrid identity and Otherness in the borderlands of the U.S.–Mexico border, and Said's Orientalism in identifying Westerncentric thinking on one hand and the ways of Othering the East that it produces. It is thus perceived "as a space of radical openness, a context from which to build communities of resistance and renewal that cross the boundaries and double-cross the binaries of race, gender, class and all oppressively Othering categories" (Soja 1996, 84). This third dimension conceptualizes the hybridity and in-between-ness of the new identity that develops in ethnic immigrant enclaves in the city. For the purposes of this project, the third dimension is the immigrants' lived space, their spatially situated social reality and spatial practice and reflects the hybridity (Soja 1996, 1999) or creolization (Argun 2003) that bridges the immigrants' multilayered identities. The Otherness of this space is often perceived and framed as problematic in the dominant policy debate but in many cases represents empowerment (Roy 2005) as immigrants create a space where they can belong. The spatialized third dimension is a fusion of the social conditions, historical context, geographic environment, and informal empowerment that newcomers find and create outside the formal realms of state institutions and dominant definitions.

Why a Spatial Perspective?

In spatially conceptualizing the visibility of the immigrant other, scholars have often utilized the private–public distinction (Göle 1996; Winter 2008). This distinction draws attention to the political factors that require assimilation of immigrants and other minorities in the public arena, but that should allow them to live their cultural individualisms (to a certain extent) in the private sphere. Although this distinction is helpful for understanding the justifications for political regulations of the public sphere and potentially unjustified interventions into individuals' private spheres of life, the spatialized third dimension opens up a different perspective. It provides explicitly spatial insights into the power differential between the dominant discourse (in this case, politics and media) and the social minorities who are the subject of such discourse. Therefore, it offers a unique avenue to look behind the scenes to question and deconstruct how social relations are dominantly conceived and portrayed. It offers a perspective that might otherwise go unobserved.

A popular example will illustrate the gap between narrative and reality. Most historians are, of course, aware that even academic portrayals of historical events are narratives within themselves. The difference between a historical narrative based on a symbolic story line and a historical narrative based on actual historical facts can be considerable. The universally known story of Pocahontas, a Native American woman, and her relationship with John Smith, an English colonizer, provides a fitting example for the gap between historical reality and the story that is presented to us.

We commonly perceive it as a story that makes us happy. In reality, however, Pocahontas stands for two stories: the historical story (that is, what actually happened), and the fictional story told in movies and novels. One story (the fictional one) is uplifting, romantic, and happy; the historical one, although maybe extraordinary, is strangely anticlimatic and complicated, maybe even bleak. Everybody is familiar with the sobering experience of leaving a beautiful movie based on a real story and being confronted with images of the real people and the real stories, apart from Hollywood scenery and makeup.

The beautiful, easy story is that conceived by the observer or by the reader of fiction; this story is generally captured by what we see as the dominant political discourse, of political framing. Lefebvre (1984) has defined this perspective as a conceived space—our imagination of a people, a story, a neighborhood, or a person. It can be so strong that it turns into a self-fabricated reality. This reality is simple and sometimes even beautiful. It is make-believe, a stand-in for reality, but in most cases, it is actually divorced from reality. It glosses over the complexities of real life, which are most often neither black nor white but instead characterized by different shades of gray. In politics, narratives and oversimplifications filled with symbolism are often utilized to convey certain justifications for policies to the public (Edelman 1988; Stone 2002). This very phenomenon—a dominant narrative about something that is imagined, something that should be, could be, or might be true—is captured by conceived space.

The other story, the one based on historical facts, is the story that has been lived. It is a bleaker, more complicated story, one that tends to be overlooked because we like to believe the simpler truth that is dominantly portrayed. A different, lived perspective provides the means to capture a more complicated social reality, one that is often overlooked or ignored.[19] The importance of differentiating between these levels of analysis is captured in the fact that this lived perspective moves beyond the narrative—beyond the dominant discourse. It is, in fact, an attempt to capture reality, the practice on the ground, and not merely the story. It provides a tool to understand that what is conveyed to us but that may not be what actually happened. It stands for what is left of the story after we strip it of the projections of our own dreams and imagination. In reality, beyond the narrative of love, war, and passion, Pocahontas really existed, someone who—naturally—sought to help her people and thus engaged in a dialogue with John Smith. This lived perspective does not take the narrative for granted; it encourages us to question it and to see what is hidden behind it.

For the purposes of understanding integration through the lived reality of Turkish immigrant citizens, the concept of the lived perspective becomes a tool that helps to capture what lies beyond the political spectacle of integration and policy discourse.

This approach has two important benefits: first, it provides an avenue to conceptually capture the binary nature of integration—literally in theory and practice—in Berlin's two immigrant neighborhoods, Kreuzberg and Neukölln. Second, it also provides unique insights into the role that power plays between discourse and reality. As noted earlier, the book eschews the political terminology on integration that would further or underline the political discourse on integration. Instead, the term *integration* in this book applies to the immigrants' lived ways of self-incorporation in the immigrant neighborhood. This redefinition points to the existence of alternative ways of integration outside the policy discourse, which are often overlooked due to the static and one-dimensional nature of the dominant approaches to integration policy.

Space as a Tool, Place as a Venue

The addition of a lived dimension, a perspective beyond the story that is told through the political discourse and spread through the media, serves as a tool for an analytic path that focuses on two Turkish immigrant neighborhoods in Berlin as places of hybrid spatial practice. The immigrant neighborhood represents an empirical unit of analysis. Space is utilized as a concept to understand the reality of the immigrant neighborhood as a place of hybridity and at the same time as a place of home. The comparison of how the immigrant neighborhood is perceived from the outside—or framed—by local policy makers, and how immigrants perceive themselves and their neighborhood highlights the gap between conceived space and lived space.

The immigrants' spatial practice of making a home for themselves in the neighborhood is related to the policy makers' debate on citizenship and identity. It is, however, not dialogical in nature. Theoretical sketches of deliberative practice, such as Benhabib's (2002) Habermasian interpretation of democratic discourse ethics, and the Gadamerian *Horizontverschmelzung* (fusion of horizons) of interlocutors of different backgrounds as they engage in a conversation, all presuppose at least some conscious engagement of both sides in process of deliberation. Immigrants, however, largely remain outside the integration debate and therefore are unable to engage in an equal dialogue with those in power. Spatial practice of hybrid identity in the lived space by immigrants is in reaction to and in spite of dominant narratives. It can be described as a minority's way of intuitive sociospatial incorporation through hybrid social practices. In other words, sociocultural hybridity develops without predetermination; it is, in fact, an intuitive state of mind and practice through which individuals consolidate the familiar traditions of their country of origin, their family, or both with the new traditions of the country of immigration (Plaza 2006). Rather than a conversation, a debate, or a discussion, the practice of hybrid identities in the lived space happens through the establishment of informal social networks and associations within the urban space that accommodate these hybrid identities. The establishment of Little Istanbul in Berlin-Kreuzberg came about through the concentration of people of immigrant background in one neighborhood and their establishment of social institutions, networks, and businesses that could cater to their needs.

De Certeau (1984) describes spatial practices such as walking, talking, and interacting with others; using a certain language; producing and selling food and drink; or simply being visibly present within a space as ways of molding the space itself, by either contesting or asserting previous identity claims to the space. Thus, the sociocultural hybridity of Turkish German neighborhood space in Berlin-Kreuzberg has been established through a multitude of daily life practices.[20] These practices challenge preexisting traditional frames of German ethnonational identity in the city. Urban space and daily life practices within it thus can serve as means of producing and contesting perceptions of mainstream national identity and integration as the immigrants infuse their identity into the neighborhood but also change in the process; the neighborhood leaves an imprint on them as well. The neighborhood—its history and sociocultural fabric—and the immigrants who inhabit it engage in a mutually constitutive process of identity formation. As the research in this book illustrates, immigrants utilize their traditional immigrant neighborhoods to pursue their own avenues of incorporating themselves into the receiving society. Although policy makers ascribe top-down approaches to integration on the basis of certain dominant frames of the national mainstream, immigrants, confronted with social reality, find different routes to integration through the safe space of the neighborhood. Their collective difference from the mainstream becomes visible in the immigrant neighborhood, upsetting the structure of the sociospatial fabric of the city as it is imagined in policy discourse.

2 TALK OF THE TOWN

Space, Visibility, and the Contestation of German Identity

The one who adapts his policy to the times prospers, and likewise the
one whose policy clashes with the demands of our times does not.
—Niccolò Machiavelli (1513)

THIS CHAPTER PRESENTS AN ANALYSIS of the political debate on
integration in Berlin by examining the frames and images employed in the
public dialogue. These frames and images serve as tools to convince the
public of the validity of certain problem definitions and the necessity of certain solutions and strategies for integration. The pattern that emerges from
the analysis reveals how policy makers and Turkish community representatives represent Turkish immigrants in Berlin as new immigrant citizens.
In other words, this analysis of political discourse provides the means for
understanding how those holding political power conceive of and imagine
the integration of Turkish immigrants as citizens on the one hand, and how
these same immigrants are represented by their own community leaders on
the other hand. An examination of the debate on integration in Berlin identifies prominent frames that policy makers use in conceiving and imagining integration and preserving certain properties that they consider to be
part of Germany's mainstream identity.

The policy makers' discourse, in this context, provides the basic information for the media and thus—more so than the media itself—is instrumental
in the creation and shaping of the views of the general public. As Berkowitz
(1994) notes,

> When considering the impact of policymakers on the news agenda, the focus is
> actually on a portion of a larger group called *news sources*, who supply news
> items and story information to journalists. Put most simply, news sources exert a

stronger influence over the news agenda than do journalists. Over and over, stud-ies have found that source-originated stories comprise the majority of a news-paper's or television station's news mix. Further, policymakers have been found to be even more influential than the overall group of news sources. (81)

Thus the lion's share of the raw, newsworthy information for the mass media comes from the policy makers themselves.[1] By dominating the media dis-course on certain issues, policy makers are in a privileged position of influ-ence with regard to the public policy discourse.

Policy discourse is a crucial tool for framing the role and image of immi-grant minorities in the receiving society. Murray Edelman (1988, 15) notes that there is a "diversity of meaning inherent in every social problem, stem-ming from the range of concerns of different groups, each eager to pursue courses of action and call them solutions." In the process of framing social problems, different actors often attach oversimplified symbolic meanings to these problems. With reference to Turkish immigrants in Berlin, this pat-tern is evident in frames that refer to Turks as unintegratable or unwilling to integrate.

On January 25, 2009, the German newspaper *Die Welt*, one of Germany's mainstream national newspapers, reflected on citizenship law and integra-tion policy in an article entitled "Migration: Warum die Türken bei der Integration nicht mitspielen" (Immigration: why the Turks do not cooper-ate when it comes to integration). *Die Welt* argued that the lack of integra-tion of Turkish immigrants in Germany and their isolation in their own ethnic neighborhood enclaves is because immigrants had no interest in settling in Germany in the first place. Furthermore, according to the news-paper, most former guest worker immigrants came to Germany from the Turkish countryside in eastern Anatolia, and their low education level has prevented them from improving their socioeconomic situation. Instead of integrating themselves into German society, Turkish immigrants isolate themselves in immigrant neighborhoods and refuse to interact with the German mainstream. The newspaper concludes that the spatial isolation and socioeconomic disadvantages of Turkish immigrants in Germany are due to the immigrants' own lack of willingness to integrate themselves into German society. This article relies on data from a 2009 study by the Berlin Institut für Bevölkerung und Entwicklung (Berlin Institute for Population and Development) entitled "Ungenutzte Potentiale? Zur Lage der Integra-tion in Deutschland" (Unused potentials? About the state of integration in Germany). By generalizing from the Berlin context to Germany as a whole, the newspaper's basic argument illustrates the negative frames prevalent in the popular media with respect to the Turkish immigrant minority in Berlin. Turks are portrayed as unwilling to adapt to German society, and thus they are held responsible for their own exclusion. The term *integration* itself remains undefined, although the text implies that it is used interchangeably with *assimilation*.

In addition, other symbolic images, such as honor killings and forced marriages, are used to define the Turkish immigrant minority in Berlin. They create a powerful negative frame for this particular group in German society. These events are rare, yet they are standard framing referents of the Turkish community for mainstream ethnic Germans.

Framing and problem definition are critical to agenda setting and policy making in general, but they are specifically important when it comes to the promotion and acceptability of policy prescriptions for dealing with Turkish immigration and integration. Policy scholars describe in detail the process in which certain issues become defined as problems, rise on the political agenda, and have certain solutions attached to them (Kingdon 1995; Baumgartner and Jones 1993). Policy makers and interested parties actively attempt to frame the policy issue in a way that justifies the proposed solutions: "Conditions become defined as problems when we come to believe that we should do something about them. Problems are not simply the conditions or external events themselves; there is also a perceptual, interpretive element" (Kingdon 1995, 109–10). The "perceptual, interpretive element" Kingdon mentions is important to framing an issue in a way that requires policy makers to take certain actions. Similarly, Baumgartner and Jones (1993) argue that social conditions do not always automatically generate public concern and thus justify policy action. Instead, a condition needs to be defined first as a public problem, which is important and at the same time solvable through policy action. Policy entrepreneurs attempt to define problems and promote solutions that run parallel to the desired definition of the problem. Media and public attention to the issue are integral in this process:

> As government officials become active on more issues over the years, media coverage, scientific research, and popular opinion are affected both by the social problem itself and by reports of government activities to solve the problem. . . . public and media attention leads to increased government activities, and these in turn lead to greater public and media attention in the future. (171)

In other words, once the problem has reached a certain level of attention, the process of public attention and government activity on the issue becomes self-perpetuating. According to Baumgartner and Jones, symbols are a key factor in this process, not only in order to promote a certain solution, but also to influence the allocation of attention to the problem.

In reference to urban space specifically, scholars have argued that the institutional public policy discourse and the mass media are central actors in attaching symbolic meaning to physical space and spatialized identity (Gottdiener 1995; Richardson and Jensen 2003):

> Spatial agents "appropriate" space in terms of ascribing cultural and symbolic attributes to their environment whilst their spatial practices are simultaneously enabled or restricted by the very quality of this spatiality. A discursive representation of space prescribes a domain of "meaningful" actions and thus at the end of the day provides a regulatory power mechanism for the selection of appropriate and meaningful utterances and actions. (Richardson and Jensen 2003, 12)

The framing of the public debate is a central process in creating these clear-cut and often black-and-white images through which social reality is narrated to the public. These images, symbols, and narratives establish and position certain issues in such a way that policy makers can attach their own clear-cut solutions to them and thus further their own political agendas (Chong 1993; Brewer 2003). As illustrated in the previous chapters, the issue of immigrant integration has moved to the center of the German political debate since German unification and the changes in German citizenship and immigration law. In the city of Berlin, the integration debate has taken on a strong spatial dimension as a result of the high visibility of immigrants in certain immigrant neighborhoods. Some German policy makers frame the presence of immigrants unwilling to integrate as a problem and propose to reclaim those neighborhoods through a kind of integration that would restore the visibility of German mainstream identity. The definition of integration itself, then, is dependent on the framing of Turkish immigrants in Berlin and explanations of their social status and socioeconomic situation. On the basis of the assumption that immigrants are unwilling to integrate and render German identity invisible in certain neighborhoods of the city, integration is defined as a reversal of this process and a requirement that immigrants become more German. Alternative assumptions, however, might reverse the causal direction: perhaps immigrants are willing to participate in German society but remain excluded from it. Integration in this case is defined as a process of helping immigrants become part of German society by, among other things, encouraging greater acceptance on the part of German society. These different policy frames and assumptions about the meaning of integration place entirely different blame for the situation of Turks in German society. In one scenario, immigrants are assumed to be unwilling to integrate and are therefore blamed for their own exclusion. In the other scenario, the host population is expected to do its part in the integration process by being more welcoming and accepting toward immigrants. Therefore, different approaches warrant different expectations on different segments of German society for remedying the situation.

By setting the political discourse in relationship to immigrants' live worlds (which will be explored in chapter 3) the social power relations between those who frame the political discourse and those who exist beyond it can be teased out: "In these 'dominating' spaces of regulatory and 'ruly' discourse, these mental spaces, are thus representations of power and ideology, of control and surveillance. This *Secondspace,* as I term it, is also the primary space of utopian thought and vision" (Soja 1996, 67).

Baum and Potter (2008) note that while it is generally assumed that the media have an independent effect on public opinion and policy as a result of their heavy reliance on official sources, the mass media often act as a relatively passive conduit of elite views and frames to the public. They suggest that this is especially true when leaders use culturally congruent, cliché-laden frames, such as, in the German case, "Muslims do not like democracy" or "Turkey has a misogynist culture." In addition, Baum and Potter argue that the public in general is at an information disadvantage on most policy issues, which makes them more susceptible to elite and media framing. The media, in its crucial role as a collector, framer, and distributor of information, not only relies on elites as central information sources, but also responds to and perpetuates elite frames: "Despite a widely held belief in the media's mission to inform, they do not consistently act to remedy the informational inequities in the . . . policy marketplace. Rather, they react in ways that tend to exacerbate the prevailing trend" (50).

Rein and Schön (1993) and Chong (1993) argue that opinion leaders (in politics, the media, or the community) attempt to frame the issue in such a way that establishes common frames of reference and restricts alternative interpretations. In this way, the public discourse, which is heavily influenced by elites, has a strong influence in determining how people think about certain issues. This is important because it suggests a dominant position for policy makers—and not the media, as is often assumed—in framing social issues. Brewer (2003) claims that frames are the central organizing elements defining an issue or controversy, and the very essence of that issue. Stone (2002, 138) notes that symbols and narratives are extremely important and effective in political life because "we often make policies based on examples believed to be representative of a larger universe." Citizens, in this line of argument, rely specifically on frames borrowed from the public debate in order to draw specific connections between general and personal values and the issue at hand.[2] Consequently, it is important to look at how integration is framed by policy makers through the dominant discourse because this also affects the general population.

The policy discourse has very real consequences for the perception of Turkish immigrants and their descendants by the (German) majority population. Edelman (1988, 89) notes that enemy construction by political elites is a useful means of framing social reality because blaming "vulnerable groups for the sufferings and guilt people experience in their daily lives is emotionally gratifying and politically popular." This is particularly obvious in policy statements, which often attribute social problems, such as violence in schools or high welfare costs, to immigrants' unwillingness to adapt to democratic norms and their dependence on social welfare.

Thus, elite frames that perpetuate or confirm dominant public perceptions of in-groups and out-groups are particularly attractive to the public. The public acts as an active consumer of frames, picking and choosing the ones that best fit their general conceptions, not necessarily the ones expanding their horizons (Blumler, Katz, and Gurevitch 1974). This is true regarding the public's support of certain policies, as well as their choice of media source, as each individual is driven to reduce the cognitive discomfort that accompanies dealing with information that contradicts your own core beliefs on an issue (Elster 1983).

The prominence of Islam in the integration discourse illustrates the power of policy frames, and the special strength of what Baum and Potter (2008) call culturally congruent frames. Turkish immigrants are often simply defined as Muslims, who do not fit culturally into the Western democratic framework of the German nation-state. For instance, the local debate about the head scarf and the public display of religious symbols has stirred intense debate among German Turks as well as Germans, and the debate is ongoing. This intense focus on Islam is characteristic of the immigration debate of many European countries and, to a certain extent, the United States. In the German state of Berlin, a 2005 local neutrality law prohibits the public display of any (Muslim, Christian, and Jewish) religious symbols for state employees (in public service and law enforcement). However, the law is controversial: some are concerned about the general implications and consequences of the law for other employment sectors, while others think that the law does not go far enough. Inside the religiously divided Turkish immigrant community, some (secular) women feel threatened by Islam and publicly lobby for more restrictions, while other (religious) women feel inhibited in their personal beliefs and religious practice by the neutrality law. The center-right parties in Germany go even further in their condemnation of Islam. Beyond arguing that it is simply incompatible with Western culture, they also address security concerns referring to the threat of Islamic terrorism in Germany through immigrants from Muslim countries.

The prominence of negative frames regarding Islam as the greatest obstacle to successful integration in Berlin evokes little cognitive dissonance and is perpetuated by policy makers and the media. However, it overshadows the fact that immigrants also face exclusion on the basis of their Turkish immigrant identity rather than their religious identity. Although many policy makers directly involved in the integration debate may recognize this issue, their parties appear to remain resistant to a more central problematization of the issue of exclusion based on ethnic difference. This underlines the fact that the integration discourse is still governed by assimilatory principles (Ehrkamp 2006).

In exploring the political debate on integration, this chapter will focus on two specific prominent groups in the discourse. First, it explores the positions of Berlin policy makers involved in the broadest sense with immigration and integration, specifically that of women. Second, this chapter examines the frames of Turkish community representatives, who actively speak for the Turkish community in a continuous dialogue with local policy makers and the public. The focus will be on the roles these two groups play in defining integration and integration policy and the meanings they attach to these terms, as well as their reactions to the concept of visibility, specifically the visibility of difference in Turkish immigrants.

Local policy makers and Turkish community representatives frame the visible spatial presence of Turkish immigrants in Berlin, and with it integration policy prescriptions, in different ways. Through the analysis of personal interviews and official party platforms of policy makers, "different [and sometimes competing] knowledge-framing processes" (Richardson and Jensen 2003, 17) emerge and direct attention to the importance of the political space as a sphere of representation. It is here that the discursive practices and use of symbols by Berlin's policy makers and Turkish community representatives shape the representation of immigrants and their place in urban space.

Women as Symbols for Integration

Sociocultural and ethnic boundaries inside and outside of minority and majority groups tend to be defined by women—their bodies, their social status. This is true in particular for the integration debate in Germany. The guest workers who arrived in Germany starting in the early 1960s are always said to have been almost exclusively men from the villages of eastern Anatolia. Women are generally thought to have joined the men later, primarily as a consequence of family reunification policies. This is not completely true: many of the textile and garment workers attracted by the garment industries in larger cities like Berlin were women. Not only that, but Düspohl (2009) notes that many of the women were not from Anatolian villages in eastern Turkey but came from middle-class families in urban Turkey. They came to Berlin not just for the money, but also for the exciting experience of living abroad. These were educated, westernized women embracing Western fashion and culture. Thus, Düspohl notes, there were actually two very different groups of women immigrants: those who arrived early as guest workers (working mostly in the textile industry), and those who arrived later, not based on employment but on family reunification visas to join their husbands in Germany. The female Turkish immigrant population in Berlin is thus actually socially quite diverse.

Regardless of their immigration stories, women now play a central role in framing integration debate. They are seen as symbolic indicators of immigrants' commensurability with modern gender roles and other premises of modern liberal democracies. Their bodies are particularly important in the context of religious markers, such as head scarves, which have led to vigorous debates in several European countries, among them Germany. Yuval-Davis (2000, 175) argues that women are often perceived as the embodiment of the nation and play an important role in the social reproduction of culture: "Gender relations often come to be seen as constituting the 'essence' of cultures as ways of life to be passed from generation to generation." Women's socioeconomic positions, including education level and career attainment, are also of particular interest when it comes to discussing the integration of Turkish immigrants into German society. This has to do with the generally accepted idea that women in Western society are emancipated, but also with a culturally congruent frame according to which Turkish or "Oriental" culture is highly misogynist.

However, it is not just the public role that Turkish immigrant women play in the integration debate. Their social position within their families is also under scrutiny. In this context, a common argument of policy makers is that the lack of success experienced by Turkish immigrant women in the German labor market is a result of the misogynism of Turkish culture. Lutz, Phoenix, and Yuval-Davis (1999, 11) refer to this frame as the social construction of the primitive Other from which "native German women" as well as "native German culture" and "German modern liberal democratic values" need to be protected. Yuval-Davis (2000) notes that the burden of representation lies with women, not just because of their central position within the nationalist discourse but also as a result of their symbolic role in pro- and antimodernist discourses and the question of emancipation.

The interviews presented in this chapter explore this symbolic role of Turkish immigrant women in the display of visual–cultural difference and the representation of national identity within the framework of integration policy. Women's bodies and the socioeconomic role of women in society often function as indicators for the success of their ethnic minority group in the integration process. The framing of the socioeconomic position of women in the Turkish immigrant community tends to overlook the diversity of Turkish immigrant women as a group. It simply serves a symbolic role in the justification of certain policy agendas on integration (Lutz, Phoenix, and Yuval-Davis 1999; Stone 2002). The depiction of Turkish immigrant women's conceived socioeconomic roles provides as an example of the symbolic identification process of the Turkish immigrant community as a whole. At the same time, it is also a means to justify integration policy in the local policy debate.

Approach

The symbolic role of Turkish immigrant women in the display of national and ethnic identity provides many questions for policy makers and community representatives about the women's specific role in the integration discourse. A number of local policy makers involved in integration policy as well as representatives from the Turkish immigrant community in Berlin were interviewed.

Local Policy Makers and Government Bureaucrats

The local political elites interviewed included members of the Berlin senate, which represents the administrative, governmental capacity of the city-state's elected mayor, among them the senators themselves or heads of the appropriate departments and their staffs. They represent the city's executive leadership. In addition, interviews were conducted with elected representatives of the Berlin parliament who work specifically on issues of integration and women,[3] representing the city's legislative branch. Berlin does not only have an independent municipal city administration but is also its own federal state unit in the federal system (Berlin, Bremen, and Hamburg are all city-states).

All individuals interviewed in the Berlin senate administration were either appointed by the mayor and were members of the parties of the "Red–Red" governing coalition in Berlin, composed of Social Democrats (SPD) and the Socialists (Die Linke, the Left Party). Other informants were administrators who were working and speaking for their superiors inside the governing coalition but who were not necessarily party members themselves. Interviewees came from three different branches of the Berlin senate that are specifically involved with issues of integration and women. Interior and Sports addresses legal issues (Interior) regarding social and political rights and freedoms in circumstances where the states have jurisdiction over the federal government. This includes certain features of visibility of difference in public, such as the head scarf and other religious symbols. Although not the only element, the legal framework around the display of religious and cultural symbols of difference is central in the local integration discourse in Berlin.[4]

Integration, Labor, and Social Issues, on the other hand, frames the integration approach of the Berlin government's governing coalition (Integration). The official integration approach of the Berlin administration is likely one of the most central and powerful elements in framing the integration debate among policy makers and the public. The local government conducts and publishes studies about the state of integration of immigrant minorities, notes which minority groups encounter specific issues in integration (mostly, according to the administration, immigrants of Turkish or Arabic background), and formulates new social strategies for integration.

The fact that a ministry for integration (along with an official integration law) is now part of the Berlin administration is highly symbolic in itself. Baumgartner and Jones (1993) suggest that policy interests try to establish control over framing their issue area and the institutional arrangements that reinforce it. In other words, policy experts try to prevent other interests from entering their issue area and challenging their control over the framing of the problem. The creation of a local government arm in Berlin responsible for integration provides policy makers with such a policy monopoly and gives them the opportunity to exert a certain degree of control over the problem and policy definitions of integration policy. At the time this research was conducted, the representative for this branch of the administration was Doris Nahawandi, an experienced veteran on the issue of integration policy in Berlin and a representative for Günter Piening, the head of the integration subsection.

Economy, Technology, and Women addresses the specific social issues of women in Berlin and formulates policies designed to improve the overall situation of women in the city (Women). This also includes women of immigrant background. Because of the central role of immigrant women in the integration debate in general (specifically in reference to the head scarf question) and the specific focus of this study on Turkish immigrant women, it is necessary to include this aspect of Berlin politics. Moreover, Turkish immigrant women in the political discourse are often collectively subsumed under the category Muslim. The German immigration debate primarily focuses on Muslims and the role of Islam in German society. Therefore, the legal debate on the head scarf as well as women's roles in Turkish immigrant families and communities are often hot-button issues in the integration debate. From this branch of the administration, the state secretary for Economy, Technology, and Women, Almuth Nehring-Venus, was interviewed.

The speakers for integration policy in the Berlin parliament represent the city's legislature. Among them, the governing coalition made up of the SPD and the Left Party is represented, as well as the opposition parties that have been voted into the Berlin parliament: the Green Party, the Christian Democrats (CDU), and the Libertarians. The speakers for integration policy in the parliament represent their parties' platforms on integration policy and are integral to revising and improving them. They all try to keep in personal contact with local communities and make connections with immigrant associations to demonstrate their local involvement on the ground. In order to capture the whole political spectrum of Berlin's multiparty system, the speakers for integration policy of all parties represented in the Berlin parliament were interviewed.[5]

The last set of officials interviewed were the representatives for integration matters at the district level from the two districts with the highest percentage of immigrants (approximately 25 percent): Kreuzberg and Neukölln. Berlin's city government itself is highly federal in nature. All city government structures are recreated at the level of the city's twelve districts. Thus, Günter Piening's two equivalents at the district level in the two most prominent Turkish immigrant districts, Kreuzberg and Neukölln, were interviewed. Both are career civil servants and not elected party members. However, they implement the integration policies of their district's governing party—the SPD in Neukölln and the Green Party in Kreuzberg-Friedrichshain. The Greens and the SPD make a serious attempt to appeal to local immigrant populations in the districts by putting up candidates of immigrant background at the local level.[6] This is reflected in the immigrant background of their speakers for integration policy.

Berlin's districts have an additional level of political involvement: local citizen councils, the *Bezirksverordnetenversammlung,* or BVV (district representative convention). Local citizens (anyone eligible to vote is also eligible to run) can run for these district-level councils. In those districts with larger immigrant populations, many of the left-wing parties' BVV representatives are of immigrant background. However, these citizen councils have no decision-making power in terms of policy making,[7] which is mostly determined by the district mayors, and the Berlin parliament, the *Abgeordnetenhaus.* Therefore, the BVV has not been included in my analysis.

The selection of interviewees in the Berlin administration, parliament, and districts was strictly limited to individuals involved in the framing and formulation of integration policy who play an active role in shaping the city's integration debate. The individuals interviewed here are central figures within the integration discourse on Turkish immigrants, and specifically women.

Turkish Community Representatives

The lines blur somewhat between local policy makers and career civil servants as well as between Turkish community representatives and other individuals of immigrant background. A considerable number of policy makers representing the left-of-center parties (the SPD and the Greens, with the exception of Die Linke[8]) in the area of integration policy matters in Berlin are themselves of immigrant background and thus have personal experiences with integration. A young, well-educated group of second-generation immigrants, who were either born in Germany or who moved there as small children, have become involved in local integration policy in Berlin. Among these policy makers and government bureaucrats involved in the policy discourse on integration are Doris Nahawandi, who has a German mother and an Iranian father. Bilkay Öney, speaker for integration policy for the Green Party in the Berlin parliament, was born in Turkey and came to Germany at the age of three. Raed Saleh, speaker for integration policy for the SPD in the Berlin parliament, was born in Jordan and moved to Germany with his family as a small child. In the fall of 2008, Eren Ünsal, speaker for the Turkish Union Berlin-Brandenburg (TBB), assumed the position of officer for equality matters for the state of Berlin. This is remarkable because it represents a merger between the Turkish community and local government, and it illustrates the close cooperation between the political arm of the Turkish immigrant community in Berlin—the TBB—and the local government. Furthermore, it demonstrates the intention of the left-of-center parties (again, with the exception of Die Linke) to want to appeal to the immigrant electorate. The local SPD and Berlin's Green Party see themselves as champions of immigrant rights and compete for the immigrant vote. However, the controversy around Sarrazin, who is also an SPD member, and his anti-immigrant book, demonstrate that political alliances with the Turkish immigrant community are more complicated than a simple for or against. Young, second-generation immigrant representatives, such as Öney, Saleh, Nahawandi, and Ünsal, wrestle with the duality of their positions: they represent the Turkish immigrant community on the one hand, and their party's political platform on the other.

All Turkish community representatives are speakers for the TBB and are central public figures in Berlin's political scene. Traditionally, they are secular, well-educated young professionals, working in different occupations in the public and private sectors and additionally functioning as representatives of the Turkish community in Berlin's policy debates. However, over time, the TBB's representatives have changed from being strictly secular to being more open to religious matters as the TBB's leadership has evolved. The older generation of representatives, which arrived around the same time as the first generation of guest workers, was not composed of guest workers, but rather of well-educated urban elites, who came to Berlin to get a Western education or foreign work experience. The younger generation of TBB representatives is composed of the children of former guest workers; they have received university educations in Germany and have thus experienced tremendous social upward mobility. They tend to be the first generation in their family to receive a formal education; many guest workers' family origins are not urban but instead are largely rural Turkish. Their outlook on religion and tradition is therefore strongly shaped by their family history. Although the TBB is certainly not the only Turkish community organization, it is by far the largest and most politically involved one in Berlin. Of all the Turkish community organizations, the TBB has the best access to the political debate and to individual policy makers, because Berlin's policy makers rely mainly on the TBB as a representative for Turkish immigrants in Berlin.

It is important to note, however, that Turkish community representatives have a much lower level of influence on the public debate than policy

Figure 4. Interviewees from the Berlin executive, legislative, and the Turkish Union Berlin-Brandenburg*

Position	Institutional/ Party Affiliation	Legislative/ Executive	Name
State Secretary, Senate Administration for Economy, Technology, and Women	Left Party	Executive	Almuth Nehring-Venus
Representative for Integration Matters for the Senate Administration for Integration, Labor, and Social Issues	SPD	Executive	Doris Nahawandi
Senator for the Senate Administration for the Interior and Sport	SPD	Executive	Ehrhart Körting
Speaker for Integration Policy	SPD	Legislative	Raed Saleh
Speaker for Integration Policy	Left Party	Legislative	Udo Wolf
Speaker for Integration Policy	Green Party	Legislative	Bilkay Öney†
Speaker for Integration Policy	CDU	Legislative	Kurt Wansner
Speaker for Integration Policy	Libertarians	Legislative	Rainer-Michael Lehmann‡
Integration Officer for the District of Neukölln	NA	Bureaucracy	Arnold Mengelkoch
Integration Officer for the District of (Friedrichshain-) Kreuzberg	NA	Bureaucracy	Regina Reinke
Head	TBB	NA	Kenan Kolat
Speaker	TBB	NA	Berrin Alpbek
Speaker	TBB	NA	Safter Çınar
Speaker	TBB	NA	Eren Ünsal

SPD, Social Democratic Party; CDU, Christian Democratic Party; NA, not applicable; TBB, Turkish Union Berlin-Brandenburg.

* This table reflects the offices and positions as they were staffed during the time of my interviews in 2009. Current staffing of Berlin's administration is available online (www.berlin.de/politik-und -verwaltung/senatsverwaltungen/, as is the current staffing of the Berlin parliament, the Abgeord-netenhaus (www.parlament-berlin.de/pari/web/wdefault.nsf/vHTML/A00?OpenDocument).

† Öney left the Green Party in 2009 and since became a member of the Berlin SPD. She has not yet been replaced. Her departure from the Green Party was an unexpected move after the SPD's Canan Bayram, like Öney of Turkish immigrant background, switched to the Green Party and thus shifted the parliamentarian majorities of both parties. Öney reacted by switching the other way, thus keeping the parliamentarian majorities between both parties the same.

‡ Lehmann left the Libertarians in March 2010 and joined the SPD, citing the "social coldness" of his party as his main motivation. He was replaced by Mieke Senftleben.

makers themselves on the national and local debates on integration in Germany. Although they advise the SPD-controlled local government in Berlin as a result of their ideological proximity to the SPD,[9] the TBB remains a niche institution that can exert only advisory influence on policy matters.

By including the framing of integration policy by Turkish community representatives from this organization, the book explores the question of how the leaders of the most prominent group representing German Turks perceive Turkish immigrants in Berlin as a group, and in how far the organization's political stances on integration are in line with the city's political left, especially the SPD, which tends to form political coalitions with the TBB on integration issues.

What Does It Take to Be German?

Integration, Identity, Visibility

Integration Policy Platforms

Berlin's major political parties and individual policy makers support a variety of official frames for integration policy that affect the formulation of the government's actual policies. They provide different definitions of integration policy and achieved integration. They also have different ideas about what the parties perceive to be the specific social challenges that integration policy approaches should target. These variations occur in spite of the fact that the SPD members in Berlin's government coalition have published an official integration concept for the city:

> "Encouraging diversity—strengthening cohesion"—the guiding theme of the integration policy of Berlin reflects both faces of a modern integration policy: on one hand, the chances arising from the cultural diversity should be recognized and utilized; on the other hand, the objectives for more equal opportunities in the main living spheres should not be neglected. If diversity exists without equal opportunities, social segregation would just be worsened; and if equal opportunity comes without consideration for the cultural diversity, the culturally dissimilar one will then be excluded. (Integration concept of the Berlin government, 2007–11)

The above statement is the introductory paragraph of the Berlin city government's integration concept "Encouraging Diversity—Strengthening Cohesion." It is also an excellent example of what Baumgartner and Jones (1993) have defined as the government's attempt of creating a policy monopoly in framing a specific policy problem. In providing a definition of integration, the local government frames integration in a way that conforms to their preferred policy approach for dealing with immigration and integration.

Although the Berlin government acknowledges the importance of supporting cultural diversity, it also seems to imply that cultural diversity may have negative effects on equal opportunity. The specific integration indicators used in most political approaches to and measurements of integration cluster around general points, such as immigrants' socioeconomic attainment, educational attainment, command of the German language, and interaction with Germans. Most of these factors are listed as important components of integration policy by local policy makers.

For most of Berlin's political parties, better integration into the labor market and an improvement of the education system to provide immigrant children with better education opportunities are central defining tenets of their integration policy. These points are listed in the different party programs as ways to ensure the alleviation of social problems, especially in districts with high numbers of individuals of immigrant background. Furthermore, the Green and Left parties emphasize the importance of immigrants' participation in the democratic process through communal voting rights for non-E.U. resident aliens and an easier naturalization process. In terms of agency, the three parties on the left side of the political spectrum—the SPD, the Left Party, and the Green Party—perceive integration to be a mutual and interactive responsibility between immigrants on one hand and policy makers and the majority population on the other. Their policy platforms frame integration as something that requires openness, concessions, and mutual understanding on both sides. Conversely, the CDU frames integration policy as a control mechanism that defines immigration policy, and upholds the basic democratic order by assimilating immigrants to it and thereby limiting isolation and the threat of terrorism.

Furthermore, both the SPD and the Green Party emphasize the neighborhood as an important unit of policy making and advocate the decentralization of integration policies from the federal and city levels to the district or neighborhood levels. Conversely, the CDU lobbies for further centralization of integration policy by creating an integration office at the district level. This suggests quite different perspectives for the center right and the center left with regard to the appropriate geographic and political level for dealing with integration policy should be located.

There are clear differences in the basic framing of integration policy between the center-right and the center-left parties. The wording of the CDU's integration policy is replete with strong references to integration as a control mechanism. The areas of control concern legal and illegal immigration, the practice and teaching of Islam, and the naturalization of immigrants living in Germany legally. On the other hand, the integration policy platforms of the center-left parties frame integration as an expansion of rights for immigrants. These contrasting ways of portraying integration policy and defining its primary purpose demonstrate the fundamentally different concepts that political parties can have of integration. The Green Party is the only party that explicitly addresses the role of immigrant women, which is framed as dually problematic. Immigrant women are portrayed as victims of discrimination by the majority population on the labor market as well as a marginalized group in their own communities as a result of domestic violence and forced marriages. Therefore, the Green Party presents Turkish immigrants as a group that should be specifically addressed and protected by integration policy approaches. This is remarkable because it indicates that the party uses two different frames. The portrayal of Turkish women as the victims of domestic violence and forced marriages within the Turkish immigrant community is a commonly used frame in German politics in connection with Turkish immigrants. It portrays their group as poorly integrated and unwilling to adapt to Western democratic and family values. In contrast, the framing of Turkish immigrant women as victims of discrimination in the labor market attributes some of the blame for the marginalized position of Turkish immigrant women in German society to discrimination by the German majority.

Figure 5 illustrates the subtle but significant differences in the official integration platforms of the individual parties in Berlin. Furthermore, it sheds light on the fact that the parties differentially emphasize integration as a political goal. Although the Left Party and the Libertarians have little to no detailed information on their definitions and goals of integration policy, the Green Party, the SPD, and the CDU make integration a central point of their policy platforms. According to these general local party platforms on integration, the dominant integration discourse is attached to general tenets of integration, or integration indicators. Among parties, perceptions of integration policy differ with regard to its overall political importance, the political approach, and who is responsible for making successful integration a reality.

The parties also have different political motivations for emphasizing or deemphasizing integration. The SPD, on the basis of the party's role as the sponsor for integration policy in Berlin and as the major political affiliation of the Turkish immigrant community, has made integration one of the central tenets of their political platform. The CDU, in trying to appeal to a conservative constituency generally critical of immigration, takes a restrictive

Figure 5. Party platforms on integration in Berlin

Party	Challenge	Integration Approach
Social Democratic Party (SPD)*	Provide equal opportunity for immigrants to employ their qualifications and stand on their own feet financially	**Education:** Focus on education and vocational training **Urban Cohesion:** Neighborhood management: support for socially disadvantaged districts **Better Service:** Integrate immigrants in local welfare and support systems **Strengthen Civil Society and Participation:** Combat discrimination against immigrants and domestic violence against immigrant women; support immigrant civic engagement **Integrate Refugees:** Grant autonomy to long-term refugees and asylum seekers **Integration Policy:** Implement a concrete integration strategy with "verifiable criteria for integration achievements"; replace identifier "immigrant nationality" with "immigrant background"
Left Party†	Persisting disadvantages for migrants in realms of education, professional training, labor market	**Reform Citizenship Policy:** Implement an active and easy naturalization policy (and dual citizenship) **Expand Voting Rights:** Expand communal voting rights for long-term residents to ensure democratic participation rights for immigrants
Green Party‡	Counteract discrimination, especially for immigrant women, on the labor market	**Priority:** Make integration policy a central topic of the Berlin administration **Decentralize:** Decentralize integration by moving policy and administration from one central office to neighborhood offices **Affirmative Action:** Ensure representation of immigrant minorities within the Berlin administration by giving preference to applicants with immigrant background **Equality:** Guarantee constitutional rights and participation to immigrants **Education:** Reform and individualize education to improve the educational background of children of immigrant background **Opportunity:** Reduce discrimination in the labor market, especially against women of immigrant background **Minority Rights:** Make efforts to protect constitutional rights of immigrants, especially women, whose cultural communities do not recognize these rights

Christian Democratic Party (CDU)§	Rising numbers of immigrants, poor integration of third- and fourth-generation guest workers Low standard of living of immigrants, low education level, high crime rates Local concentration of migrants, "disintegration," Islamic terrorism, formation of parallel societies and radical Islamic groups	**Citizenship:** Ease naturalization for long-term residents, introduce communal voting rights for non-E.U. resident aliens **Legal Residency:** Ease the path to permanent residency for asylum seekers and refugees **Specialized Labor Immigration:** Integration into the labor market through better education of immigrants and limiting immigration to Germany to well-qualified and well-educated immigrants **Control Religious Leaders:** Limit the admission of imams to the ones educated at German universities instead of accepting imams certified abroad **Coordinate and Control Immigration:** Coordinate immigration and by introducing an immigration law that welcomes qualified immigrants **Stricter Enforcement:** More strictly enforce immigration law for those whose visas have expired; financial support for immigrants who voluntarily return to their country or origin **Civic Education:** Control naturalization by implementing citizenship tests and thus a basic understanding of and identification with the German democratic order **Islamic Fundamentalism:** Zero tolerance for Islamic extremism by deporting suspects **Political Centralization:** Further centralize integration by incorporating the integration office into the mayoral office
Libertarians (FDP)¶	No official platform on integration	**Language Skills:** Markus Löning, head of the Berlin Libertarians, "highlighted learning the German language as the main building block for [successful] integration" **Dialogue:** Markus Löning also emphasized the importance of a dialogue between German and Turkish Berliners about "religious and social conflicts"

* The Turkish Union Berlin-Brandenburg states in its activity report for the time period from March 3, 2007, through May 24, 2009, that it is generally in support of Berlin's "Red–Red" coalition's integration policy (TBB Berlin, 2007–9, www.tbb-berlin.de/downloads_tbb/Vorstandsbericht_2007-2009_deutsch+tuerkisch.pdf). The TBB has been an integral part of developing the current local administration's integration concept. Data for the SPD are from "Encouraging Diversity—Strengthening Cohesion," Berlin's concept for integration; available at the website of Berlin's office for integration matters (www.berlin.de/lb/intmig/publikationen/index.en.html).

† Data from a press statement by Dr. Hakki Keskin commenting on integration policy for *Die Linke* (www.die-linke-berlin.de/nc/politik/presse/detail/artikel/integration-verlangt-taten-statt-worte/)

‡ Green Party platform for the 2006 communal elections (Program grün 2006, gruene-berlin.de/site/fileadmin/dateien/2006/Wahlprogramm_2006.pdf).

§ Christian Democratic Party program for the 2006 communal elections in Berlin: Berlin kann mehr (2006) (www.cduberlin.de/image/daten/Diskussionspapier_Wahlprogramm.pdf).

¶ Data from FDP Berlin Press Release (2008).

stance on integration policy, with an emphasis on control. The Green Party, with its rather left-wing activist constituency, has created an integration agenda that is similar to the SPD in its local approach but that has a specific focus on women's rights. The Libertarians and the Socialists lack any special emphasis on integration in their party platforms. This indicates that their target electorate does not have significant stakes in the integration debate.

Party platforms represent general positions of the party base and leadership on certain issues. However, individual policy makers who deal with the issue of integration on a daily basis have individual firsthand experiences with integration that are often different from what is written on paper. Exploring their personal statements provides an avenue to understand the dynamics of integration policy on a deeper level—and to see how firsthand experiences may affect policy makers' definitions of integration.

The policy platforms also reflect diverging opinions regarding the centralization or further localization of integration policy. Decentralized approaches to integration allow policy makers and bureaucrats to design a more individualized approach to integration that is in line with the conditions of immigrants in specific localities. More centralized approaches, on the other hand, provide more central political control but are necessarily less targeted at the specificities of individual localities.

Excursus: Integration Policy and the Neighborhood

On the basis of the official party platforms on integration, parties do in fact differ in the level of implementation they envision for their policies. As noted earlier, the parties on the left of the political spectrum tend to see integration as a hands-on local issue that should be addressed at the district and community levels, whereas the center-right CDU is in favor of a centralized approach to integration policy at the city and state levels. These different conceptions of the appropriate level of centralization of integration policy partly reveal the parties' underlying goals of integration policy. Immigrants tend to have strong emotional and family roots in the neighborhood. A localized approach to integration, as suggested by the SPD and the Greens, demonstrates personal engagement and concern with immigrants and an emphasis on catering to their personal needs. A more centralized approach provides more control over issues such as religious fundamentalism and terrorism, and illegality—major concerns for the CDU and its supporters. The approach of exerting centralized control over immigrants by means of an integration policy also demonstrates that conservative policy

makers imagine national identity as an ideal type of homogeneous mainstream identity that requires protection through central political organs.
Deviations from the norm of this idealized national identity usually focus
on individual neighborhoods. Kurt Wansner, the speaker for integration
policy of the CDU, perceives the neighborhood of Kreuzberg specifically
as an example of a problem area when it comes to integration:

> I once demanded—that's now about ten years ago—that Germany has to remain
> visible in Kreuzberg. Germanywide this led to an outcry, and they all said—"if
> Wansner says something like that he has to be a right-wing radical." But this
> debate is crazy! This policeman once said that no German life takes place in
> Kreuzberg anymore. And that guy was almost strangled by the Social Democrats
> and the Greens . . . but I think he is totally right, there is really no German life
> left in Kreuzberg—you don't even have to know any German anymore. So when
> I cross the street right here and go over to Mercedes, everything there is in Turk-
> ish. The price lists are in Turkish, they even have a Turkish salesman, and they
> even have a Turkish head mechanic. And when you go shopping on Görlitzer
> Strasse, you won't be able to see any German stores anyway. Well, when I look at
> Oranienstrasse—the German stores there have been gone for years—that envi-
> ronment is hostile to integration![10]

Wansner ties the challenges to German ethnonational identity to the visibility and cultural presence of Turkish immigrants on the local level. In his
view, the strong presence of people of Turkish immigrant background in
Kreuzberg leads to the necessary conclusion that "no German life is left
in Kreuzberg." He perceives a direct spatiovisual challenge to his conception of German ethnonational identity in Berlin, especially in Kreuzberg.
The fact that stores and even traditionally German businesses like Mercedes
have no German signage and no German employees is, in Wansner's view,
a consequence of the concentration of people of Turkish immigrant background in the neighborhood. In other words, the visible concentration of
Turkish immigrants in the neighborhood challenges his ideal-type German
national identity.

Individual Stances on Integration

In practice or in individual opinions, integration can be interpreted in a
myriad of different ways. Individual definitions of integration policy may
be more volatile than the rather rigorous general definitions of integration
within official party platforms. However, they may also be more flexible and
informed as a result of policy makers' more direct confrontations with social
reality.

This section explores the individual frames of policy makers on integration as opposed to their parties' platforms on paper. Although the party platforms on integration emphasize certain aspects and indicators over others, individual policy makers may have individualized and more nuanced conceptions of the meaning of integration. This section examines in more detail the actual interview statements by policy makers on the topic. Figure 6 provides a sample of representative statements on integration from the individual interviews.

Some larger themes in the definitions of integration by policy makers and Turkish community representatives stand out: linguistic integration (learning the language of the receiving country to able to communicate), equal opportunity in terms of education and access to the labor market, and equal access to democratic participation in local and national politics. These themes reflect some of the integration indicators introduced in chapter 1.

However, the individual interview statements provide deeper insights on how these themes are also connected to the challenges that Turkish immigrants face in the integration process. Important additional factors of the integration process emerged in the individual conversations with policy makers and Turkish community representatives. These factors are rarely part of the public debate, but are at the same time are strong contingency criteria for successful integration. They include socioeconomic integration (in terms of equal access to education and the labor market) as well as democratic participation, which is often dependent on factors that find little to no mention in party platforms on integration, such as the visibility of religious and/or ethnic difference in immigrants. Policy makers involved in integration policy tend to be aware of these factors. The statements of policy makers and community representatives below shed light on important aspects of the integration debate that are easily overlooked. These aspects provide crucial insights into the inherent difficulties of the integration process in Berlin and Germany.

Achieving Integration: Difference as Self-Fulfilling Prophecy?

Policy makers, such as Raed Saleh and Doris Nahawandi, note that socioeonomic advancement in education and professional attainment, which are generally framed as central indicators for achieved integration, are in themselves highly problematic. The main concern of these policy makers, therefore, is not with socioeconomic integration indicators, but rather with the acceptance of difference. They note that the so-called markers of difference—a different name, a different skin color, a foreign accent—could be the actual obstacle to social upward mobility for immigrants, even if they are educated and highly motivated to succeed. For them, integration indicators that measure socioeconomic achievements alone are missing the point. Instead, they argue that the focus should be on whether the majority population is appropriately tolerant of the markers of difference to allow for true equality of opportunity for immigrants, and not on whether the immigrants can assimilate according to the majority population. As Raed Saleh (SPD), speaker for integration policy, says,

> You probably heard this about a hundred times already but you cannot compare integration with assimilation—assimilation is the shedding of your own culture, and I disagree with that. Integration must be the participation in society along with retaining some factors that simply have to be different, such as religion, such as culture, such as skin color. Those are just some differences that come along with the whole package, and those differences cannot be eliminated. You don't need this kind of homogenization [in order for integration to work].

Saleh's colleague, Doris Nahawandi (SPD), speaker for Berlin's representative for integration matters, adds that it is often precisely these cultural and religious differences—and Islam in particular—that make it difficult for immigrants to reach complete equality in German society.

> There are strong inner-party conflicts [on the meaning of integration] where the more tolerant voices are unable to gain any ground. There is strong prejudice against Islam, no matter in which party—among the conservatives as well as within the left.

Nahawandi's statement provides a glimpse into the conflicts on integration policy that take place within the various political parties despite their seemingly firm and coherent party platforms and political goals for integration. Conflict from within arises especially on polarizing topics such as how to treat markers of difference in the integration process. Nahawandi ties the local debate on immigrant integration in Berlin closely to the central role of Islam as a marker of cultural and religious difference and a lack of integration.

The statements by former German president Christian Wulff and German chancellor Angela Merkel on Islam, multiculturalism, and integration illustrate that Islam in particular presents an extremely polarizing topic in the national-level debate on German identity. Another local policy maker who asked to remain anonymous noted in an interview that markers of ethnocultural difference in general, and Islam in particular, are highly polarizing political issues that policy makers are afraid to touch. Instead of taking

Figure 6. Definitions of integration by local policy makers and Turkish community representatives in Berlin

Representative	Name (Institutional or Party Affiliation)	Office	Integration Definition
Representatives from Berlin Senate Administrations	Almuth Nehring-Venus (Left Party)	State Secretary, Senate Administration for Women, Labor, and Technology	Integration should not be measured based on religious or cultural symbolism
	Doris Nahawandi (SPD)	Representative for the Officer for Integration Matters, SPD, for the Senate Administration, for Integration, Labor, and Social Issues	Contested definition of integration, strong inner-party conflicts on the topic
	Ehrhart Körting (SPD)	Senator for the Interior	Ability to integrate into receiving society; ability to communicate
Berlin Parliament, Speakers for Integration Policy	Raed Saleh (SPD)	Speaker for integration policy	Integration is not assimilation. It should be defined as ensuring participation in receiving society while being able to retain some differences, such as religion, culture, skin color
	Udo Wolf (Left Party)	Speaker for integration policy	Equal rights, equal opportunity apart from heritage, social background, religious and cultural preferences.
	Bilkay Öney (Green Party)*	Speaker for integration policy	Equal opportunity
	Kurt Wansner (CDU)	Speaker for integration policy	Coexistence with Germans in the city instead of "the Turks just being among each other and integration not working"
	Rainer-Michael Lehmann (FDP)†	Speaker for integration policy	Linguistic integration, equal opportunity

Integration Officers at the District Levels	Arnold Mengelkoch (District of Neukölln)	Integration officer	Higher levels of intercultural competence of job center employees, teachers, and city administrators
	Regina Reinke (District of (Friedrichshain-) Kreuzberg)	Integration officer	Equal social upward mobility for immigrants in spite of their heritage and identity; the ability of immigrants to retain their own culture
TBB	Kenan Kolat (TBB, Turkish Community in Germany	Head of the TBB and the Turkish Community in Germany	Democratic participation and representation, linguistic integration, acceptance
	Berrin Alpbek (TBB)	Speaker	Opportunity for participation
	Safter Çınar (TBB)	Speaker	Feeling of acceptance and integration vis-à-vis the majority population
	Eren Ünsal (TBB)	Speaker	Move away from thinking in categories, specifically when it comes to women; ensure participation, encourage women to get involved and get an education

SPD, Social Democratic Party; FDP, Libertarian Party; CDU, Christian Democratic Party; TBB, Turkish Union Berlin-Brandenburg.

* Öney left the Green Party in 2009 and since became a member of the Berlin SPD. She has not yet been replaced. Her departure from the Green Party was an unexpected move after the SPD's Canan Bayram, like Öney of Turkish immigrant background, switched to the Green Party and thus shifted the parliamentarian majorities of both parties. Öney reacted by switching the other way, thus keeping the parliamentarian majorities between both parties the same.

† Lehmann left the Libertarians in March 2010 and joined the SPD, citing the "social coldness" of his party as his main motivation. He was replaced by Mieke Senftleben.

the initiative and publicly problematizing the challenges that immigrants face in the integration process, policy makers are primarily intent on appealing to their party's voters, the source said.

This sentiment aligns with Baum and Potter's (2008) argument that culturally congruent frames, such as Islam's supposed incompatibility with German democratic values, are extremely difficult to challenge. Thus, the media as well as policy makers are highly reluctant to take a nonconformist stance on these issues and possibly end up on the wrong side of majority opinion. Therefore, the policy debate rarely confronts what appear to be the key issues of the integration process. Instead, policy makers tend to pander to the public and perpetuate negative feelings among the public about immigrants for political reasons. The immigrants' ethnocultural markers of difference continue to validate the irreconcilability between host and immigrant cultures for the general public.

The visibility of ethnocultural difference is not mentioned in any party platform on integration. Yet on the basis of my interviews, it is a central aspect of Berlin's integration debate. It is also likely to be the key factor in determining whether immigrants can achieve successful integration according to the main tenets of the national mainstream: socioeconomic attainment and participation. Visibility of difference serves as a primary reminder of the presence of an Other. The interview quotes of Berlin policy makers make evident that conflicts about integration are often closely tied to the immigrants' cultural–visual representations of difference. The visibility of immigrant minorities on the basis of phenotypical traits and cultural and/or religious practice presents one of the main challenges to traditional conceptions of German ethnonational identity, which still rest on assumptions of its ethnocultural homogeneity (Faist 1994).

In contrast to party platforms, the visibility of religious and cultural differences is of high relevance in the public policy makers' integration discourse, especially with regard to Turkish immigrants, who are often perceived and portrayed as coming from different cultural traditions than immigrants from within the European Union or the rest of the Western world. Most center-left parties, according to their official political platforms on integration, support policies that grant immigrants the space to keep practicing their own religion and culture. However, representatives from the Turkish immigrant community find that despite these official platforms, little is done to help immigrant women, who are in particularly vulnerable positions when it comes to religious symbolism and integration. In fact, Eren Ünsal, speaker of the TBB, contends that policy makers on both sides of the political spectrum often perpetuate discrimination and point to religious symbolism as an example of the lack of ability to integrate on the part of Turkish women. Left-wing policy makers tend to do so often in spite of their parties' official platform, as noted by Eren Ünsal, speaker for the TBB:

> The visibility of certain markers [of difference]—skin color, gender, the headscarf—increases direct discrimination. In this context, it is not surprising that these markers are adopted in the political discourse as well. Especially in a country that is still strongly influenced by Christianity.

Ünsal notes that visible markers of difference play an important role for the lack of acceptance of certain immigrants as part of the mainstream. She emphasizes the particular difficulties that immigrant women encounter. These markers of difference are highly relevant in the political discourse—not just in terms of ethnonational difference, but also culturally, despite the fact that secularization is taking a stronger hold in Europe. Only 47 percent of Germans believe in a god (Eurobarometer 2005), but Christian cultural traditions nevertheless are perceived to be a defining cultural trait of German society because Christianity in the second half of the twentieth century has remained the most dominant religion in the country. It appears that many Germans perceive Christian cultural values and traditions as divorced from actual religious practice, and apply this same reasoning with regard to Turkish immigrants, whether they practice Islam or not.

Similarly, Jürgen Habermas (1995) has suggested that the liberal state is blind to individual differences or culturally neutral, as long as these cultural practices do not impinge on the basic democratic values of the liberal nation-state. However, while many nation-states conceive of themselves as neutral with regard to religious culture, or as even secular, this category hardly exists in reality. According to Andrew Davison (1998), even explicitly secular societies are often strongly shaped and deeply affected by religious traditions. The introduction of new religious practices or cultural traditions via the influx of immigrants can evoke rejection of these practices even in liberal nation-states, which have previously defined themselves as secular. Faced with high numbers of immigrants from Muslim countries, many nonreligious Germans tend to react by emphasizing their Christian roots, which seemed irrelevant before. As a consequence, immigrants with highly visible and different cultural and religious traditions are often subject to exclusion.

Germany's history of denying the fact—until the ascension of the SPD–Green Party coalition in 1998—that Germany was a receiving country of immigration has delayed the debate about symbols of religious and cultural difference, according to Nawahandi:

> We have long moved away from a homogeneous society. Because we have not realized that, we have this big debate now [about religious symbols and the head scarf].

This denial occurred in the presence of approximately one million Turkish guest workers who had arrived in Germany by the early 1980s (Kappert, Haerkötter, and Böer 2002) and remained in the country permanently. Almuth Nehring-Venus of the Left Party, the state secretary for the Berlin senate administration for Economy, Technology, and Women, identifies the immigrants' visibility as an Other in the city as a central issue in the debate about religious and cultural difference in Berlin. She notes that if society cannot accept the existence of visible cultural–religious difference, those who are in fact visibly different might become completely excluded from the mainstream population, and integration will have failed permanently because the immigrants' opportunities for social upward mobility will be permanently blocked:

> Of course the head scarf debate concerns women primarily, women become particularly visible and have to tolerate questions and are "partly not normal."
>
> ...
>
> The central question is as follows: How does our society treat people with a different religious, traditional or cultural background? If you just start prohibiting things, families with a different cultural and traditional background will find other ways [to practice this difference]—they become [socioeconomically] invisible.

To counteract alleged discrimination based on religious symbolism and cultural practice, the Berlin Senate Office for Integration, Labor, and Social Matters and the State Office for Equal Treatment published a brochure in 2008 that informs immigrant women with head scarves about their legal rights and encourages them to report cases of discrimination (Figure 7). This brochure was rejected by prominent sociopolitical activists in the Turkish immigrant community, most notably Seyran Ateş and Serap Çileli, who argue, "The pamphlet is much too one-sided and does not say one word about the fact that Muslim women who do not wear a head scarf are being discriminated against by those women who do wear a head scarf" (Ateş in *Der Tagesspiegel* 2008b). The two women claimed that the Berlin senator for Integration, Labor, and Social Issues, Dr. Heidi Knake-Werner, was betraying "secular Muslim women" (Ateş in *Der Tagesspiegel* 2008b) in this brochure. Çileli argues in the German magazine *Focus* (2008a, 16) that

Mit Kopftuch außen vor?

Schriften der Landesstelle
für Gleichbehandlung –
gegen Diskriminierung

2

Figure 7. Cover of the informational brochure Excluded with Head Scarf?*, Berlin Office for Integration and the Berlin Office for Equal Treatment, 2008. Published by Landespressestelle Berlin.*

there are people in the Islamic world who think that the head scarf is irreconcilable with modern times. She also notes that women in modern societies do not have to cover up in order to prevent sexual harassment. She further says that the brochure could be interpreted as "a bow to [Islamic] fundamentalists" by the Berlin government.

Çileli's and Ateş's statements illustrate that the conflict over religious symbols and cultural practice does not just take place between the German majority population in Berlin and the Turkish immigrant population. Rather, it demonstrates that an ongoing debate about religious symbolism also exists inside the Turkish immigrant community. This also has consequences for the citywide political debate on integration: Turkish community representatives are generally more careful than activists like Ateş and Çileli to not take a side in the integration debate regarding the public display of religious and cultural difference. Although important divisions exist within the Turkish immigrant community along the lines of religion, there is also a considerable amount of mutual loyalty in the face of a polarizing integration debate in which many Turkish immigrants think that they are not allowed to be participants but merely subjects. However, as we shall see here and in the following sections, the importance of religious symbolism in the integration debate overshadows the fact that immigrants experience exclusion apart from these religious and cultural markers of difference.

It is often not just the religious and cultural practices but rather the phenotypically visible differences of immigrants that can present the biggest challenge to immigrants in the integration process. The political debate focuses on religious symbols, but many Turkish community representatives note that other markers of difference, such as accents or skin color, are also difficult to overcome and hinder immigrants from attaining socioeconomic equality. Berrin Alpbek, speaker for the TBB, notes,

> Well, if a woman says that she is experiencing discrimination because of the head scarf, she may be right, but in the end one doesn't even know whether the employer doesn't want her only because of the head scarf. She would probably experience discrimination also if she didn't wear a head scarf because she is an immigrant. So there are two things that come together.

Alpbek alludes to the possibility that the ethnic visibility of Turkish immigrants can put them at a disadvantage on the labor market. Along the same lines, Bilkay Öney, speaker for integration policy, a Green Party parliamentarian, and a Turkish immigrant herself, suggests that the visibility of ethnic difference causes immigrant women in particular to be defined as not integrated, which leads to their exclusion:

> Sociologists have found that those who are considered very well integrated are the ones whose immigration background is invisible, those who speak German, those who have a Christian name, and so on. And all others who don't fit this picture have to fight prejudice—that does not only concern Turkish women but Vietnamese women or Greek women and so on. If someone has a darker skin color, a darker hair color, a different name, they will fall prey to prejudices or generalizations. This is the case unfortunately. . . . But I would say that integration means reaching equal opportunity.

Brader, Valentino, and Suhay (2008) note that often the largest, most visible immigrant community in a country experiences the highest levels of discrimination in the labor market as a result of the visibility of its ethnonational identity. Thus, Turkish immigrant women in particular may not experience discrimination because they wear a head scarf, but simply because they look like or talk like Turkish immigrants. Indeed, Regina Reinke, representative for integration matters in the district of Kreuzberg, notes:

> When they [people of immigrant background] apply somewhere and speak good German . . . , you can often hear [by the way they speak that they are immigrants]—it is no problem, I mean in general when I meet someone I always think it is great when he has an [interesting] accent. But they [immigrants] are often told, "Well, you should go and learn proper German first"—that happened to a colleague, when he applied for [graduate] school. And he speaks perfect German! But unfortunately this happens over and over again. It's not just the accent—looks [darker hair and skin] might spark similar reactions. European foreigners, however, have a different [better] status.

Reinke points to yet another central marker of difference: language. Local policy makers from all major parties in Berlin consider encouraging immigrants to learn German as paramount to successful immigrant integration. Notably, linguistic integration is perceived as a central tenet of successful integration across party lines. Yet it is often not a perfect command of the German language that is most important to potential employers, but rather the ability to speak it without any markers of difference—essentially accent-free German. It is therefore not the inability to speak German but rather the linguistic exhibition of ethnocultural difference that leads Germans to consider Turkish immigrants to be not integrated.[11]

According to the individual statements of policy makers and Turkish community representatives, integration is strongly tied to the visibility of ethnic, cultural, and religious practice and symbolism. Some individual local policy makers, like Reinke, recognize this as a problem, but no general consensus exists among the local political elites in Berlin that discrimination based on ethnic markers of difference might present an obstacle to integration. The challenge that immigrants encounter in the integration process simply because they look like or talk like Turkish immigrants points to the prevailing strength of the assimilatory element in the German policy debate. This implies that the change in terminology from *assimilation* to *integration* in the contemporary immigration debate is still largely symbolic. Real political changes may be more incremental as the debate goes on.

Diverse Experiences:
Turkish Community Representatives

In the integration debate, the majority German population often overlooks the internal fragmentation of the Turkish immigrant community on the topic of religion. It is common to perceive groups of Others as more similar and internally homogeneous than they are in actuality. The political debate is based on the assumption of a German–Turkish cultural binary. Turkish immigrants are simply defined by basic markers such as religion, ethnicity, accents, and culture. In reality, the Turkish community is composed of different national (Turkish, Kurdish), religious (Sunni Muslim, Alevi, secular), and—just like the German majority—educational (high, low) segments.

These internal group differences are less obvious at a time when Turkish immigrants are lobbying for improved representation and equal opportunity and thus feel a stronger group identity, but they may become increasingly relevant as the Turkish immigrant community further establishes itself in the city. The TBB is a group of mostly white-collar, highly educated German Turks who tend to define themselves as secular. However, the TBB explicitly aims to be a political representative for the Turkish immigrant community as a whole. None of the representatives of the TBB see themselves as advocates for any particular subgroup within the Turkish immigrant group. Nevertheless, Turkish community representatives, like local policy makers, possess and are affected by their own personal viewpoints and ideologies. My conversations with the four speakers of the TBB, who are all powerful figures in Berlin's local political landscape, particularly highlight the generational and class differences between Kolat and Çınar on the one hand, and Alpbek and Ünsal on the other. Alpbek and Ünsal are the descendants of guest workers, whereas Kolat and Çınar are from upper-middle-class Istanbulite families. Kenan Kolat is not only the head of the TBB, but also the head of an organization called Turkish Community in Germany, the national umbrella for all Turkish immigrant organizations in Germany. Kolat was born in Istanbul, where he attended the Austrian high school Sankt Georgs Kolleg (St. Georg Avusturya Lisesi ve Ticaret Okulu), a bilingual (German–Turkish) and bicultural private school. He went on to study at Istanbul Technical University and later at Berlin's Technical University, where he received a master's degree in engineering with a specialization in marine technology. Since moving to Germany, Kolat has been strongly involved with the Turkish community in Germany.[12] He does not share the guest worker background of most German Turks. He holds dual Turkish and German citizenship. Kenan Kolat is married to Dilek Kolat, an SPD parliamentarian in the Berlin parliament.

Safter Çınar, speaker for the TBB, was born in Brussels while his Turkish parents were temporarily living in Belgium on business. He grew up in the white-collar Istanbul neighborhood of Nişantaşı and attended Istanbul's German high school, Alman Lisesi. After his graduation in the late 1960s, he went to the former West Berlin to study economics, and he eventually married a German citizen. He has been politically active in Berlin since his arrival in the late 1960s and is a founding member of the TBB. As a dual German and Turkish citizen, he sees himself as an advocate for Turkish immigrants to Germany, but like Kolat, he does not share their guest worker identity.

Berrin Alpbek, speaker for the TBB, is also the head of the Föderation Türkischer Elternvereine in Deutschland (Federation of Turkish Parents' Associations in Germany). She was born in Turkey. Her parents moved to Germany as temporary guest workers. They initially left the children behind because they assumed that they would return to Turkey. Alpbek's sister followed her parents as a teenager and was put into special education for children with mental disabilities as a result of her inability to speak German—a common practice at the time for dealing with the non-German-speaking children of immigrants. Alpbek was deeply affected by her sister's experience and did not follow her parents until she finished high school and obtained a basic command of German in Turkey in order to be able to attend university in Germany. On the basis of her own (and her sister's) experience, Alpbek is a special advocate for improving educational support for the children of Turkish immigrants in Germany. Alpbek's résumé in particular illustrates the crucial role that the host country of immigration must play in the integration process. The compelling story of her sister provides a glimpse into the obstacles that immigrants can face if the receiving society fails to provide opportunities for integration.

Eren Ünsal, the youngest of all four speakers, was also born in Turkey but immigrated with her Turkish guest worker parents to Germany when she was only four years old. She studied education, psychology, and sociology at Berlin's Free University and has been actively involved with the Turkish immigrant community since 1996. She is the only one of the four speakers who explicitly identifies herself as a Muslim. In 2009, Ünsal became the head of Berlin's Office for Equality Against Discrimination.

These four résumés provide a glimpse into the diversity of backgrounds of Turkish immigrants in Berlin and also indicate the generational split in the political leadership of the Turkish community. The first generation of guest workers was highly disempowered as a result of strong class and educational disadvantages, as well as their temporary status in Germany. When it became clear in the late 1960s and early 1970s that many guest workers would remain in Germany for longer than anticipated, the initial political leadership of the Turkish immigrant community was composed mainly of white-collar students from Istanbul's urban elite, many of whom had received a bilingual education at one of Istanbul's European high schools, and had come to Germany to attend university.

For readers not familiar with Turkish society and culture, it is important to note that the rural–urban divide in Turkish society is still more pronounced than in many other industrialized countries. After the foundation of the Turkish Republic in 1923, the lives of the urban elites became the model for Turkish modernization, which included adoption of elements of a Western lifestyle (Erman 2001).[13] The rapid development and modernization of cities led to an increasing rural–urban divide, with urban secular elites becoming the new center of political and social life. This also affected the Turkish community in Germany because its initial representatives were not guest workers but part of the Turkish urban elite.

Increasingly, however, the children of the first guest workers established themselves within the community. They grew up in Germany and have first-hand experiences of the hardships that blue-collar guest worker families and their children encountered as immigrants in Germany. The vast majority of guest workers were not a part of Istanbul's middle class. Instead, they were former blue-collar workers or farmers from eastern Turkey. Their identities were shaped by different factors than the identities of the urban, Western-educated Turkish university students who came to Germany in the early 1970s. These different identities are crucial for future (and often contested and contradictory) self-definitions of the Turkish community as a whole, which is highly fragmented along ethnic and religious lines to begin with. All four representatives make a strong effort to represent the Turkish community as a whole, regardless of religious convictions. Kolat and Çınar, despite their backgrounds, are aware of the problematic position of Turkish Muslims in Germany and have repeatedly stated their support publicly. However, they do not see themselves as advocates for Muslims. In comparison to Ünsal, who emphasizes the additional hardships for Muslim women with head scarves, Kolat and Çınar keep their distance from the head scarf issue. In the interviews, Alpbek repeatedly emphasized that the head scarf issue must not overshadow the challenges that non-Muslim Turkish immigrant women face solely on the basis of their ethnicity, apart from religious factors, implying that she is concerned with supporting Turkish immigrants first and Muslims second. Ünsal was the only one who explicitly drew a connection between ethnicity and Islam, suggesting that Turkish immigrant identity and Islam are often conflated in the Turkish immigrant debate in Germany. In her view, German policy makers use Islam as a marker of ethnocultural difference to frame Turkish immigrants as an explicit outgroup incompatible with German cultural values.

These accounts demonstrate that the TBB, while trying to provide all-encompassing support and community representation for the Turkish community in Berlin, is affected by the social, political, and economic factors that shaped their experiences in both Turkey and Germany. Just like local policy makers, the TBB's speakers are influenced by their own experiences and their personal and social backgrounds in the process of representing the Turkish community and defining and emphasizing its needs. Despite the Turkish immigrant community's fragmentation, however, Turkish community representatives appear to make a strong effort to represent the community as a whole.

Intercultural Competence

Understanding the identities of immigrants is essential to understanding the reality of the challenges that immigrants face in the integration process. One primary way to obtain this kind of insight is through personal experience. Arnold Mengelkoch, the city official in charge of integration issues in Neukölln, is fully aware of this fact and has emphasized the importance of intercultural competence as a basis for approaching and successfully integrating newcomers into the city, the education system, and the job market:

The job centers and the schools have to provide their employees with intercultural schooling. That is part of the integration effort that Germany needs to provide. . . . Intercultural competence develops in exchange with others and not by passively reading a book. And Neukölln here is full of migrants, about 38 percent [immigrants] but in the district administration there are only three out of fifty-two people with an immigrant background. That is a joke!

Mengelkoch suggests that there is a general lack of understanding of the identity and cultural background of immigrants within the policy-making community. In his view, the German government needs to ensure that those Germans working in the public bureaucracy in job centers and schools have enough active exposure to and interaction with immigrants that they can acquire intercultural competence—that is, the ability of individuals to understand both German and immigrant (in this case, Turkish) culture, language, and customs. This dual understanding provides individuals with the capacity to see both sides (German and immigrant) of the integration process and allows them to function as a mediator when problems arise.

Mengelkoch's statement implies that immigrants should not the carry sole responsibility for successful integration, but that both sides need to work together in order to ensure a positive outcome. Mengelkoch also notes the lack of political representation of immigrants in a district like Neukölln, where more than 50 percent of residents have an immigrant background. In his view, to successfully integrate immigrants, policy makers must take significant steps toward allowing immigrants to be properly represented politically.

Policy makers and Turkish community representatives in Berlin have different ways of perceiving the integration process. However, many of them understand that integration is a process that requires the cooperation of both immigrants and the host population. A large number of policy makers and Turkish community representatives interviewed recognize the problems immigrants face and the contested meaning of integration policy. Despite differences in the different parties' platforms on integration, most policy makers and Turkish community representatives seem to agree on some basic tenets of integration. Furthermore, most of them recognize the potential barriers to socioeconomic integration immigrants face based on certain ethnic and cultural markers of difference.

Others, such as Kurt Wansner of the CDU, interpret integration solely as the immigrants' responsibility. Successful integration, in this view, requires immigrants to actively integrate themselves socioculturally, and most importantly linguistically, into the host society. There are few expectations of the host society to facilitate the integration process. On the other hand, some policy makers, such as Erhard Körting of the SPD, support the idea that the host society carries a responsibility for integration in the sense that it is expected to educate immigrants in respecting basic Western democratic values. Along the same lines, Öney of the Green Party suggests that German society has a responsibility to educate newcomers, but that change will come incrementally:

> In terms of ethnicity, we also have problems such as honor killings and forced marriages, but these things are culturally conditioned. Well, so we have to educate and hope that these views will change someday. But, you see, traditions are things that have grown over centuries and we can't just change the points of view of people, just like that. That is very, very difficult. This means we will always have certain problems and they will also always be related to a certain ethnic or cultural background, but we have to deal with that.

This argument is in line with what has been stated by scholars like Wimmer (2002) about the tendencies of certain societies to justify integration policy with the need to educate immigrants in proper democratic values, which merely serves as a cover for assimilation. Öney, who is of an immigrant background herself, echoes what many conservative policy makers frame as the dominant cultural values of Turkish immigrants. She notes that honor killings and forced marriages are still a crucial issue in the community and an illustration of the long way ahead toward integration. Öney tries to appeal to a German audience while simultaneously advocating for Turkish immigrants. This type of dual message has important implications for the key role of intercultural competence in the integration debate. As a traditional supporter and an important lobbyist for Turkish immigrant rights, Öney, who grew up in Germany, understands the side of the immigrants but also appeals to popular German frames about the challenges of integration. Thus, in her conversation with me, a German, she appealed to what Baum and Potter (2008) describe as culturally congruent frames about Muslims, who, according to German majority opinion, support forced marriages and honor killings. Aware of her specific audience, Öney did not try to question or reverse popular German conceptions of Muslim culture, but rather suggested that incremental change and reeducation are possible.

On the one hand, Öney's stance illustrates the advantages of intercultural competence, as individuals like Öney have dual cultural understanding and can easily navigate and mediate between both ethnic Germans and German Turks. On the other hand, Öney's statement demonstrates the political pressure on policy makers to frame polarizing political issues in the public debate. Even minority policy makers do not attempt to publicly question culturally congruent frames. In order to be politically credible, Öney thinks that she has to insert typically German points of view about immigrants in order to be able to appeal to all voters, not merely to immigrants. However, Berlin's political landscape in the area of integration policy is changing. Because of the heightened role of integration policy in an immigrant metropolis such as Berlin, more highly educated Germans of immigrant background are getting involved in local politics and seeking to shape the policy dialogue. Other policy makers of German heritage, such as Reinke and Mengelkoch, have long been actively involved with grassroots immigrant organizations in the local neighborhoods and have thus personally acquired the intercultural competence Mengelkoch calls for. These individuals have the ability to shape the integration debate in Berlin and foster greater understanding of the special challenges that immigrants encounter in the integration process. However, they are not unaffected by the political pressure to appeal to voters, a majority of whom are ethnic Germans.

The Berlin city government also recognizes the need for more interculturally competent policy makers. On August 3, 2010, the Berlin administration ratified a new integration law *(Integrationsgesetz)*. Berlin is the first state in the German federal system to pass such a law. This law stipulates, among other things, an intercultural opening of the Berlin government administration, and explicitly mentions the importance of intercultural competence among its employees. The law suggests a quota in order to adequately represent immigrants in the local administration based on their percentages among Berlin's urban population. However, the law curiously avoids determining and legally requiring a specific quota, even though, according to Berlin's census, roughly 25 percent of the city's population has an immigrant background (Bömermann, Rehkämper, and Rockmann 2008).

The integration law also officially recognizes the importance of the host population in contributing to the success of the integration process, noting that

> the integration policy of the state of Berlin aims to provide individuals of immigrant background with the possibility for equal participation in all areas of societal life and at the same time eliminate any special advantages or disadvantages. . . . Thus, integration is understood as a societal process, whose success depends on the cooperation of all citizens—the population of immigrant background as well as the general population. (Article 1, *Gesetz zur Regelung von Partizipation und Integration des Landes Berlin*)

This is an important point because one of the key arguments that dominates the public debate on integration in Germany is the role of immigrants themselves in the integration process: general media attention still focuses on the supposed unwillingness of Turkish immigrants to integrate into the German majority population. The new integration law challenges this focus with its acknowledgment of a certain amount of responsibility for the host population in the integration process.

Berlin's integration law remains controversial, however, because of its lack of concrete policies and procedures, such as a minority quota. The mayor of Mitte, a Berlin district, Christian Hanke (SPD), notes that the law is merely a symbol that does not engage with or attempt to solve the real issues (*Berliner Morgenpost* 2010).

Conclusions from the Political Debate

An important finding of this chapter is the disconnect between official party platforms and the opinions of individual policy makers. A large number of policy makers show strong sympathy and understanding for the immigrants and their role in the local and national integration debates in Berlin and Germany. Although the party platforms appear to be rather static policy prescriptions, individual policy makers' opinions tend to be shaped not only by their party's stance on integration policy, but also by their personal opinions, experiences, and exposure to immigrants.

Despite their dependence on political opinions and popular majorities, the appearance of interculturally competent policy makers in the political debate on integration provides a new perspective on immigrants and integration, as Öney remarks:

> I often get complaints from Turks who say "I was insulted by the police" or treated badly. I mean, how are you going to prove that, right? I am sure there are nuances, I can really imagine that well. Why? Because I have been pulled over by the police myself, and I know that if I had been a sixteen-year-old Turkish boy, I would have gotten into a fist fight with that guy. I know that. But because I am a woman and already thirty-eight and a little quiet and a little German, I said, OK, and I discussed things [with the police]. But not everyone has that kind of peace of mind to deal with certain situations. And that is why there is more trouble for certain groups. And those are the Turkish and Arabic kids.

Öney's statement is an example of the kind of intercultural competence demonstrated by some of the political representatives who have come to influence the policy debate on integration in the city in recent years. As a result of their immigrant background and their simultaneous exposure to German party politics and administrative bureaucracy, these policy makers have the ability to understand the issues of immigrants while at the same time recognizing the prevalent (mis-)perceptions of the dominant population about the minority group. This dualism in their perception of social reality is also reflected in their ways of approaching integration policy. Thus, these culturally competent policy makers could become a potential bridge between the new immigrant citizens and the majority policy discourse.

Berlin's policy discourse on integration is evolving. The increasing involvement of educated young elected or appointed policy makers and civil servants of immigrant background in local integration policy is changing the integration discourse. The general policy discourse on integration and the discourse within politically involved immigrant associations such as the TBB are converging. There is a notable increase in policy makers and government bureaucrats of immigrant background who have their own direct experiences with the challenges of integration. Those policy makers who are not of immigrant background themselves, with some exceptions, have been active in the realm of immigration in the so-called problem areas of the city for years. Thus, many of them have acquired the needed intercultural competence. The influx of individuals of immigrant background with higher levels of intercultural competence into local politics, either as elected officials or as government administrators, is opening up the heretofore stagnant policy debates. Policy makers directly involved in integration policy are beginning to recognize and act on their knowledge of the problems immigrants experience in the integration process.

Despite this recent evolution of the integration discourse in Berlin, an important caveat remains. Culturally competent Germans still remain a minority within the political party bases, as well as among the general population. Culturally congruent policy frames remain a powerful presence in the political discourse; they are rarely openly questioned, even by culturally competent policy makers. In addition, the political parties broadly are still reluctant to publicly problematize the exclusion of immigrants, fearing a decrease in voter support. These caveats, which are related to the strong connection between public opinion and political framing, demonstrate that despite the influx of culturally competent policy makers, profound change in the integration debate can only come about incrementally.

Turkish community representatives have been influenced by their personal experiences, as much as policy makers have. Their experiences as immigrants in Germany and their inherited roles in Turkish politics and society provide important clues about the dual forces that drive Turkish immigrants in Germany in shaping the debate on integration while simultaneously living it. They are not merely acting as an immigrant minority in Germany, but are (at least in the first and second generation) also influenced by their (or their family's) position in Turkish society and politics. These factors become highly relevant in understanding the diversity of the Turkish community and the inner tensions it experiences. In addition, we can assume that the leadership of the Turkish community may be changing from within in the near future as one generation replaces another. Such a development may also affect the Turkish community's political alliances with certain parties, such as the SPD.[14] Although the political influence of Turkish community representatives is not comparable to local policy makers, they nevertheless play an important role in Berlin politics, representing a significant Turkish immigrant community, which is still growing in size.

The Neighborhood

The importance of implementing a neighborhood perspective with respect to integration policy was emphasized in the party platforms of both the SPD and the Green Party. Although both local integration representatives—Mengelkoch in Neukölln and Reinke in Kreuzberg—are extremely knowledgeable regarding the problems immigrants face in their districts and sensitive to the strategies that immigrants use to make a home for themselves in the neighborhood, they do not have much say when it comes to policy making at the city level. The district of Neukölln has, overall, been quite active in implementing certain measures on the district level to help its immigrant residents, women in particular, in battling unemployment and discrimination. Reinke specifically mentioned and praised the implementation of employment measures in Neukölln and expressed her regrets about the fact that Kreuzberg, despite its Green Party–led district government, abstained from funding similar measures. However, the alleged effectiveness of the specific programs implemented in Neukölln is controversial and has been questioned by a considerable number of representatives in the Turkish immigrant community.

It is also remarkable that so few of the interviewees mentioned the neighborhood. Those that did include Reinke and Mengelkoch, who report directly from the district level, and Wansner, who portrays the influence of immigrants on the neighborhood in a negative way. This lack of mention of the neighborhood as a basis for creating and reforming integration policy in the city implies that integration policy making still takes place at the level of the city government in Berlin. In contrast to the centralized level of the political debate, the immigrants' personal associations and identity formation are strongly tied to their neighborhood. The next chapter examines the concept of lived space further by exploring actual territorial spaces of intercultural competence in the city of Berlin. Through the voices of Turkish immigrant women of different religious, social, and cultural backgrounds in the districts of Kreuzberg and Neukölln, the chapter examines how integration is (re-)interpreted and lived inside the immigrant neighborhood, which highlights the mutually contingent relationship between identity and space. Chapter 4 continues the exploration of the spatial dimension by focusing on the spaces of Neukölln and Kreuzberg themselves and by tracing the potential influences of differences in history and political structure on the immigrants in both places.

3 *MEIN BLOCK*

The Neighborhood as a Site of Identity

Insan doğduğun değil doyduğu yerdendir.
One is not from where she was born, but from where she meets her
expectations.

—Common Turkish saying

THIS CHAPTER TAKES THE READER to two of Berlin's densest immigrant neighborhoods and shows how integration is practiced in spaces beyond the public gaze. Viewing the immigration debate from the point of view of the immigrants within their neighborhood opens up a new perspective on how the immigrants themselves, the subjects of the policy makers' efforts, are living their own ideas about integration in these selected multiethnic neighborhoods. This is reflected in the chorus of "Mein Block," a 2004 song by the popular German singer and songwriter Sido, who sings of becoming one with his block:

Meine Stadt, mein Bezirk, mein Viertel, meine Gegend, meine Strasse, mein Zuhause, mein Block
Meine Gedanken, mein Herz, mein Leben, meine Welt reicht vom ersten bis zum sechzehnten Stock.

My city, my district, my quarter, my area, my street, my home, my block.
My thoughts, my heart, my life, my world reach from the first to the 16th floor.

Sido, a German of mixed German and Roma ancestry, expresses his affection for his own dilapidated block full of drug addicts and prostitutes in an area full of urban-renewal-style high-rises. He does not care that it is poor and dirty. It is his home, his identity. This close identification with one's block holds true even more for Turkish immigrants, especially women. They identify closely with their neighborhood and their block. For them, their block is a significant factor for helping them to find and negotiate their own individual identities between Germany and Turkey. Many Turkish immigrants strongly identify with the neighborhood space they occupy, not just because they live there and shape the neighborhood through their presence, but also because the neighborhood comes to represent their identity and shape their lives in return.

Immigrant identity is constituted spatially, and space is constituted by the people who live within it. This mutually constitutive process between space and immigrant identity represents a hybrid third identity in between, one that is neither purely German nor purely Turkish. This hybrid identity manifests itself in a kind of lived integration that may not be congruent with dominant policy definitions of integration. Instead, it represents the way in which immigrants make themselves at home by establishing an identity that is neither here (Germany) nor there (Turkey). More so than their country or city of residence, the neighborhood they live in represents who they are. In order to understand how Turkish immigrants in the immigrant neighborhoods "live" integration, it is critical to explore the self-perceptions of Turkish immigrant women in Berlin's immigrant districts of Kreuzberg and Neukölln. The women's life histories give insights into their individual feelings of identity as well as the obstacles they have encountered in Germany in negotiating between their Turkish and German identities.

The chapter is organized as follows: First, a brief conceptual overview emphasizes the importance of the immigrant neighborhood as a place of alternative integration practices. The second section discusses the importance of visibility in analyzing approaches to immigrant integration, both for policy makers and immigrants. In this process, spatial arrangements are strongly interconnected with the identity formation of Turkish immigrant women. The third section explains the methodological approach used to gather data and reports on the obstacles to field research in the Turkish immigrant community. The next section presents ethnographic interview data that provide insight into the fragmented identities of Turkish immigrant women, the challenge and stigma of being a Turkish immigrant, and finally the meaning of the immigrant neighborhood for Turkish immigrants in practicing their own ways of integration and identity.[1] The ethnographic data indicate that scholars and policy makers often overlook the fragmented and multifaceted character of immigrant identity.

What's Space Got to Do with It?

As certain immigrant neighborhoods in Berlin have become intersections between German and Turkish identity, as well as places of family and child-hood memories for the women of immigrant background, who grew up here, they have acquired special meaning in their inhabitants' identity for-mation. The immigrants' knowledge of Turkey is shaped by their parents' stories, memories, and summer vacations. It is the mythical home of their family and their ancestors. Their German home is the location where they have grown up, even though they lack a complete sense of belonging. The Thirdspace of the immigrant neighborhood provides a hybrid home zone that these second-generation immigrants identify with more strongly and personally than with either Turkey or Germany. At the same time, the immigrant neighborhood is neither Turkey nor Germany but rather, like its inhabitants, a place that symbolizes a new third identity that combines elements of German and Turkish identity. The multiethnic neighborhood becomes a place of peaceful coexistence and mutual exposure to different lifestyles and cultures. Hence, the fragmented immigrant identity finds an approximation of a home in this third or lived space. The neighborhood as an enclave of diversity in this scenario becomes a place of identity. In this place, there is no clash of rigid and conflicting understandings of German and Turkish identities. Instead, the third identity as Kreuzberger has the capacity to incorporate and consolidate the differences and contradictions that neither national identity could consolidate. "Hybridity and diversity serve as the building blocks of Third Spaces" (Gutiérrez, Baquedano-Lopez, and Tejeda 1999, 287). The immigrant neighborhood becomes a place of the lived integration practices of Germans and German Turks.

Exploring Visibility and Identity Formation: The Biographical Approach

Turkish immigrant women are at the intersections of the integration discourse. How they live their lives often serves as a political yardstick for measuring successful integration. If the social positions of immigrant women and their appearances correspond with policy prescriptions for inte-gration, then they are considered well integrated and a model for others. At the same time, these women, especially those of the second generation, still function as visible indicators for their communities' loyalty to the life-style and culture of their country of origin. Moreover, because women play central roles in child rearing, they also find themselves at the intersections of the clashes that their children may experience between home and host culture. Burdened with their own visual symbolism, women find their own ways to reconcile the traditions from the country of origin with those of the country of immigration.

The application of the conceptual lens of lived or Thirdspace to the Berlin context draws on the personal observations and interpretations of neighborhood space and of personal and national identity gathered from biographical interviews with seventeen women of Turkish immigrant background. These women are from different socioeconomic, educational, religious, and cultural background. They are between twenty and fifty years of age, and they are all either second- or one-and-a-half-generation immigrants to Germany.[2] The biographical, semistructured, open-ended interviews are an approach to understanding the social context in which the women negotiate their personal and national identity, as well as a way of exploring how their identity formation is tied to urban space. Bertaux (1981) argues that the exploration of life stories through biographical interviews provides a thick, in-depth description of social processes. In-depth interviews can provide insights into the perspectives of minorities that are often overlooked by large-scale quantitative studies. Negotiation of identity takes place on a group level within the public sphere; identity is also negotiated on an individual level on the basis of personal impressions and experiences. Benhabib (2002) notes that identities are inherently dialogical in nature. This implies that identities are shaped through engagement in and exposure to social interaction and dialogue.

Identity formation through dialogue and interaction is an incremental process. Findlay and Li (1997) state: "This [biographical] approach suggests that the meaning of migration and the perceived identity of the 'other' place and society is established over long time spans. Therefore the 'seeds of migration' lie in the individual's life course rather than just in an external trigger event" (35). The life stories of individual immigrants provide a glimpse into the way they negotiate their identities. Of special importance in the process of identity formation and negotiation are the immigrants' contacts with and personal experiences within the receiving society. For second-generation immigrants, this means negotiating their own identity by reconciling the conflicting impressions and lifestyles of their parents and their imported memories of the home country, the country of origin, and of the receiving country and German society. It is here that the role women play as national symbols (Yuval-Davis 1997) in the process of national and group identity formation becomes most pronounced. Both their German and Turkish identities incorporate different ideas of who these women are and what they should stand for. Political discourse and stereotypes in Germany also influence the identity formation and negotiation of the Turkish immigrant women. Their life stories serve as their own demonstrations and justifications for the opinions, values, and standpoints they have about German and Turkish societies, and their position in both. Thus, mapping the process of immigrant identity formation is facilitated by looking at women, how they talk about themselves, their identity, and their feelings about neighborhood space.

Thick Description: Notes from the Field

Although in-depth, open-ended interviews are the best approach for capturing the variety of the Turkish immigrant women's practices and self-perceptions, this methodology presents high barriers to the researcher. The primary challenge is that the field researcher herself plays a role in the outcome of the interviews. She cannot claim to enter the world of the research subjects as a neutral observer, but whether intended or unintended, as a member of the majority population, she becomes an element of the dynamics inherent in the power relationship between minority and majority groups. The action of the researcher as an interviewer asking questions, her gender, her nationality, her skin color, and the nature of questions she asks will all provoke a reaction in the research subjects. In other words, the researcher becomes part of the story she is writing. England (1994) argues:

> I see field work as a dialogical process in which the research situation is structured by both the researcher and the person being researched. Two issues flow from this point. The first is that the dialogical nature of research may be transformed by the input of the researched. The second is that dialogism means that the researcher is a visible and integral part of the research setting. (84)

What does that mean for the purposes of this research? It is impossible for the researcher to extract herself from the specific reactions to her person by the research subjects? Stanley and Wise (1993) argue that research is carried out through the medium of the researcher's consciousness. This process is impossible to deconstruct retrospectively, as every researcher, no matter how neutral she may intend to be, will be affected by her own feelings in carrying out and interpreting the research. Hence, as the investigator, I must situate myself as a researcher within the dynamic of actions and reactions between informants and other forces of social life and be aware of my own central role in framing the research.

England (1994) also acknowledges the presence of the power relations, which are always inherent in carrying out field research. In order to be honestly accountable for the research and its conclusions, these power relations and their possible effect on the outcome of my field research need to be made transparent.

On Trust

As an ethnic and native German, a power relationship was implicit for my informants by the way in which I spoke (High German with no foreign or regional accent) and the way I look (a white woman with freckles). For them, I was initially—and by association—just another German trying to observe them to give them bad press. Thus, many women were initially hesitant to agree to an interview. I quickly learned that contacting potential Turkish interviewees by e-mail was completely unsuccessful. The less personal the medium, the less initial trust the women extended to a stranger. I was more successful when I contacted informants by phone. I was most successful in gaining their trust when I asked whether I could visit them at their workplaces—a less personal location, which meant I would not intrude on their private spheres right away—and have an informal conversation with them. This method ensured that they could get to know me before I asked them for an actual interview. Actually seeing me, the researcher, in person and being able to ask questions about the research project and my motivation for the specific research topic helped build trust among the informants. My own immigrant identity and experiences as a German living in the United States helped my informants to better identify with me. They did not merely see me as a German asking them questions about integration, but came to conceive of me as a different kind of immigrant with whom they could compare notes.

Meeting women through personal connections in the Turkish immigrant community—being introduced to them by someone they trusted—provided me with an ideal entry point: my informants trusted my personal friendship ties with members of the Turkish community. My connections demonstrated their trust by calling up their friends and acquaintances and telling them that I was looking for interviewees for my research. They always added that I was trustworthy and that they could vouch for me.

I met most women whom I interviewed repeatedly and often in informal settings, such as cafés, and, occasionally, at community gatherings or parties, where we would socialize together. I realized at these gatherings how tightly knit the Turkish immigrant community in Berlin really is. No matter whom I was invited by, I ended up running into the same people at the gatherings, and many of them were personally connected with each other. This, however, was only true for the white-collar informants, who, as it turned out, are much more visible thanks to their political involvement and their awareness of the importance of social alliances within the community. Their connections with one another, and their political engagement in the public sphere, are conscious steps that open doors to stronger political representation. Although the blue-collar immigrants develop complex social networks as well, their social life takes place in more traditional, private spaces. The women of blue-collar immigrant background tend to be more religious, conservative, and traditional and would not necessarily participate in social gatherings that involve drinking, dancing, and networking. Their social gatherings took place during the day instead of in the evening; they took place at somebody's home and not in a public space, though occasionally they would gather socially at work; and the gathering involved drinking tea and informally chatting about their families, vacations, and community. The white-collar immigrant women participated in public gatherings that included men. They got together to be social, but also to create new political and professional connections to further their careers by expanding their professional networks in the community.

On Informality

Although interviews are a highly formal medium for conducting research, the qualitative nature of my interviews proved to make them more informal. They often took place in an informal setting—a café or a restaurant, or somebody's kitchen, though others took place at or near the workplace, during lunch and coffee breaks. Many of them were conducted over the course of more than one day, which meant that I met many informants more than once. The open-endedness and lack of rigid structure of my interviews also helped to give them more of an air of a conversation instead of a formal interview. Thus, although the relationship that ensued between me as the researcher and my informants cannot be characterized as personal in all cases, our encounters went beyond a merely formal interview.

On Representation

Despite the rather informal and friendly relationships that ensued with the majority of my informants, I remained an outsider to their community. This may mean that in some cases, informants were attempting to frame their own social reality in a certain way in order to appear to me, the researcher, in a certain light. The fact also remains that I, the researcher, processed the information obtained in ethnographic field research through a personal lens based on my own experiences. In social science research, none of these biases can be completely avoided. However, conversing with other Turkish German and Turkish American colleagues about my experiences in the field proved to be an effective strategy to put certain biases into perspective.

On Power

The power relationship inherent in the interview process is unavoidable. The fact that I, as the interviewer, represented part of the dominant population group vis-à-vis a minority immigrant group is an inescapable truth, and it leaves its mark on this research project. As everything else inherent in the relationship between interviewer and interviewee, this power relationship does not remain external to this project but is also incorporated into it in some way through the interviews. It therefore needs to be acknowledged. The power imbalance may have been adjusted somewhat by the relationships of trust that evolved between the informants and myself, and also helped by my identity as an immigrant woman living in the United States. Although this fact is unlikely to make the researcher an equally visible ethnocultural minority, at least it establishes some points of trust, commonality, and relatedness between researcher and interviewee. These points cannot dissolve the inherent power relationship, but they may alleviate certain aspects of it.

Which Block? Berlin's Neighborhood Space

Interviews and life stories are the ideal method to identify the connections between space and identity because different people imagine space and identity in different ways. The political debate on integration in Berlin as presented in chapter 2 represents the different ways in which policy makers and government officials in general imagine urban space and integration in Berlin.

The neighborhood space, however, is not merely a space the immigrants imagine. The immigrants actually practice their life worlds—their social existence—within the space of the neighborhood. Thus, for Turkish immigrant women, parts of the immigrant neighborhood become a lived space. The interviews capture the essence of the life worlds of these immigrant

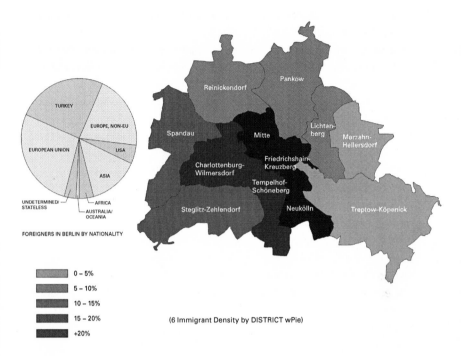

Map 2. *Berlin after the 2001 district reform—densities of immigrant populations by district.*

women and the way these life worlds are actually practiced or lived embedded within the neighborhood space. This link between life world and place—such as a block, a street corner, a teahouse, a restaurant, a corner store, a supermarket—within an urban space becomes evident through the exploration of the immigrants' daily lives within the neighborhood. Their life practices, which are embedded in the neighborhood itself, link the neighborhood space and immigrant identity. The immigrants' life practices within the immigrant neighborhood in essence represent a reaction as well as an alternative to the political debate, which often creates or enhances the (exclusionary) conditions under which immigrant enclaves form in the first place.

The distribution of Turkish immigrants across Berlin's central districts shows a remarkable resemblance with the earlier residential patterns of Turkish guest worker settlement, despite some changes in recent years. The moving bans of the 1970s and 1980s, which were implemented by the local government to prevent a spatial concentration of immigrants in one neighborhood, no longer apply because many Turkish immigrants became naturalized German citizens when the new citizenship law took effect in 2000. Few Turkish immigrants have moved to the districts located in the former East Berlin. Ayşe Çağlar, who has conducted place-based research on Turkish immigrants in Berlin, attributes this phenomenon to the Turks' strong communal, familial, and spatial attachments to certain districts in Berlin, as well as to anxieties about incidents of racism and discrimination in the former East (Çağlar 2001; White 1997). More recently, many lower-class German Turks from Kreuzberg, Mitte, and Schöneberg, affected by gentrification, have begun to concentrate in the working-class district of Neukölln, seeking employment or cheaper rents.

The women who speak through this chapter live in either Kreuzberg or Neukölln. Their different socioeconomic and educational backgrounds, experiences, and occupations provide them with different perspectives. Nevertheless, patterns emerged regarding their relationship with the neighborhood space. Their names have been altered to guarantee their anonymity, and this is also the reason why no biographical information can be revealed about them beyond the stories that emerge from their interviews. They are briefly introduced below.

The Women from Kreuzberg

The Kreuzberger women come from different backgrounds and have had a broad range of experiences living in a German society. Two primary subgroups emerge from among them: there are women with a university education who have overcome the obstacles that keep Turkish immigrant children from higher education, and women who continue to struggle without adequate education and training. The women without adequate job training survive on local government employment initiatives, but many of them have also experienced long-term unemployment. Those women who could be described as middle class have completed or are pursuing a university education. They are also outspoken political activists. All of them are strongly motivated by their personal experiences as immigrant women.

Deniz, a law student, who by the time of this book's publication had become a successful lawyer, is a young woman who is part of the middle-class, university-educated group. Her story, which is told in the pages that follow, is possibly the most disturbing of all the women's stories. Her path to a university education resembled an extraordinary obstacle course. She almost did not make it—not because of a lack of knowledge or skills, but because of her immigrant identity. It was through Deniz's own resourcefulness and persistence that she was finally able to complete the German college-track high school *(Gymnasium)* and attend university. Her story has become her political message as well: she is deeply involved in local and national politics, where she uses her experience to make a political difference in integration policy.

Esin, another university student is, like Deniz, heavily involved in local and national politics, with an emphasis on immigration and integration policy.

Elif, a university graduate, is deeply involved with the Turkish community in Berlin. Like Deniz, she has personally experienced the lack of equal educational opportunities for Turkish immigrant children in Germany. Her experiences have motivated her to help build and maintain programs that improve educational opportunities for immigrant children.

Betigül obtained an academic degree in pedagogy, psychology, and sociology, and is working for the local government.

Özge came to Germany as a small child. She grew up in a working-class family and chose to go into local politics after finishing her university education. She is an advocate for immigration.

Senem is enrolled at a technical college.

Bilge, a social worker, lives and works in Kreuzberg and has an intimate connection to the neighborhood. Her formal university education in social work enabled her to start her own office, which she operates almost exclusively on the basis of state funding in the form of grants.

Ceyda and *Ayşegül* both work in Bilge's office and live in the neighborhood.

Ayşe is *Senem*'s mother. Ayşe works as a secretary for a local Turkish immigrant women meet-up group.

Zeynep and *Melike* are temporary social workers in a government office. Both have been in and out of work, and with little formal educational background, they are happy to have work as part of a state-sponsored employment measure for long-term unemployed immigrants. Zeynep and Melike know each other from work and are now close friends. Zeynep is married to a German man, but her bonds with Turkey are still quite close. Like all other women interviewed, they regularly visit their families in Turkey.

None of the Kreuzberger women wear head scarves.

The Women from Neukölln

The Neukölln group is considerably smaller than the one from Kreuzberg and therefore serves more as a comparative example to the better-represented

Kreuzberg case. Generally, the women from Neukölln are less formally educated than the women from Kreuzberg. This does not mean that no educated, white-collar Turkish immigrant women live in Neukölln. However, the majority of the intellectual and social leadership of the Turkish community is clustered in Kreuzberg. The Kreuzberg women therefore take on an additional responsibility because they represent the engines of community empowerment and representation, and they have an active part in shaping the Thirdspace. Their relative absence from the local context in Neukölln makes it harder for the community there to forge a Thirdspace for itself.

Gülen is employed as a social worker in Neukölln, where she also lives. She does not have a university education, but she has proven her competence by coordinating the part-time work of Fadik, Binnaz, Latife, Mutlu, and Sibel. Gülen is in her thirties and wears a head scarf. She says it is her own choice, and she feels more comfortable this way. In her stories, she implies that it has not always been easy for a Turkish immigrant woman with a head scarf to be taken seriously in the realms of employment and education.

Fadik is in her forties, and her children are in middle and high school. She was unemployed for a long time and is happy to have found work. She does not have a formal education; she has mostly seen herself as a housewife until her children were older. She is from Kreuzberg and had to move to Neukölln for work and cheaper rent. She misses Kreuzberg and her social networks there, but she enjoys having found new friends at work. She also wears a head scarf.

Latife and *Binnaz* are middle-aged. Both came to Germany as teenagers and have lived in Berlin ever since. Both of them have lived in various districts of the city, but always inside immigrant communities.

Mutlu also wears a head scarf. Her children are grown, and she also arrived in Berlin as a teenager. She has lived in Neukölln for a long time but thinks it is too dirty, too cramped, and too poor.

Sibel is probably in her early thirties. She has lived in Neukölln for quite some time, but she dreams of moving to the suburbs, where there is more green and recreational space. She also doesn't mind the more gentrified immigrant neighborhoods in the heart of Berlin, but she thinks that Neukölln, especially its northern parts, where most immigrants live, is just too dirty.

The women in Kreuzberg and Neukölln appear to have had similar experiences in their educational and professional lives. The obvious difference that does exist across districts is primarily related to socioeconomic factors. The women who have made it in terms of education and a professional career tend to remain in Kreuzberg. Overall, the Turkish community in Kreuzberg is more heterogeneous, with a better-established leadership in the form of socially aware German Turks, who have often struggled for better educational attainment and who are actively working on improving conditions for the Turkish immigrant community as a whole. The women in Neukölln are more homogeneously from lower-income families with little to no formal education. They are more dependent on local government initiatives for work. The majority of interviewees from Neukölln describe themselves as religious and wear head scarves. This difference is significant in the sense that lower-income, less educated Turkish immigrants tend to have stronger religious attachments. This makes the community in Neukölln more homogeneous, not just in socioeconomic terms but also in religious and cultural terms, further isolating it and feeding into German stereotypes about Turkish Muslims.

Döner or Currywurst?
Negotiating Turkish Immigrant Identity in Berlin

A food metaphor accurately describes the choice of identity Turkish immigrants in Berlin face: Should they opt for Currywurst,[3] a traditional Berlin specialty, or Döner Kebap, a Turkish specialty sold at every street corner in Berlin? Exploring Turkish immigrant identity through interviews with women of Turkish immigrant background living in Berlin-Kreuzberg and Berlin-Neukölln lies at the heart of this book. The fragmented nature of Turkish women's perceptions of their personal and social group identity leads to an understanding of the inherently hybrid nature of their identity and its embeddedness in alternative integration practices that are constituted by and inextricably tied to space itself—the neighborhood space.

Not All Turks Like Döner

A shared immigration background and hybrid identity, however, do not warrant a conclusion of homogeneity among the Turkish immigrant population. Turkish immigrant identity is highly contested along the lines of religion (Sunni Muslim, Alevi) and secularism as well as Turkish and Kurdish ethnic identities and language:

> Yesterday, we had a conversation where somebody said, "Well, the Turks don't stick together." First of all, "the Turks" do not exist [as a group identity]. Secondly,

for this very reason, because we have so many people with different views, they cannot stick together. The only common denominator is that they [the German Turks] all don't belong to the majority population, but that is too little, too thin [to create a common identity]. It is complicated, very complicated. . . . But it can't be that way [that not belonging to the majority population is enough for a Turkish group identity] because then we would stigmatize ourselves. And reduce our identity to merely being Turkish. (Deniz)

Identity negotiation is personal and can be different for everyone. Turkish immigrant women are aware of the diversity of their own minority group in Germany and often feel like this diversity is not sufficiently addressed or recognized by the majority population:

The thing with Turkish women is that you have to categorize [among them]— there are women that came here later, or, for example, women with head scarves, and then there are women who don't really want to be Turkish and don't want to be supported in that way; there are women who have made their way, who have an individual identity for themselves, and women like me maybe, who can function in both [German and Turkish] societies and want to exist and remain in both. (Esin)

This implies also that identity formation and integration are in part individual processes. Integration strategies designed by policy makers to target generalities (such as visual–cultural difference), cannot capture these individualities. Policy platforms tend to streamline integration policies, addressing not only German Turks as a homogeneous group but often grouping them together with Germans of Arabic descent from different countries. This approach reduces the diversity of the Turkish immigrant population in Germany to the only trait the immigrants do have in common: their country of origin. In contrast, most immigrants are aware of their own identity, which they often place within a specific subcategory that cannot be accurately described solely as simply Turkish immigrant. Furthermore, immigrants often see Turkey as more of a symbolic home, which most of them cannot completely relate to either.

In sum, Turkish immigrant identity is far more complicated and multi-layered than is commonly described and addressed in the political discourse. Instead of being a homogeneous category, Turkish immigrant identity in Germany exists within a number of different subcategories. The identity, especially of the second generation, is not attached to the real country of Turkey, but rather to a mythical place of home that only exists in the nostalgic stories of the older generations, and that has never been experienced in daily life except during summer vacations visiting relatives.[4]

Neither Here nor There

Immigrants further struggle with the fact that minority group identity is devalued in many communities. Immigrants feel the pressure of assimilation from the country of immigration, and their "strong ties to [their] ethnic group and extended family, [which] may be part of an essential and valued core of personal identity" (Goodenow and Espin 1993, 175) are challenged by the majority population. The immigrant community itself, in addition to family members and friends who remained in the country of origin, may also devalue their relatives and acquaintances for selling out or for abandoning the traditions of the country of immigration.[5]

Turkish immigrant women feel the dual pressure of cultural assimilation (Ehrkamp 2006; Faist 1994) and loyalty toward their culture of origin, their homeland. The second generation of Turkish immigrants to Germany, in search of a place of belonging, idealizes this homeland, even though for them the homeland is no more than a myth, in the sense that they can only recover its reality from the stories of their parents. Their parents' experiences there may not always generate the happiest memories. Nonetheless, the stories these women have grown up with are pregnant with nostalgia for a lost homeland—a homeland that Germany, as their new home country, is unable to replace. The parents' nostalgia often transfers to the second generation and expresses itself with phrases like "Turkey is our real home," although the younger generation has never known the kind of homeland their parents have. They were never accepted as Germans in Germany, and they never felt the kind of belonging experienced by their parents in Turkey either. In fact, when visiting the homeland, most women also reportedly experience rejection that is based on a visual–cultural difference within Turkey itself:

We feel at home neither here [in Germany] nor in Turkey. We are stateless, so to say. *(laughs)* They have [in Turkey] a different way of dressing, and they speak differently too. They can hear by the way we speak that we are from Germany. But here [in Germany] we are not accepted either. (Aysegül)

My mother says you are at home where you eat. I think that is true. Because otherwise we would not really be at home anywhere. Neither here in Germany, nor at home in Turkey, where we are being looked at in this way—"Look at those Germans." (Senem)

Well, we are emigrants . . . from Turkey. We are in the middle—when we go to Turkey it is boring after four weeks and we don't want to be there anymore . . . *(laughs)*

For vacation, yes, but if you stay there [in Turkey] longer. . . . [it gets boring].
But when we come here, we are foreigners too. Despite the fact that our children
were born here, and my husband was born here too and they [husband, children]
don't want to go back to Turkey. I once jokingly suggested that [we go back to
Turkey]—I said, "Enough! We have no real work here, we can return to Turkey."
And they [children, husband] said, "Are you sure, mother? But what are we supposed to do there?" *(laughs)* Here I know the school, I know the laws and I can
move around freely everywhere. No! I don't want to [go back to Turkey]! Yes,
that [returning to Turkey] would be hard for me because I have been here for
more than twenty years. (Binnaz)

To be honest, I feel in the middle. Why? Let me tell you. For example, when we
are in Turkey, they [the Turks in Turkey] often say, "Yeah, those are Germans,
well, German Turks who live in Germany"—well, like tourists, so to say. When
we come here [to Germany], we are foreigners. . . . So, where are we supposed to
live, this is our state—for example, I am a German citizen. But still I am a foreigner because my name is different and my family, and Islam [my religion],
everything. So even when I say I am a Berliner, that's not true. When I travel to
Turkey and say I am Turkish, that's not true either—I was born in Berlin. And
went to school here. And I can speak German. . . . So because of all this I have no
idea where we [German Turks] belong. (Ceyda)

Aysegül's statement documents the dual rejection that immigrants feel on
the basis of their "neither here nor there" identity. Ceyda's account describes
the utter confusion German Turks feel in regard to their identity. Germans
in Turkey, foreigners in Germany, dual citizens legally—Turkish immigrants
often feel like they do not belong anywhere but belong everywhere at the
same time. This notion of "neither here nor there" is a universal sociological description of the second generation of immigrants, who belong in both
the country of origin and the country of immigration while they are simultaneously permanently unable to reach a sense of complete belonging and
acceptance anywhere (Soysal 2002).

The accounts of the other women display confusion and inner conflicts
as well. Binnaz clearly expresses her desire to belong to German society,
but she notes her frustration with being perceived as a foreigner in Germany. Senem's attempt to describe her own definition of belonging (or lack
thereof) is particularly indicative of the contradictory and complicated way
in which Turkish immigrant women in Germany negotiate their identity
and belonging. Although she mourns the fact that she and her family are not
really at home anywhere, she utilizes the nostalgic German term *Heimat*
(home, homeland) in reference to Turkey.[6] She also declared at the beginning of the interview, which included her mother, that she did not have

much to say about Turkish immigrant identity because she feels German. Thus, although Germany is the country of Senem's everyday life, a country she seems to identify with in a general way, Turkey remains a strong mythical homeland, and her identity and loyalties are divided between both places. Other women feel similarly divided in their loyalty and identity:

> ZEYNEP: Well, I also feel German, seriously! Both [German and Turkish]—I adapt.
> MELIKE: It depends on whom you are talking to.
> ZEYNEP: And in Turkey you feel different, of course, because you grew up here [in Germany]. Of course you are in the middle—do I belong here, or do I belong there? In the middle, this thing, that's true. But when your parents, for example, when you still have your grandma and grandpa in the country [in Turkey], a house and a yard, then we do say, yes, we belong here [in Turkey].
> MELIKE: Yes, because in your heart you know that you belong there [Turkey]. You might live in Germany but you belong there.

Zeynep's and Melike's statements demonstrate the confusion and contradiction of living with and in between both identities at the same time. Zeynep hints at personal and material circumstances, such as family and property in Turkey that make the country more of a home to her. This suggests a spatial materialization of the mythical homeland in Turkey through the existence of a house and a yard.

Melike clearly feels the same mythical connection with Turkey as *Heimat* that Senem senses. In that sense, the literal meaning of *almancı* becomes true in Melike and Senem: business and everyday life are in Germany, but Turkey remains a mythical homeland.

> I definitely don't feel like a German, I know that for sure. . . . Then, in a second step, I don't feel like a Turk—but my first response is more secure—I don't feel like a German. . . . I also don't feel like a Turk but I play with my identities, I have to admit. . . . [When I travel] sometimes I am a Turk abroad, sometimes a German. . . . [But here in Germany] I am best [described as] a German Turk or simply Deniz with a German background or something like that. But I cannot remember ever having said, "I am German." Maybe I said, "I am Turkish," or at least I say that in Turkey. Even though in that case, I always add in the next sentence that I come from Germany, I always underline that right away, that is important to me, even abroad. Abroad I always say, well, my parents, not me, but my parents are from Turkey and I live in Germany . . . so what actively belongs to me is Germany, and what I have adopted is Turkish . . . I always have to say these two sentences because it really reflects me the best. . . .
> This is an emotional response, so it is not at all a legal response. And that's all good but I also want to . . . connect these points because some also ask, "What

citizenship do you have?" Great, I have both citizenships. "Where do you vote?"
I could theoretically vote in both places. These are not the indices that help me
to decide about the way I have to feel because there is no "must" or "have to" but
it's a real subjective and emotional thing. . . . I don't know, everybody has to
decide that on her own. (Deniz)

Deniz describes the stark difference between (emotional) identity and
(legal) citizenship. Citizenship as a concept oversimplifies the much more
complicated notion of belonging. As a (future) lawyer, this distinction has
become a fundamental part of her reflections on her own identity. Deniz's
dual analysis of her identity provides a glimpse into the multilayered complexity and the personal nature of this concept. The personal nature of the
concept of identity is underlined by the statement by Deniz's friend, Esin:

I simply say that I am a German with a Turkish background. . . . I mean, I don't
have to have been raised in a certain way to say I'm a German Turk, right? . . .
But I almost never say I am just Turkish. No, that's very, very rare, it always
depends on the situation, or when there are maybe . . . some older people from
Turkey that you might say quickly, yeah, I am Turkish, or my father comes from
this and this town. (Esin)

As opposed to Deniz, who almost never simply says that she is a German,
Esin states that she almost never simply says that she is Turkish. She is German with a Turkish background, unlike Deniz, who says she is—at most—
of "German background," but under no circumstances German. This is particularly remarkable because the two women are friends. Deniz is about the
same age as Esin, has a comparable educational background, and, like Esin,
grew up in Germany. These fundamental perceptional differences show
how individual and experience based the process of identity formation is,
even for immigrants of comparable background. Unlike Deniz, Esin states
that she feels challenged in her German-ness not so much by her own feelings of identity, but rather by the reactions of the Germans around her,
who constantly question this German-ness. This also becomes clear in the
way she describes her relationship to Turkey:

I have been asked several times now—because I still travel to Turkey a lot—
"Well, how was it in the home country (Heimat)?" And I always respond, "Well,
staying with my grandma was nice." Somehow they [the Germans] just don't
want to realize it [that Turkey is not the Heimat] and . . . I have heard this six
times already—"How was it in your home country?" Then I always say, well, it's
nice here [in Germany] but staying with my grandma was nice too.

OK, of course one has to remember that many [people] just ask that question
and are not aware at all that it bothers me or what it is that bothers me [about the

question]. It just shows that somehow for forty years this integration [of Turkish immigrants] into the neighborhood hasn't been working. (Esin)

The statements by Deniz and Esin indicate that individual identity formation and definition are strongly tied to personal struggles and experiences of immigrant women. Despite their similar demographics, their individual experiences are completely different. Although Esin encountered some prejudiced comments by Germans growing up, she faced no unusual obstacles on her way to the university. Deniz, on the other hand, was treated like many of her immigrant classmates in Germany's rigidly tracked education system: her teachers channeled her into a non-college-track high school,[7] a decision her parents could have protested successfully if they had been familiar with the system. Deniz's goal was always to study law at university. She tried to get her teachers to provide her with the recommendation needed to transfer to the *Realschule* and from there to the college-track high school, the *Gymnasium,* to obtain a university-entry diploma. However, every year she tried to get the recommendation, her teachers refused, arguing that her German was not good enough. When I spoke to Deniz, her German was perfect and accent-free, and I would not have been able to tell her language skills from that of a native German. Finally, Deniz graduated the *Hauptschule.* The teacher wrote on her diploma that Deniz could not be recommended to move up to a *Realschule* or a *Gymnasium* because her German language skills were inadequate for the material taught in these academically more demanding schools.

Frustrated and angry, Deniz decided to go a different route. She moved to Istanbul and enrolled as a nondegree student at a German *Gymnasium* there.[8] She took a regular course load and did so well that after one year, her German teachers in Istanbul wrote her letters of recommendation for the *Gymnasium* in her German hometown, asking the school to allow Deniz to enroll. In response, the principal of the *Gymnasium* in her hometown told her that he would let her enroll, but that he did not think she was going to make it even through the first year. Contrary to his predictions, Deniz graduated and went on to law school. At the time of the interview, she was in her final years of law school and has since graduated. However, her identity as a Turkish immigrant in Germany, as well as her identification with the country, was deeply affected by this negative experience. In contrast to Esin, she is no longer able to identify herself as a German because despite her best efforts to fit in, she was treated like an outsider throughout her high school career. Deniz's story, and the comparison of her self-identification with that of her friend, show how the individual experiences of these women shaped them into the personalities they are today, and it indicates to what extent they perceive themselves to be a part of both German and Turkish societies.

These experiences have greatly affected how the women I interviewed actively and passively pass on their notions of identity to the next generation:

> My older son is now sixteen years old, and my little one is ten. They say— . . . my little one has always said right away "I am German." *(laughs)* [He says] "My parents are from Turkey but I was born in Berlin, I am German." For a long time, I was unable to accept that *(laughs)*, but now I say, "OK, we have German passports," but I want him to learn that he is not German because in this society I am afraid that he will get problems one day—psychological problems—with this identity because German society is not going to accept him as a German. . . . So I say to him, "You have got that right, we—your parents—come from Turkey, you were born in Berlin and you belong to both societies. You are a Turk and also a German—you are in between, OK?" (Bilge)

Bilge is afraid of the rejection that her son, who identifies himself as German, may experience from German society because of his ethnic background. Her fears are based on her own experiences as a Turkish immigrant in Germany. In order to protect her children from a similar rejection, she tries to instill a sense of dual identity in them, to signal to them that even if they are told they are neither a German nor a Turk, they are still something—they are both, or they are in between.

The process in which immigrants attempt to make a home for themselves in the new culture is a complicated and often contradictory process. Goodenow and Espin (1993) argue that

> it may result in complete marginality in or segregation from the new society, or in total assimilation. The best alternative may be biculturalism—the development of an identity that integrates aspects of both worlds in a way, which enables the individual to function satisfactorily in the two cultures. . . . The development of an integrated bicultural identity must necessarily be an active rather than a passive process, since choices must be made about which elements of each culture to retain and value, which to modify, and which to reject. (178)

The different accounts of Turkish immigrant women in Berlin show that the process of individual negotiation of ethnonational identity and cultural belonging is highly individual and experience based. In their efforts to define their personal identity and belonging, Turkish immigrant women show deep emotions. They attempt to negotiate and reconcile their often contradictory German and Turkish identities, culture, and lifestyle, forcing them into a constant process of self-reflection.

Sharing a Home: A Thirdspace and the Turkish Immigrant Experience

The immigrant neighborhood space provides a place where immigrant women experience a less conflicted sense of their personal identity. An exploration of the neighborhood, with its spatial arrangements, thus results in a better understanding of the contradictions that necessarily define the social and personal identity of Turkish immigrant women. The immigrant neighborhood reconciles immigrant identity and visibility. Turkish immigrant women do not stand out visually in this neighborhood in terms of their looks, names, clothes, and cultural practices. Their difference is not as strongly visible as it is, for instance, in an ethnically German neighborhood. Within the hybrid and heterogeneous framework of the neighborhood, this difference ranges from small to nonexistent. To phrase it another way, while in the larger German society (as in the larger Turkish society in Turkey), Turkish immigrant women and their in-between-ness stand out visually, in the immigrant neighborhood, they fit in. The neighborhood provides the cultural framework of home and belonging for Turkish immigrant women that neither Turkish nor German overarching national identity can provide.

To See and (Not) to Be Seen: Visibility and Difference of Turkish Immigrant Women

Visible difference matters. Previous chapters have addressed the fact that some Berlin policy makers see the dominant definition of German national identity challenged by the immigrants' visibility. Kurt Wansner, a local parliamentarian of the Christian Democratic Party and a long-term Kreuzberg resident, states, "Germany needs to be visible in Kreuzberg again." The intense focus on visibility by both immigrants and policy makers in Berlin is remarkable because it clearly demonstrates how strongly visibility in this context is tied to how the majority population conceives the German mainstream identity, and how the immigrants' visible difference from that German identity affects their lives in Germany. Some women of Turkish immigrant background report that they find more acceptance among Germans when they do not look Turkish, even though an accent or a darker complexion makes them appear foreign.

From the outside, I do not look like a Turkish woman. You can see that—at least not Turkish-Turkish. I am somewhat lighter, and with my blue eyes I am never assumed to be a Turkish woman. Nobody says that to me—and it's also the way I dress—I have not experienced any discrimination so far—rather acceptance. That is positive. I have not been discriminated against as a foreigner here. As long as I don't speak. When I start talking with my accent then you will realize that I am a foreigner, but I am not being discriminated against because of that either because many people think I am from Poland or from France, from Italy. [As long as they think that,] they are OK, they accept me. When they find out that I am Turkish that changes completely, 180 degrees. Call it Turkophobia, hatred, I don't know. (Bilge)

Maybe that [the lack of discrimination I have experienced in Berlin based on my looks] is related to the fact that I don't look Turkish because these Turkish looks have such a negative connotation. Well, Turkish looks mean, so to say, that you are in a forced marriage. That is the stuff they say [about Turks]. And I live here in Kreuzberg and, seriously, almost all Turks even speak German to me because they think that I am—I don't know—from Latin America. Well, like I said, neither the Turks nor the Germans get the idea that I have Turkish heritage. So maybe that's why they treat me in a more neutral way. That definitely is an advantage. Because, I mean, a Brazilian woman is more sympathetic [than a Turk]. *(laughs)* To them [the Germans], at least. I mean I don't think that's a good thing that they have created a scale like that for Turks and non-Turks. . . . But my whole life I was never addressed as a Turk. And most people act surprised [when they find out that I'm Turkish], like, "What? Turkish?" and all that and I don't like their surprise either [when they find out]. I mean, what did you think Turks were like? (Deniz)

I know women who have changed their first name . . . when they received [German] citizenship . . . as in, "I don't want to be, I don't know, Ayşe anymore but Celina" and married a German man so that they would have a German last name, but does it have to be that way? The person stays the same. Nothing changed there [on the inside], just on the outside. Just like with me sometimes [when they say], "Oh, you don't look like a Turk and your German is so good!" But there are many whom you would not recognize on the street as Turkish women. Believe me, I am not unique, it happens all the time. . . .
    Yes, it happens like this: "Oh, you are Turkish?" "Yes." "But that can't be!" [because I don't wear a head scarf] "Yes." *(laughs)* That is really so ridiculous. Not even my mother wore a head scarf, so I don't have to wear one either. There are many women in Turkey who don't wear a head scarf. This [prejudice] is really only because of the media, this image—migrant, Muslim, head scarf. . . . When I watch the news, there are always only those pictures [of Turks with head scarves]. . . . [and they say], "Go, go to Kreuzberg, there you will see all these Turkish women wearing their head scarves." Not true! Most women I see there who are Turkish are without head scarves, but people are just following their prejudice, so they only notice those ones [with head scarves], not the others. (Elif)

All three women are aware of their visibility (or lack thereof) as Turkish immigrant women, and its significance. They all think that it is not necessarily the visibility of difference, but rather, and specifically, being visibly Turkish, that has strong negative connotations in Germany. Deniz and Bilge both think that they receive better treatment in German society because although they may exhibit difference, they do not look Turkish. The implication is that a specific negativity is tied to the image of the Turkish immigrant in Germany—more so than to the image of immigrants in general.

Bilge describes herself as more or less invisible in German society because her light skin and light eyes make her blend in in the same way that a Polish, French, or even Italian woman does; being associated with a European background does not denote difference per se. Immigrants from European Union member states are generally not negatively stereotyped as Turkish immigrants in the popular discourse, and they receive different treatment in Germany. Unlike Bilge, Deniz does not fall into the category of European invisibility. But like Bilge, Deniz does see herself as non-Turkish looking. Instead, she is stereotyped in a different way: like someone from Latin America. In Germany, being Latina is not attached to the same negative stereotypes that being Turkish carries. Deniz argues that a Brazilian woman would get a much friendlier reception in Germany than a Turkish woman because of the specific negativity associated with Turks. Despite her visual difference, her visibility, Deniz claims to have benefitted from her non-Turkish looks in the sense that she can pass for a Latina and get friendlier treatment from ethnic Germans.

Importantly, it is not necessarily the starkness of the contrast to German society that creates the highest levels of rejection. Deniz, while certainly not German or European looking, notes that she receives better treatment than those who look Turkish. Turkish looks are often conflated with Middle Eastern or Arabic looks, which evoke specific cultural stereotypes, specifically in connection with Islam, which leads to an even more stringent rejection. Brader, Valentino, and Suhay (2008) find that ethnic cues alone do not trigger rejection of or negative opinions about immigrants. Rather, specific stigmatized out-groups—who are often associated with a lack of assimilation or integration into the host society—provoke strongly negative and emotional reactions toward immigrants. For example, in Brader, Valentino, and Suhay, the Latinos in the United States are stigmatized. Similarly, it is not the visibility of difference in general but what is stereotypically considered Turkish visibility that seems to be the factor triggering the stigma that Turkish immigrant women in Berlin have experienced.

Elif points to specific negative connotations that are associated with
Turkish identity in the popular discourse in Germany. One important connotation is Islam. According to Elif's account, Muslim identity is not only
strongly associated with Turkish identity in Germany, but it is also conflated
with Islamic fundamentalism. For example, Turkish immigrant women are
often stereotyped as veiled women in forced marriages. Elif also hints at
the possibility that the difference of Turkish immigrant women in German
society may not be only associated with the visibility of certain clichés such
as the head scarf, but also with names and language.

German Turkish policy makers confirmed this observation. In my interview with her, Eren Ünsal from the Turkish Union Berlin-Brandenburg
argued that the visibility of certain traits of difference heightens discrimination. Along the same lines of argument, Bilkay Öney (formerly a representative of the Green Party but since 2009 a member of the Social Democrats)
states,

> People are being perceived as successfully integrated when you cannot see their
> immigrant background, those who speak German and have a Christian name and
> all that. And the others that don't fit that picture have to fight prejudices. . . . If
> someone has a darker skin color, a darker hair color, a different name, then she
> is exposed to prejudice and generalizations.

Visibility of difference, as this example demonstrates, is relative and strongly
dependent on the properties of the space in which individuals live and
(inter-)act. German Turkish women, though visible by difference in both
places, indicate that they are differently visible in Turkey than in Germany.
Turks in Turkey or Germans in Germany who fit the dominant definition
of being Turkish or being German are comparatively invisible; they present no visual challenge to the dominant stereotypes of national identity.
Those (physical or visual) traits that are not generally accepted as part of
the national identity become visible. Because they differ from the mainstream identity, negative connotations become attached to them. In other
words, difference from the national mainstream becomes negatively visible.
In Germany, the rejection of difference is experienced as specifically related
to what is stereotypically considered Turkish or Middle Eastern displays of
difference, and to Islam in particular. Thus, it is not difference per se that is
rejected, but rather difference specifically in association with Turkish (and
Muslim) identity.

The specific rejection of Turkish identity may also be related to the cliché
of Turkish immigrants as the largest group of immigrants in Germany.

Similar to Latinos in the United States, Turkish immigrants in Germany have become the stereotypical immigrants. In the eyes of the public, they are seen as largely working class, with low education levels and the strongest visible presence of all immigrants. They are also consistently perceived as the least well integrated group of immigrants in socioeconomic and cultural terms. The inherent momentum of the largest immigrant group in any country presents, ipso facto, the largest threat to mainstream identity (see Brader, Valentino, and Suhay 2008). The perceived negative effects of and clichés about immigration among the majority population are therefore often tied specifically to the largest group of immigrants in a country.

Turkish immigrants in Germany bear the additional burden of a religious cliché that has been attached to them, which complicates their situation even further. Even though a majority of Turkish immigrants in Germany claim to be nonpractising Muslims (Von Wilamowitz-Moellendorff 2001), they are perceived as Muslims in the public eye. Ethnic difference is conflated with religious difference and its associated clichés. Along with the elevated visibility of being the largest immigrant group in the country comes the increased visibility of their neighborhoods and enclaves.

My Block: Neighborhood Space and Identity

The immigrant neighborhoods in Berlin, including the neighborhoods of Kreuzberg and Neukölln but also parts of the districts of Mitte and Schöneberg, represent places where immigrants, particularly those of Turkish origin, become visible to the German majority population by means of clustering. On the other hand, it is precisely those visible immigrant neighborhoods in which Turkish immigrants can become invisible as individuals. Their individual visual–cultural difference does not stand out here in the same way it does in the strictly German parts of the city. Thus, while the individual immigrant becomes invisible in the crowd of immigrants, the neighborhood becomes visible as a result of the very presence of this immigrant crowd.

In academic texts, Kreuzberg in particular has been praised as a functioning multicultural enclave dominated by its Turkish minority (Çağlar 2001; Kaya 2001) and is famously dubbed "little Istanbul" (Kaya 2001; Koopmans 2003). Germans in Berlin have mixed feelings about these immigrant neighborhoods. Although some people enthusiastically move to more multicultural neighborhoods and embrace their diversity, others, like local parliamentarian Kurt Wansner, a Christian Democrat, are more critical and find the visual presence of difference and diversity worrisome. The *Hertie*

Berlin Studie, conducted in 2009, is one of the most extensive studies on urban life in Berlin (Hertie Stiftung 2009). The study's findings indicate that the German majority and the immigrant population generally have good relationships with one another. In Berlin, 61 percent of native Germans and 77 percent of immigrants perceive their intercultural relationships as positive.[9] Even in so-called problem areas, like the district of Neukölln, more than half of the native German residents (54 percent), and a large majority of the residents with an immigrant background (86 percent) are reported to interact with one another on a regular basis.[10]

Turkish immigrant women for the most part have strong personal affiliations to certain places within their neighborhood; they see their personal and family histories as well as their personal identities as inextricably tied to their neighborhood. More importantly, although most women describe a feeling of fragmented loyalties and only partial belonging to German and Turkish national identities, their relationship to their local neighborhood is not at all fragmented but rather characterized by the belonging they could not find in either country (see maps for the places described below):

AYSE: Well, I lived in West Germany[11] for a while but I am so happy in Kreuzberg.

SENEM: Well, here in Kreuzberg it's like Kottbusser Tor, Görlitzer Bahnhof, Schlesisches Tor[12]—I simply know everybody here! Seriously everybody!

AYSE: I am really at home here, I can say that. When I go out I always run into friends and acquaintances. I find that wonderful. And Kreuzberg is also always a little *multikulti* [multicultural]. I like that too.

ZEYNEP: I am from Kreuzberg—from the very beginning. . . . *(laughs)*

MELIKE: Me too!

ZEYNEP: Well, I came to Germany [as a child] and we lived at the subway station Möckernbrücke [which is in Kreuzberg], Grossbeerenstrasse, that was seriously my favorite area; and then I moved with my husband to Potsdamer Strasse [which connects the districts of Schöneberg, Kreuzberg, and Mitte]. . . . then I moved back to Kreuzberg, right there by the Berlin Museum, and then I moved to Lindenstrasse, so I always stayed in Kreuzberg.

MELIKE: Since I moved to Berlin I have always stayed in this area around Anhalterstrasse/Wilhelmstrasse [which is in Kreuzberg, close to Mitte].

ZEYNEP: I have been here for thirty-seven years! It is really nice. For example, around the subway station Hallesches Tor, where I live, there is Kaisers [a German grocery store chain], there is the subway, the atmosphere—seriously, I would never get any ideas of moving anywhere where there are no stores, no subway . . . It is very centrally located. . . .

MELIKE: When you know everything, when you get along with the people [in the neighborhood] . . . when I go outside here, I do not feel like I am in Germany, it is as if I was in Turkey. I can go shopping here and I have no problems, nothing. I don't feel like a Turk, I just feel like a human being.

ZEYNEP: . . . Back in the day when my parents moved here [to Kreuzberg], there were Italians, Yugoslavs, Turks. And then the Arabs came here from a bunch of different countries, and everything mixed together, and what happened? Our children learn a little from everyone *(knocks on the table)* and that is great.

Well, of course the architecture is somewhat important, but the social conditions are more important. Or the way of living together and the atmosphere, well, definitely for the people here [in Kreuzberg], who have different qualities, or different, multilayered identities is much more becoming. I don't think that's just the case for the children of migrants but generally for people who are open or have to be open, I don't know, because they are gay, because they are migrants, so they don't belong to the majority—because they are looking for something different. . . . For people who are different, this city is simply more comfortable. (Deniz)

Zeynep and Melike emphasize the importance of the neighborhood as a place of acceptance. It is not necessarily the presence of other German Turks in the neighborhood, but rather the coexistence, mutual acceptance, and friendships that develop between Germans, German Turks, German Arabs, and other immigrants in the neighborhood. This friendship conveys to everyone a sense of normalcy: Melike and Zeynep are not, as they would be in a purely German neighborhood, the Turkish women on the block. They are merely other Berliners, friends, acquaintances. This is what makes the neighborhood a home.

Deniz hints at the deeper meaning of space beyond architectural structure and the built environment. Thus, it is not just the architectural and geographical dimension of place, but the mental importance of the neighborhood space to the immigrants. Because of Deniz's identification with Kreuzberg's identity as a place in which those who are different from the norm can coexist, she can be at home there.

The immigrant neighborhood provides a specific identifier for women of immigrant background when they lack other ways of describing who they feel they are:

Well, I think first and foremost I would describe myself as a Kreuzberger Berliner. . . . Because when I recently told people that I was a German Turk, they would always say something like 'But your parents are originally from Turkey, aren't they? . . . And so I say German Turk just for provocation. (Esin)

Those children [our children] will not leave because they did not come from Turkey, so they're not going to Turkey, they may not see Germany as their home [their *Heimat*] but they relate to the [specific] place—for example, I can tell you about the children [of Turkish immigrants] in Berlin, who say, "We are Berliners, not Germans, Berliners!" That is their identity. It's place related, not nation related. . . .

I grew up in Turkey and I have changed over the last thirty years [in Germany] and now I don't feel completely comfortable in Turkey either. I have changed in Turkey to the Turks. My personality has developed differently. I have my own identity. I also belong to this society—and I feel comfortable in Kreuzberg. I like to go for walks on the Hasenheide [street connecting Kreuzberg and Neukölln, which is next to a large city park that carries the same name] in Berlin . . . , and I like to go on vacations in Turkey. I have to go on vacation to Turkey every year; I cannot do without that. *(laughs)* But to forever live only in one society—always here [in Germany], always in Turkey—that's impossible. I belong to both societies. That is something new, a new identity really. . . .

Seriously, when I spend five, six weeks in Turkey I start missing Kreuzberg and my home and—like I said—drinking coffee on the Hasenheide. *(laughs)* (Bilge)

You know, I would never leave Berlin. . . . Even when I go on vacation, for three weeks, I get homesick and want to come back to Berlin. Because you get used to things; I was born here, I have friends here, I know all the streets, for example, and everything—much better than in Turkey. You get so used to all that, so I would never leave all that. (Ceyda)

These accounts underline the key importance of Kreuzberg and Berlin in the women's lives and identity formation. Some women hint specifically at the fact that they cannot identify with German or Turkish national identity but have strong local ties to their city and neighborhood. The strong local identity becomes a substitute for the lack of national belonging. Specific places acquire an almost mythical status, as life stories and memories, family, and personal identity are tied to them. The immigrant neighborhood represents a safe haven where immigrants acquire the status of belonging and acceptance that they fail to find in either German or Turkish society. Melike bluntly states that in her neighborhood, she feels like a human being instead of a Turk in Germany. Bilge finds a space in her neighborhood that corresponds with her own hybrid identity. Whether the women identify most strongly as Turks, Germans, or German Turks, their highest loyalties lie with the city of Berlin and the neighborhood of Kreuzberg. The place of the immigrant neighborhood most accurately reflects the women's personal identities that seem so irreconcilable with German, Turkish, or both national identities. The neighborhood allows the women to map their mental life world onto a physical space and to practice their identities.

A Home in Neukölln?

Importantly, Neukölln does not acquire the same status as Kreuberg as a place of home and belonging for Turkish immigrant women. Most women I spoke to moved to Neukölln for employment or cheaper rents after their families had initially settled in one of Berlin's more traditional immigrant neighborhoods, such as Kreuzberg, Schöneberg, or Mitte. Generally, those parts of Neukölln that border Kreuzberg, where most of the immigrants live, are poorer and more working class than even the poorer parts of Kreuzberg, which have gentrified rapidly over the past fifteen years. However, the border line between both districts marks no stark social contrast. Yet the women who live in Neukölln, beyond this invisible border line, do not have the same strong way of identifying with their neighborhood:

In the beginning I cried for two months [after moving from Kreuzberg to Neukölln]. I was supposed to work here [in Neukölln], and it was not that easy for me. I went outside and went for walks, and still I said, "No, I can't live here." In Kreuzberg I had huge circles of friends, and here I had no one but when I started my job, I had so many colleagues, met so many people, so I quickly forgot [about how unhappy I was], and now I am content to live here. Kreuzberg was a little different, but this is also related to my job. I now have a permanent job, a better job, so I always say, Neukölln brought me luck. (Fadik)

We don't really like Berlin, there are too many weird comments [directed at us], too much aggression, too much mistrust, no acceptance. (Gülen)

LATIFE: I came from Turkey, and in Berlin, I first came to Schöneberg. Then I moved to Kreuzberg and then to Neukölln. The next time I move, it will be to . . . Zehlendorf![13] *(laughs)*
MUTLU: It is too much here, too many people, too crammed. The apartments are—everything is so close, the houses are too close together to breathe. . . .
SIBEL: Yes, it is nice in the East or the South [of Berlin]. It is very nice there, my brother bought an apartment there. It is very beautiful, very clean, and not too many people, that is nice.
BINNAZ: I don't like it, I don't like Neukölln, but I have been in Neukölln since I was born. I used to like it, but not anymore because now there are so many people here and they are all alcoholics and stuff. You can see that when you are walking along the street and there is all that dog poop on the way. . . .
MUTLU: Seriously, here in Neukölln we say "poop street" *(laughs)*. . . . because everywhere you go there is dog poop. . . .
SIBEL: I was in Zehlendorf, and there it was clean everywhere—you can sleep on the ground, it was that clean. No dirt at all—nothing. I tried to move a few times but we have a job here—so I couldn't. I work here in Neukölln—and there is also a [specific area] where you get assigned to work, and [if you

move] you can't continue with your job.[14] . . . My husband does not want to
move away from Neukölln either.

MUTLU: When we moved here from Schöneberg, we always missed it, and we
always drove over to Schöneberg, a nice area, where it was quiet—beautiful!

SIBEL: Schöneberg is nice too! And Kreuzberg! . . . Well, I'd like to move away from
Neukölln—somewhere else. Because the school is not good in Neukölln—we
have many problems there.

The effort through which immigrants create a home for themselves in the
neighborhood is a long-term process, and their statements reveal that they
have faced, and in many cases overcome, some initial difficulties. Others still
wish to move on or move back to their traditional neighborhoods where
they enjoy established social networks, but, as Sibel mentions, they are tied
to Neukölln as a result of the district's employment regulations.

Jurgens (2005) has noted the traditionally strong ties that Turkish immigrants have formed with their neighborhoods in the city since their settlement in Germany. The women living in Neukölln complain about the
density of the area, which makes them feel uncomfortable. At the same
time, they romanticize traditional immigrant areas such as Schöneberg and
Kreuzberg, which are just as dense and dirty as Neukölln and do not resemble the rich district of Zehlendorf, which Latife dreams of as the ideal
place to live. The women in Neukölln, it seems, mourn the absence of the
social networks that provided them with comfort in Schöneberg and Kreuzberg. Their mourning of these networks is reminiscent of their mourning of the faraway homeland. Just as the homeland provides a mythical
place of belonging and identification for Turkish immigrants in Berlin,
their original neighborhood of settlement provides a real place of belonging. Moving to a different neighborhood means losing this place of belonging. Neukölln seems to not yet have replaced this place of belonging, but
Fadik's statement implies that it has the potential to become a home in the
long run.

The women's social worlds often still do not revolve around their lives
in Neukölln, but instead continue to be associated with the social networks
they participated in the districts they moved away from, such as Kreuzberg
or Schöneberg. However, the strong local measures for creating (temporary)
immigrant employment, especially for long-term unemployed, unskilled,
or blue-collar immigrant women in Neukölln, have brought many women
like Fadik, Binnaz, Latife, Gülen, Mutlu, and Sibel together at work. They
have made friends at work and may, in the long run, be able to transform
these friendships into new social networks.

My Home Is My Block:
Immigrant Neighborhoods and Identity

The comparison between Neukölln and Kreuzberg shows that they are similar with regard to the percentage of immigrant settlement. The differences between the two districts, however, are important for understanding the immigrants' lived experience and the development of a place-based third identity between their German lives and their Turkish roots. The interviews with Turkish immigrant women have highlighted one significant difference. The women's attachment to Neukölln as a place of home is considerably weaker than that of Turkish immigrant women in Kreuzberg. Neukölln also lacks the presence of a group of strong, politically involved, and well-educated Turkish immigrant women. This is yet another feature that distinguishes it from in Kreuzberg. As in gentrifying neighborhoods in the United States,[15] the in-migration of gentrifiers who belong to the same ethnic or racial minority groups as those people already present in the neighborhood leads to better organizational structures among the grass roots in Kreuzberg. In other words, those German Turks who have made it up the social ladder in German society have a dual effect on the neighborhood. On the one hand, they become part of the gentrification movement in Kreuzberg and contribute to rising rents and property values. On the other hand, their loyalty to their community and their political engagement can become empowerment tools for the entire ethnic minority community (Pattillo 2007). Those who are priced out of Kreuzberg, however, move to Neukölln, where they live with other immigrant women in similar socioeconomic circumstances. The women from Neukölln have yet to create new social networks and develop their potential for political organization and representation similar to the powerful voices from Kreuzberg.

The traditional immigrant neighborhoods in Berlin have provided immigrants with important social networks composed of family and kin, in which they could escape the intimidating role of being foreigners in Germany and simply belong. Yet this commonality cannot hide the fact that the women understand and perceive their identity as individuals with significant differences between them. Bilge understands herself as a hybrid and sees her identity as something new that is neither German nor Turkish. She senses that the neighborhood can reflect her own hybridity and give her comfort in her differences from both Germany and Turkey. Melike, at the other end of the spectrum, defines herself as Turkish and feels at home in the immigrant neighborhood because it provides her with a feeling "as if she were in Turkey." Nonetheless, she also claims a strong local Berlin identity and describes her Turkish as a typical *almancı* Turkish. Life in the immigrant neighborhood, as the place of belonging, can take on meanings and connotations for different individuals that range from one end of the spectrum to the other.

Overall, regardless of individual interpretations, the traditional immigrant neighborhood has established itself as a place of hybrid belonging that neither the German nor the Turkish identity can provide. The immigrant neighborhood becomes a spatialized representation of the different ways in which Turkish immigrant women integrate themselves into the city, reconciling the seemingly irreconcilable differences between German and Turkish identities.

At the same time that the neighborhood becomes visible through the presence of immigrants, individual immigrants' Otherness—a constant companion in their lives in Germany—becomes invisible in the hybrid space of the neighborhood. The immigrants' cultural difference is often perceived as negatively visible outside the immigrant neighborhood because immigrants challenge the composition and definition of the German mainstream, as Bilge's and Deniz's statements about the stigma of Turkish identity indicate. However, inside the immigrant neighborhood, these same individuals melt into the crowd because here, the practice of diverse and alternative ways of living is the norm.

The Turkish immigrant women whom I interviewed recognize that integration as defined by policy makers and government officials is still inextricably connected with visibility based on imagined ideal types, dominant perceptions, and clichés about Turks in Germany, and they seek refuge in the diversity of the immigrant neighborhood. The public perception in Germany continues to be that not being visibly different equals well integrated. Instead of having abstract political and theoretical debates on the meaning of integration, Turkish immigrants practice their own lived integration within the Thirdspace of the immigrant neighborhood. Instead of visibly assimilating, the Other becomes visible through the collective practice of difference. Immigrants incorporate themselves and make themselves at home in the neighborhood in ways not conceived of by integration policy strategists. This practice appears threatening to those who hold traditional ethnic perceptions of German ethnonational identity. Consequently, Wansner of the Christian Democratic Party in Berlin argues that Germany—in the traditional ethnic perception of German ethnonational identity—"is not visible in Kreuzberg anymore."

Turkish immigrants in Berlin recover a feeling of belonging in the traditional immigrant neighborhood. The neighborhood becomes a substitute unit of identification for them because they do not think that they can identify with either German or Turkish national identity. The significance of this process is emphasized by the observation that immigrants who remained in traditional immigrant neighborhoods, such as Kreuzberg, to which they are connected through their own personal histories and experiences, exhibit stronger personal ties and loyalties to their place than immigrants who moved to a different neighborhood. The women living in Neukölln who moved to the neighborhood from other districts such as Schöneberg and Kreuzberg experience a weaker personal identification with this more recent immigrant neighborhood. They still feel sentimental attachments to their former home neighborhoods. Nevertheless, the opportunity to benefit from Neukölln's employment measures, which specifically target immigrant women, has convinced many Turkish immigrant women to remain in Neukölln and build new personal ties there in the hope that it will eventually become another place of belonging—another home.

Schiffauer (1997) has noted that strong neighborhood affiliations generally exhibited by Turkish immigrant women are also prevalent among Germans in German cities. He proposes that Turkish immigrants in Germany have adopted their neighborhood attachment from the Germans, a commonality between the two cultures that has not yet been fully explored. Mills (2010), however, points out that Turks in Turkey have equally strong attachments to their neighborhoods and localities across the city. Therefore, the neighborhood is a place of identification for Turkish immigrants but also for Germans. The recent German Kreuzberg residents often have made a conscious choice to move to this area because they identify with its diversity and enjoy living in a neighborhood that personifies a certain openness and cultural variety. As Düspohl (2005) notes, Kreuzberg's population is a rather random mix. It is composed of approximately a third each of retired 1968 student movement revolutionaries; members of the educated, politically aware, and leftist younger generation; and Turkish guest worker immigrants and their descendants. Therefore, local attachment is not a specifically German phenomenon but rather a general notion among people in urban areas, who identify with the special character of their neighborhood. In the case of Kreuzberg as a lived space for individuals of Turkish immigrant background, however, this attachment goes beyond a mere local patriotism. As the women's personal accounts make clear, Kreuzberg has become the sociospatial context that embodies their own hybrid identities.

It renders them invisible in a country in which they constantly feel visible as the Other. In Kreuzberg, they are not the Other but instead find a real home, one right between Turkey and Germany. Immigrant neighborhoods become places of hybrid identities and alternative integration practices. Different immigrants identify in individual ways with their neighborhoods and have different perceptions of the specific properties that personify them within their neighborhood. Overall, immigrants have a strong connection with their neighborhood in the sense that they personally identify with the space and the way of life that they lead within it. Thus, their ways of incorporating themselves into German society are strongly tied to the neighborhood. Although they may not define their identity as German, most of them, in one way or another, strongly define themselves as residents of their neighborhood. German–Turkish residents may not appear to be properly integrated according to the dominant political definitions of the term, but they nevertheless have adopted strategies and lifestyles via the neighborhood space that help them incorporate themselves into life in Germany in a certain way and that help them function and survive in their new surroundings. In a similar vein, Kasinitz et al. (2008) find that immigrants in New York City perceive the city as an intermediary stage of identity that provides means of identification especially for the second generation, which is caught between the country of the parents' origin and the new homeland, and therefore is literally speaking "neither here nor there." The city—or in the case of Kreuzberg, the neighborhood—becomes the home between homes. In the case of Neukölln, the attachments of women to their home in the district are notably weaker than they are in Kreuzberg.

These lived ways of integration and identification with the neighborhood apart from dominant definitions are what characterizes the neighborhood as a Thirdspace (Gutiérrez, Baquedano-Lopez, and Tejeda 1999; Soja 1996, 1999). The lived practice of integration within the immigrant neighborhood stands in contrast to the dominant discourse on integration reflected in the policy platforms portrayed in chapter 2. However, it is occasionally reflected in the policy positions of many of the culturally competent policy makers, parliamentarians, and government officials, such as Mengelkoch, Öney, and Ünsal, who shape the local integration discourse in Berlin.

The lived or Thirdspace of the immigrant neighborhood takes different forms. Kreuzberg as a residential neighborhood exemplifies a way of living and an identity that has moved beyond the rigid characterization of mainstream (German) national identity. Its specific local character and attitude attract residents who on a personal level identify with that character.

Kreuzberg as the traditional immigrant neighborhood is not necessarily perceived as a multicultural paradise, but rather as a place where being different is a bit more accepted than elsewhere. Jurgens (2005) notes that Turks, as Berlin's primary immigrant group, dominate the image of the immigrant. Despite this, however, Kreuzberg as a place of lived integration is neither merely a Turkish neighborhood nor a place of complete multicultural existence. Rather, it has become a place of home for many people who, in other places of the city, would be considered different. In Kreuzberg, however, they become friends or acquaintances—Berliners. In Kreuzberg, they are at home.

Kreuzberg is experiencing a wave of gentrification, which, while making Kreuzberg more attractive to a diverse crowd of middle-class Turks and residents from all over the world, is displacing many of the original blue-collar Turkish immigrant residents who made the neighborhood a multiethnic and multicultural place in the first place. Gentrification will continue to affect the neighborhood and its composition. This is also worth keeping in mind when we speak of Kreuzberg as a model multicultural neighborhood. The future will show in which direction the neighborhood will develop.

Neukölln, on the other hand, though not a very recent immigrant neighborhood, has become a more recent place of residence for those who were unable to afford Kreuzberg's rising rents. It has also become a haven for many immigrant women who, after battling long-term unemployment, were able to take advantage of Neukölln's various employment measures specifically targeting immigrants. The personal identification of many immigrant women with their new neighborhood may still not be as powerful as in Kreuzberg; however, because many women are tied to Neukölln by their work, they are unlikely to leave. Furthermore, because the district's current government is pushing for further measures to improve the situation of the large Turkish immigrant minority, employment for many immigrants is secured over longer periods of time, so they will be able to establish new ties. The examples of Kreuzberg and Neukölln demonstrate how the Thirdspace as a home space takes different forms and goes through different stages of evolution.

The next chapter will delve deeper into the meaning of these spaces. While the focus of this chapter was on the individual, sketching out commonalities and differences between individual Turkish immigrant women in Kreuzberg and Neukölln, the next chapter will explore the neighborhood spaces themselves. It will provide some insights into the history of both places, and examine the effect of these histories on immigrant identity and the integration process.

4 LOCATION AS DESTINY

Integrating Kreuzberg and Neukölln

Man kann mit einer Wohnung einen Menschen genauso töten wie mit
einer Axt.

You can kill a human being with an apartment just as much as with
an ax.

—Heinrich Zille (1924)

THE PRECEDING CHAPTERS HAVE EXPLORED the policy discourse
on immigrant integration and the immigrants' lived integration. This chapter focuses on what scholars (Abbott 1997; Kasinitz et al. 2004; Orum 1998;
Soja 1996) have called the social context and thus explores the spatial
dimension that lies between the policy discourse and lived integration: the
immigrant neighborhood which has, in the previous chapters, emerged as
a powerful bastion of identity formation, particularly for second-generation
Turkish immigrants. In exploring the historical and social context of the
neighborhood itself, this chapter sheds light on the interaction between
identity and space. The following discussion centers on the hypothesis that
a specific neighborhood affects the reciprocal dynamic between policy
making and immigrant identity, as presented in the previous two chapters,
sui generis. The historical and social culture of the neighborhood affects
the mentality of the people that live in it while simultaneously the residents
shape and change the way the neighborhood is perceived from the outside.
A historical–sociopolitical analysis at the neighborhood level reveals a new,
additional layer of interaction and unveils important supplementary information on the context in which immigrant identity formation occurs.

Beyond the boundaries of the immigrant neighborhood, the role of local
identity is also highly relevant in Berlin politics because of the city's highly
decentralized administrative structure. Administratively, most of the city's

formal governing institutions are reproduced at the district level, and district mayors in turn have a relatively large amount of autonomy in designing their own policies. Specific policy realms have a particularly strong local dimension and are administered at the district and/or community level through local representatives who answer to the districts' mayors.[1] This is especially the case for integration policy, an issue that is highly salient in Berlin's inner-city neighborhoods, in which immigrants have clustered over generations.

Furthermore, Berlin's neighborhoods have traditionally harbored powerful localized identities, shaped by their historical development as part of the larger city. In recent years, the reunification of the city and economic developments have caused uneven waves of gentrification. Thus, in gentrifying neighborhoods, such as Kreuzberg, blue-collar immigrants are now in direct competition with what Richard Florida (2002) has called the creative class for downtown urban space. In Neukölln, this phenomenon is much less pronounced because the downtown parts of the district where immigrants cluster have remained more strictly blue collar and are much less affected by gentrification than neighboring Kreuzberg. In other words, Neukölln is gentrifying in its less centrally located areas, while its downtown areas have remained blue collar. In that way, Berlin differs greatly from Paris, for instance, where minorities and immigrants cluster in the infamous low-income housing projects in the *banlieues,* at the outskirts of the city.

In addition to contemporary social developments and political and administrative structures, the social history of the particular districts and neighborhoods is highly relevant for their individual social identity. The history of incorporation into a rapidly growing greater Berlin *(Gross Berlin)* in the early twentieth century has left lasting marks on Berlin's different districts' identity within the city. The types of settlement and development, be it working-class tenement housing or fancy villas; be it industry, department stores, or brothels, have affected the districts' identity along with the prevailing contemporary social culture, such as grassroots organizing or the existence of a protest culture. Furthermore, historical developments in the spatial structure of the neighborhood, such as housing policy, urban renewal, and other general results of urban planning, have had a strong effect on its social fabric, as they have had in any other city.

A closer look at the history of the Kreuzberg and Neukölln neighborhoods, as well as their current integration policy and local- and community-level governance, reveals considerable variation in the two districts as a result of a number of important microdynamics on the ground: the districts and communities within them have adopted different patterns with respect to community organizing, housing structure, gentrification patterns, and integration policy. An analysis of these factors when located solely at the city level leaves these important dynamics unobserved. This chapter presents a micro-level neighborhood analysis of both policy discourse and immigrant integration patterns in Kreuzberg and Neukölln within each district's historical context.

At first glance, Neukölln and Kreuzberg do not appear to be that different. Both neighborhoods exhibit the highest concentration of Turkish immigrants in Berlin, with up to 40 percent of residents having a Turkish immigrant background.[2] Furthermore, both Kreuzberg and Neukölln are comparable in per capita income level as the second poorest and poorest district in the city, respectively.[3] However, Berlin is a city of cities, and each locality is characterized by its own particular history and identity, which are based on the historical developments of the local urban fabric itself. In the wake of industrialization and urbanization, independent communities around the city had grown disproportionately faster than Berlin itself. For the city to benefit from this growing tax base, these suburban communities had to be incorporated into the city. The discussion about incorporation went on for about a hundred years, until, after the end of World War I in 1920, the Prussian parliament, Preussischer Landtag, enacted the Greater Berlin Law *(Gross-Berlin-Gesetz)*.[4] Greater Berlin was now an agglomeration of eight cities (Old Berlin, Old Charlottenburg, Köpenick, Lichtenberg, Neukölln, Schöneberg, Spandau, and Wilmersdorf), fifty-nine communities, and twenty-seven manors (Wernicke 1998). In terms of sheer size, this meant that the city of Berlin officially grew to thirteen times its original size from September 30 to October 1, 1920 (Wernicke 1998).[5] Judd and Swanstrom (2011) note that as cities grew explosively during the time of the industrial revolution, the definition of *community* changed fundamentally. Where previously the term had denoted the socially (and ethnically) diverse agglomeration of people who populated the preindustrial towns and cities, urbanization changed this perception completely. In the big cities of the industrial age, communities became increasingly homogeneous neighborhoods, segregated along social and ethnic lines. This further increased individuals' identification not with the city, but specifically with the neighborhood.

The phenomenon described by Judd and Swanstrom (2011) is all the more prevalent in Berlin because of the city's history and urban administrative structure. Berlin's special character as a spatially dispersed city made of cities still affects the way its residents identify with the area they live in. The historical events of the twentieth century, such as, among other things, the post–World War II separation of the city, additionally shaped local identities and emphasized location and place even more strongly. Not all districts of the city have an equally prominent identity and history. From historical circumstance, the inner-city districts of Kreuzberg and Neukölln have maintained distinct and notorious identities within the city that shape their residents to this day.

Kreuzberg and Neukölln in the Context of Guest Worker Immigration

The early distribution of guest worker immigrants throughout the city of Berlin centered on Kreuzberg, but it also included other working-class districts, which offered cheap tenement housing, such as Neukölln, Schöneberg, and Wedding.

Kreuzberg quickly became a stronghold of guest worker immigration. Hartmann, Hörsch, and Neujahr (1998) note that while Kreuzberg became and remained the center of Turkish immigrant settlement almost from the beginning, Neukölln's northern parts (which border Kreuzberg to the west) also experienced considerable influx of Turkish immigration in the early years of guest worker recruitment. By the early 1970s, when the German government put an official stop to guest worker immigration, approximately 20 percent of all foreign guest workers residing in the city of Berlin lived in Kreuzberg, 16 percent in the working-class district of Wedding, and 10 percent in Neukölln, Schöneberg, and Charlottenburg. These districts were attractive to guest workers because they held the majority of Berlin's working-class tenement housing stock, which was the only housing available to and affordable for the guest workers:

> Until this point, there had been little concern with the situation of the foreigners, but now [the local government] realized hat the old tenement quarters of the city had turned into considerable colonies [of immigrants]. . . . The available hostel space [for guest workers] was still much too small, and it was not designed for longer stays or family reunification. . . . [Ethnic] German migrant workers, who were still being recruited to come to Berlin, had much better chances on the housing market. . . . The foreigners' only choice in most cases was move into the cheap, condemned working class quarters. (Hartmann, Hörsch, and Neujahr 1998, 341)

Political concerns about immigrant enclaves in Berlin's downtown areas surfaced as early as the late 1960s and early 1970s. The Berlin administration feared that an increase or concentration in immigrant population in certain areas of the city would force out locals (Hartmann, Hörsch, and Neujahr 1998). By 1975, the districts of Kreuzberg and Wedding, which at that time had experienced the highest levels of immigrant settlement, implemented a local migration ban *(Zuzugssperre)* to limit the spatial concentration of immigrants in certain localities of the city. Turkish immigrants, banned from settling in those areas, started to join others in Neukölln and increasingly settled in Schöneberg as well.

Economic Downturn, Gentrification, and New Dynamics

After German reunification, the city of Berlin lost much of the government subsidies that West Berlin had received from the federal government throughout the Cold War.[6] In addition, West Berlin ceased to be a spatially isolated island, and many local businesses moved away from the city into the cheaper suburbs, taking important tax revenues and jobs away from Berlin. Together, these factors contributed to an economic downturn, heightened unemployment, and slowed structural development in the former western part of Berlin, especially in the central working-class areas of the city, such as Neukölln and Kreuzberg (Hartmann, Hörsch, and Neujahr 1998).

Throughout the 1990s and early 2000s, the demographic distribution of the city of Berlin, which had been relatively stagnant and frozen by the Cold War, became increasingly dynamic. This development affected the immigrants and their neighborhoods. After the fall of the Berlin Wall, students and artists flooded into the cheap apartments in the downtown areas of East Berlin, abandoning the West for more affordable and cutting-edge housing.[7] The district of Kreuzberg, formerly bordering the Berlin Wall, now once again became the center of the city, and like other new downtown districts of the former east, such as Mitte and Prenzlauer Berg, experienced high levels of gentrification. The large Turkish immigrant population living in Kreuzberg experienced mostly the negative effects of gentrification. By the early 2000s, downtown East Berlin and Kreuzberg had been largely gentrified. Rents soared, increasingly forcing many Turkish immigrants to relocate to cheaper Neukölln. The composition of the Turkish immigrant neighborhoods in Kreuzberg and Neukölln changed as a result. Those who could afford it stayed in hip, multicultural Kreuzberg, whereas lower-income German Turks were increasingly forced to relocate to working-class Neukölln. Whereas Kreuzberg increasingly surfaced in Berlin tourism guidebooks as the best example of a functioning multicultural neighborhood (Hertie Stiftung 2009) and became a hot spot for flea markets, bars, and restaurants throughout the late 1990s and early 2000s, Neukölln became known as a problem area, particularly in connection with failed immigrant integration.

Kreuzberg: Antiestablishment and Gentrification

Historical Background

Kreuzberg is not officially an autonomous administrative unit. With the 2001 *Bezirksreform* (district reform), the district was fused with the (very different) former eastern district of Friedrichshain and consequently lost its independent administrative capacity. Kreuzberg and Friedrichshain remain divided, not just culturally, but also geographically by the Spree River and are connected by only one bridge, the Oberbaumbrücke (Map 3).

Kreuzberg had acquired its status as an independent district of Old Berlin as a consequence of the Greater Berlin Law.[8] The old Berlin communities of Friedrichstadt and Luisenstadt were combined into the new administrative district Hallesches Tor on October 2, 1920. In 1921, it was renamed Kreuzberg. After World War II, with the reorganization of Berlin into Allied zones, and finally with the construction of the Berlin Wall in 1961, Kreuzberg turned from an inner-city district to a district at the outskirts of the "island" of West Berlin (Map 4).

Kreuzberg has always been culturally divided. The postwar postal codes became a distinguishing feature between Kreuzberg's two cultures. Berliners today still refer to the two different Kreuzbergs. The eastern part, Kreuzberg (*Süd-Ost,* "southeast," abbreviated S.O.) had a designated postal code of 36.[9] This area, bordered by the Berlin Wall, was one of the poorest communities in the city, and it became widely known over the last three decades of the twentieth century as having developed a strong antiestablishment identity. The western part of Kreuzberg (*Süd-West,* "southwest"), with a postal code of 61, represented a typical West Berlin middle-class community. The southeastern section of Kreuzberg, or Kreuzberg 36, evolved into the home of many immigrants.

The edgy geographical position of Kreuzberg 36 at the center of Berlin and simultaneously at the outskirts of what was the sociopolitical enclave West Berlin spawned significant political and cultural developments. Throughout the second half of the twentieth century, Kreuzberg 36 developed its position as a location of resistance and counterculture. It eventually rose to notorious Germanwide prominence when it became a center of the punk music movement in the late 1970s and early 1980s. Several key

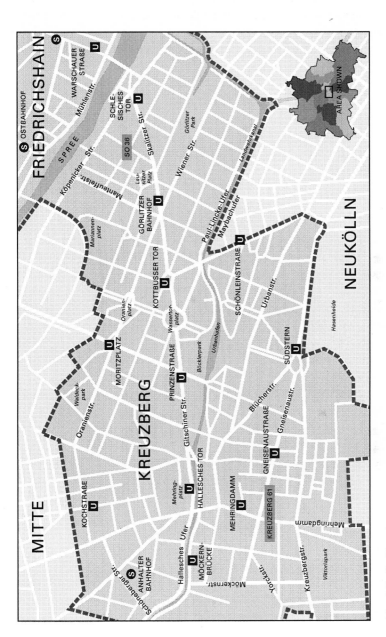

Map 3. Berlin-Kreuzberg.

= location of wall

Map 4. Berlin's district before the 2001 district reform, divided by the Berlin Wall.

developments during the 1960s, 1970s, and 1980s fundamentally shaped Kreuzberg 36 into what it is today, including the impending threat of urban renewal, which made the area affordable for Turkish immigrants and students; its growing counterculture identity, which was spurred on by the consequences of and resistance to urban renewal; and finally the 1968 student protest movement and its successors, which also contributed to Kreuzberg's resistance identity today.

Interwar Berlin from Weimar times well into the 1930s had been one of the uncontested centers of the urban renewal movement (Klemek 2011) and modernist architecture, which resurfaced in postwar Berlin. City planners and administrators designated certain areas of the city as blighted and decrepit—as old—and condemned them to be torn down in order to make space for the new. The renewal process was excruciatingly slow, however, and urban neighborhoods were often condemned years before the buildings were actually torn down (Düspohl 2009). The result was a further dilapidation of neighborhoods as businesses and investors turned their backs on condemned neighborhoods, landlords and housing authorities stopped fixing buildings that were to be torn down anyway, and tenants moved away as soon as they could afford to.

Kreuzberg's old working-class tenement housing stock was a prime urban renewal target beginning in the late 1950s. During the long wait for the wrecking crews to tear them down, the condemned, dilapidated tenement houses provided homes for a West Berlin version of a bohemian culture, the first bastion of local subculture in the district (Düspohl 2009). By the late 1960s, a younger clientele of alternative-minded university students discovered the cheap, morose buildings of Kreuzberg 36. Even though Kreuzberg was not the center of the 1968 student movement, which organized closer to the location of Berlin's Free University in the affluent south of the city, its local culture was nevertheless deeply affected by the movement. The fact that the notorious Axel Springer Press was located in Kreuzberg brought the protesters of the student movement there eventually, especially after the horrendous assassination attempt on the student Rudi Dutschke.[10] The student movement blamed Springer Press and its aggressive rhetoric for the assassination attempt.

The new presence of the student movement changed southeastern Kreuzberg dramatically (Düspohl 2009). Kreuzberg's old tenement buildings housed only a minority of original, mostly blue-collar Kreuzbergers by the early 1970s. Most of them had moved away from the condemned buildings and found housing elsewhere in the city. Students and artists who moved into the district in pursuit of the city's cheapest available housing brought along their counterculture spirit and political activism. The new Kreuzberg residents were now a mixture of Berliners and non-Berliners. Aside from the Turkish immigrants, many students from West Germany, according to Düspohl (2009), felt drawn in by the revolutionary, Marxist spirit of the Free University and the unconventionality of life in Berlin. Young men from West Germany flocked to West Berlin to be exempt from the mandatory military service.[11] Their different lifestyle, characterized by activism, music, theater, drugs, and free love, started to significantly shape the image and daily life of southeastern Kreuzberg.

Turkish immigrants had started moving to the district in the early through mid-1960s. They lived side by side with old blue-collar Kreuzbergers, who had resisted the outmigration and the new, unconventional residents, who had arrived more recently. They were attracted by the cheap housing in the district and encouraged by the local administration. The administration acted for a simple reason. As in Neukölln, the presence of Turkish guest workers in Kreuzberg was considered temporary in nature, and thus it seemed logical for the local administration to encourage them to move into the old, soon-to-be-torn-down tenement buildings in southeastern Kreuzberg. In other words, the presence of the cheap, available housing was considered to be just as temporary as the presence of its residents (Düspohl 2009). The guest worker immigrants were more attracted by low rents than by the neighborhood itself (Düspohl 2009) because at the time, they intended to save most of their money for their return to Turkey and spend as little as possible on their stay in Germany.

"Soon Conditions Like in Harlem?":
The Renewal Ax Casts Its Shadow on Kreuzberg

In the 1970s, urban renewal efforts threatened to become a reality in southeastern Kreuzberg as the city started tearing down the first of the condemned buildings. In 1973, the German center-right daily *Die Welt* (published by the notorious Springer Press) published an article titled "Bald Zustände wie in Harlem?" (Soon conditions like in Harlem?), referring to the poor southeastern part of Kreuzberg. By 1977, even the center-left weekly *Der Spiegel* bemoaned the poor living conditions in Kreuzberg 36:

> Kreuzberg is the quarter with the highest number of ancient buildings, the quarter of basement apartments and kitchenettes; the bathroom halfway down the stairway or in the courtyard. . . . Younger Germans are leaving the district; those who remain are the older and weaker ones, the outsiders and lunatic crackheads,

and most of all the foreigners. Berliners already call the elevated train that runs through Kreuzberg the "Orient Express." Every fourth Kreuzberger is a foreigner, every fifth Kreuzberger speaks Turkish [as a first language]. Some blocks are up to 70 percent Turkish.

The presence of immigrants or foreigners and the poorest segments of the city's population in the southeastern part of Kreuzberg, which the construction of the Berlin Wall had fenced in and robbed of its former exquisitely central downtown location, seemed to provide city planners and modernizers with even stronger reasons to bulldoze what was left and start over. However, the government's plans ran into strong opposition from the newly arrived young, alternative-minded Kreuzbergers, who had had sufficient exposure to protest and resistance to feel inspired to spearhead the local response.

The opponents of urban renewal policy claimed that it was destroying affordable housing and neighborhood structures, replacing them with "anonymous concrete fortresses" (Klitscher 2001, 150). Kreuzberg's new activist residents staged protests and sit-ins and resisted intensely—all under an intense media gaze. By the end of the 1970s, vocal protest among community activists, alternative groups, and churches pushed the Berlin senate to grant local residents more inclusion into local decision making.

At the same time, local activists founded a citizen's initiative *(Bürgerinitiative),* named after the neighborhood, SO 36, which sought to alert the urban administration to severe mismanagement and code violations in existing city-owned social housing, urging the local government to become involved. When the city officers did not react to their protests, members of SO 36 became squatters, occupying several empty apartments and renovating them in February 1979 (Klitscher 2001). This initiative, according to Klitscher, was not only successful, as it got the city administration and apartment managers to react, but it also gained popularity among the local population. After its initial success, squatting became a strategy to actively influence housing policy in Kreuzberg. By 1981, squatting had become a daily practice among activists in Kreuzberg. As the number of squatter activists steadily grew, there was also more fear of police removal, which sparked occasional violent clashes with police (Klitscher 2001). The situation grew increasingly tense over the next three years; it calmed down slowly as negotiations between the protesters and the city administration grew more fruitful.

By 1983, the controversy about urban renewal in Kreuzberg had not been completely resolved, but the city had made concessions promising to take local residents' concerns into better consideration in the process. By 1987, the urban renewal projects in Kreuzberg had grown so cooperative that the city of Berlin won the European and Regional Award for its urban renewal strategies, called "Careful City Renewal in Kreuzberg" *(Behutsame Stadterneuerung in Kreuzberg)*. At the same time, however, Kreuzberg's enduring poverty sparked a strong socially motivated protest movement among its residents, which culminated on Labor Day, May 1, 1987, when riots broke out in Kreuzberg 36, and several stores and cars were burned. With its poverty unalleviated, Kreuzberg 36 would become the site of violent protest and rioting on May 1 for the next twenty years.

Guest Workers Become Permanent Workers

With its abundant cheap housing, Kreuzberg turned into an immediate haven for the first Turkish guest worker immigrants in the 1960s. Since then, it has, like Neukölln, developed into one of the city's highest-density immigrant neighborhoods. Düspohl (2009) notes that West Berlin had a particular need for guest workers after the construction of the Berlin Wall, which cut off worker migration from the eastern to the western part of the city. He adds that Kreuzberg's Turkish guest workers in particular stand apart from the cliché that most guest workers were uneducated, unskilled workers from small villages in eastern Anatolia. On the contrary, Kreuzberg's first guest workers were largely educated, liberal, and urban women[12]:

> The young women [from Turkey] who arrived in the sixties were urban oriented and had secular values. They dressed in the contemporary mini[-skirt] fashion and saw their desire to earn a living [in Germany] also as an opportunity to get to know the world. (Düspohl 2009, 147)

The increasing Turkish presence in southeastern Kreuzberg was registered as almost exclusively negative by almost everyone—city administration and local residents alike—and was perceived by the general public as another symptom of blight and urban decline. Urban renewal plans for Kreuzberg are symbolic of this attitude. Already by the 1970s, local Kreuzberg activists recognized that Turkish social networks were taking root in the neighborhood. Pastor Klaus Duntze, who founded the 1977 grassroots initiative Strategien für Kreuzberg (strategies for Kreuzberg) to promote sustainable planning with strong involvement of the local residents, described the new presence of Turkish immigrants in Kreuzberg 36 as follows:

> The socially disadvantaged or: The presence—that includes those who have no other relationship to the quarter than this: It provides cheap living space. This

growing group consists of foreigners—predominantly Turks—and the socially disadvantaged who come to the quarter from the outside and who are only looking for one thing only: a roof over their heads. They accommodate most strongly those owners and administrators who exploit the houses of the quarter, as they can identify neither with the quarter's past nor with its future. To them, it means pure present tense, no past, no future. . . . But still: among the Turks, there has even over these few years developed an independent and fully functioning subculture with its own meeting points, information systems, and civic organizations. . . . The German residents have perceived this [development] with distrust and skepticism and increasingly aggressive fears: they no longer feel that they are the masters in their own house. (Duntze 1977, quoted in Düspohl 2009, 136)

Duntze identified a trend that was increasingly manifesting itself in high-density immigrant quarters, but especially in Kreuzberg: the development of social structures tied to the neighborhood. For the Turkish residents, this development represented the first step beyond a mere guest worker identity and a step toward the creation of a new home in the country of immigration. Their social networks, as well as the formation of a local subculture, signaled more than just temporary residence. It was a first step to establishing a permanent community.

Back at the Center of Things: Kreuzberg 36 after Reunification

When the Berlin Wall finally fell in November 1989, the social location of Kreuzberg 36 within the city of Berlin changed fundamentally. It was no longer located at the edge of the city but had, literally overnight, reclaimed its space at the center of the Berlin. With memories of urban renewal battles in mind, its residents feared further upgrades of the housing stock through gentrification, coupled with increasing rents and subsequent displacement. Kreuzberg, however, did not immediately become a target of the gentrification movement. Instead, yuppies claimed the district of Mitte, located at the historic heart of the city, and younger students moved into the old tenement buildings in the former East Berlin districts of Prenzlauer Berg and Friedrichshain. Instead of gaining the attention of the city's upper classes, Kreuzberg completely lost the attention of the local administration. Financial aid, which had been directed at Kreuzberg as one of West Berlin's poorest districts, was now redirected to restore and modernize infrastructure and housing in the districts of former East Berlin. Kreuzberg also seemed to lose its human edge. Artists, students, and intellectuals who had been contributing to the diversity and cultural edginess of Kreuzberg 36 moved to cheaper apartments in more interesting neighborhoods in East Berlin, and families moved away to pursue cheaper housing in better school districts. Civil society organizations shut down because they were dependent on government funding, which had been redirected to the eastern part of the city (Düspohl 2009). According to Düspohl, government attention did not refocus on Kreuzberg and its growing problems until 1999.

The blue-collar German Turks in Kreuzberg were hit particularly hard by the postreunification decline. Unlike the artists, students, and intellectuals, they had nowhere else to go. Their identity was anchored deeply in the fabric of this particular neighborhood and the grassroots social networks that it provided. Unlike their fellow (native German) Kreuzbergers, they could not blend into the eastern part of the city, but their ethnic difference would always be noticed. Furthermore, they were now competing with workers from former East Germany for employment, who did not carry the same stigma of being foreigners as did the German Turks and were generally cheaper to employ, as wage differentials between East and West were not immediately adjusted. German reunification, for many former guest workers, brought unemployment:

> The social and ethnic diversity was soon non-existent in the eastern part of Kreuzberg, in SO 36, on many blocks, and especially within the schools. Those who were left [behind] were . . . those people who did not have the means to leave, among them many Turkish migrants and the true Kreuzberg-lovers, who did not want to live anywhere else. (Düspohl 2009, 152)

Not until the late 1990s and early 2000s—about a decade after reunification—did Kreuzberg recover somewhat. As the districts in the East, such as Mitte, Prenzlauer Berg, and Friedrichshain, had become largely gentrified and rents in those districts soared in comparison to those in the old West, many students and artists returned. Kreuzberg was once again changing.

The End of Independence: District Reform and Kreuzberg-Friedrichshain

In 2001, Kreuzberg lost its administrative independence with the city's *Bezirksreform* (district reform), which reduced the number of citylike government entities from twenty-three to twelve and merged previously separate districts (Map 5).

Düspohl (2009) points out that even though Kreuzberg-Friedrichshainers initially felt like they were in a forced marriage, they increasingly collaborated on political issues that were decisive for the future of the district. For example, since the early 2000s, Kreuzbergers and Friedrichshainers have

Map 5. Berlin's twelve districts after the 2001 district reform.

united in supporting a direct democracy movement that encourages citizen activism on community issues. Kreuzberg's unique activist past has certainly been a major contributor to the district's current culture of citizen activism and involvement, especially because other districts in the city did not share its unusual activism.

Until Kreuzberg lost its status as a district of Berlin in 2001, the alternative Green Party, whose top leadership grew out of the 1968 student movement, dominated the district's local elections and government positions. However, the administrative fusion with the former East Berlin district of Friedrichshain into Friedrichshain-Kreuzberg has not affected the Green Party's local majority. In fact, the district was even able to send the Green Party's only directly elected member of parliament, Hans Christian Ströbele,[13] to the German parliament, the Bundestag.

The mayor of Friedrichshain-Kreuzberg is Green Party member Franz Schulz. He had been district mayor of Kreuzberg before the fusion in 2001 and was elected mayor of Friedrichshain-Kreuzberg in 2006. Schulz himself embodies the Kreuzberg protest culture. In 2008, the local district attorney's office sued Schulz for violating the constitutional right to freedom of association by participating in a blockade of the Kreuzberg town hall, where the right-wing social movement Pro-Deutschland (pro-Germany) had registered a protest. In fact, a January 5, 2009, article in the Berlin daily *Der Tagesspiegel* critiques Kreuzberg's perpetual protest culture:

> Protest? Any time! There are always reasons for protest and resistance in Kreuzberg. Administrative procedures are always cause for suspicion. Whether office buildings are to be constructed or trees to be cut down—just because they are politicians doesn't mean they should make those decisions here. In Kreuzberg, the people decide. And the people always find a way to help those in city hall or the [Berlin] senate understand the Kreuzberg way of grass roots democracy and citizen participation. . . . Someone always rebels in Kreuzberg, some battle is always in process. . . .
>
> Kreuzberg wants to remain Kreuzberg. Kreuzberg resists against an overall renewal, which makes the proletarian–anarchist milieu too expensive, too interesting for speculators and tourists. This attitude is supported neither by the "Green [Party]-leftist" district administration, nor by the "left-leftist" [Berlin] senate. Kreuzberg's antipolitical politics is still left [wing] at heart, proletarian, anarchist. But more than anything it is structurally conservative. The past was nice. We don't know anything about what the future may bring. We can only assume that it will be expensive.

This article describes how Kreuzberg's protest culture fundamentally shapes social relationships within the district, as well as the way the people in the district react to top-down policy making and outside influences: they create strong grassroots movements, subcultures, and social networks. The effects of these social phenomena have in turn shaped the Kreuzbergers' mentality.

The simultaneous development of immigrant social networks and a local counterculture is unique to Kreuzberg, where the local culture of resistance unintentionally helped preserve the space for Turkish immigrants by actively protesting urban renewal efforts that would have ultimately led to the displacement of the immigrants and the destruction of their social networks. Furthermore, the activist social context, which enabled Turkish immigrants in Kreuzberg to forge their own lived integration in the German society, appears to have had an effect on the immigrants as well. Esin, Deniz, and Bilge, immigrant women who live in Kreuzberg, appear have adopted Kreuzberg-style political activism and incorporated it into their daily lives.

Kreuzberg, unlike Neukölln, does not have an official integration platform or program. The district government states on its website (www.berlin.de/ba-friedrichshain-kreuzberg/verwaltung/org/intmigbeauftragte/index.html) that it is ready to lend support to immigrants as they engage in the process of adjusting to life in the city and foster intercultural understanding. This approach was echoed by Regina Reinke, the district's integration officer. The lack of a strong district government integration policy, as has been implemented by the local district administration in Neukölln, seems puzzling at first, especially in view of Kreuzberg-Friedrichshain's general liberal politics and political openness.

However, it is actually not surprising, given Kreuzberg's history and culture, that Kreuzberg's dominant counterculture image implies that political solutions to problems are not appreciated and are therefore unnecessary. The *Tagesspiegel* article about Kreuzberg's protest culture bears witness to that: Kreuzbergers do not appreciate political, top-down decision processes. Instead, they demand direct democracy solutions, created and deliberated directly within their lived space. This approach to political decision making is novel and relatively rare in Germany. Therefore, its overall effect should not be generalized. Kreuzberg's local identity is simultaneously rooted in its unique history as a place of immigration and resistance.

In addition, political involvement and participation have increasingly become an instrument of educated and privileged residents, as the interviews I conducted with the Turkish immigrant women show. The ones who are vocal, self-reflective, and political about their identity are also the ones with the highest levels of education. That statement is not meant to minimize the tremendous struggle for social upward mobility, which many of these women have experienced. Deniz's disturbing experience with the German education system, described in chapter 3, bears witness to that.

The less privileged Turkish immigrant women, on the other hand, do not participate in politics at the same level as the educated women, and the political activism of white-collar Turkish immigrant women in Kreuzberg may be of limited benefit to them because Kreuzberg's gentrification and soaring rents are driving the less educated and less upwardly mobile immigrants out.

The absence of an overall integration policy may be due to the perception by Kreuzberg's local government that top-down integration policy is not necessary and not appreciated by Kreuzberg's residents. However, the blue-collar Turkish immigrant women who work in Kreuzberg-sponsored employment programs for long-term unemployed immigrants look jealously toward neighboring Neukölln, where the district's programs are much better funded and offer immigrant residents who have little formal education permanent instead of temporary employment.

Is Kreuzberg becoming a lived space for the privileged only? The evidence is mixed. The somewhat more privileged—students and political liberals—have fundamentally shaped Kreuzberg's culture of resistance. However, their presence and resistance has in the past also created spaces for those with less political clout and less privilege, such as immigrants and workers, to benefit from and to be able to create a lived space for themselves in Kreuzberg. After all, it is not just the highly educated Turkish immigrant women who feel at home in Kreuzberg and have an intimate connection to the space; the less privileged and less educated women do too. It remains to be seen whether Kreuzberg can find a way to include them in the future, in spite of gentrification and rising rents.

Neukölln: Blue-Collar Traditions, Party Bosses, and Integration

Background

Neukölln has always been a blue-collar working-class district, seemingly far removed from the bourgeois amusements of the city's downtown. It became part of the ever-expanding Greater Berlin as the city's fourteenth administrative district on October 1, 1920. In the early twentieth century, when the city of Berlin was rapidly industrializing and growing in size, the Neukölln district suffered from a particularly severe lack of housing for the quickly expanding working class. The housing shortage affected the entire city and led to the construction of extended tracts of large apartment buildings in Neukölln. Although World War II destroyed many of these buildings across Berlin, the cityscape of Neukölln is still characterized by massive *Mietskasernen* (tenement houses), with their endless dark courtyards, harking back to the city's quick expansion of working-class housing during the industrial age. Home to predominantly working-class residents in the early twentieth century, Neukölln quickly became a stronghold of socialist movements and witnessed many working-class riots, most of which ended in bloodshed (Bowlby 1986).

After World War II, most of Neukölln's remaining old tenement housing was preserved and renovated. Once again, it became a cheap-rent district for the city's working class. Neukölln still maintains its working-class reputation today, but the district's southern outskirts underwent some redevelopment in the 1980s and are characterized by predominantly middle-income housing. The district's working-class communities also border the Hasenheide, a large inner-city park, adding to the appeal of the district. The Hasenheide features positively in the minds of the women from Neukölln and Kreuzberg because it lies at the intersection of both districts. Several of them describe it as a popular place for taking walks, a place they long for on long visits to Turkey. The Hasenheide belongs to their dreams of making a home in Berlin. This is interesting because even though the Hasenheide is a beautiful park, it is also known as one of Berlin's central locations for drug trade, and it is not unusual that unsuspecting pedestrians will be offered drugs to buy even in broad daylight when innocently strolling through the park. Neukölln, despite its continued existence as a working-class, blue-collar district, in the early twentieth century escaped the protest and social activism of the 1960s and 1970s. During those postwar years, there was little to no influx of students and intellectuals into Neukölln, the two groups who were responsible for jump-starting the social activism, protest, resistance, and direct democracy in Kreuzberg. In other words, politics in Neukölln did not develop in a bottom-up fashion, but largely as a political program, created and implemented from the top down by the district government. Unlike in Kreuzberg, there are no local initiatives and no protest movements, and there is no insistence on grassroots and direct democracy.

Neukölln Blows Up: Rütli and the Coming of Neukölln's Integration Policy

In the years after the implementation of the new 2000 immigration law and its modification in 2005, which led to a stronger political emphasis on the need for an integration policy, several local events propelled Neukölln unwillingly to the top of a nationwide integration agenda. In early 2006, a collective letter written by a number of teachers from Neukölln's Rütli school, a *Hauptschule* educating students in the lowest tier of Germany's traditional, three-tiered school system, reached the Berlin government and was also distributed to the Berlin news media.[14] In the letter, the teachers demanded that the government take action by fundamentally rethinking the school system and providing more funds to "problem schools" like Rütli. The teachers noted that the level of violence and offensive behavior by Rütli students in class and on school grounds had become unbearable to them, and they were unable to continue teaching. A key fact: at the time the letter was written, the total percentage of immigrant children (from mostly Turkish and Arab families) had risen to 83.2 percent of all students enrolled at Rütli (*Die Zeit* 2006). At the heart of the letter—and the public debate that followed—was, once again, the issue of immigrant integration, this time specifically within a school environment: "Children of German origin, who are being mocked as 'pork-eaters,' try to adapt to the customs of the majority at Rütli and are increasingly speaking broken German [mimicking the accent of the immigrant children], in order to avoid standing out too much" (*Die Zeit* 2006). The immediate response by the Neukölln government was to increase security around the school in order to prevent conflict, as many Rütli students were said to be bringing small weapons, such as knives, into school. The school experienced an increased police presence in and around campus and found itself besieged outside the school grounds by large numbers of reporters, camera teams, and photographers. The Rütli letter also prompted an uproar in the entire German media. Reporters and pundits, as well as some politicians, claimed the Rütli situation was substantial proof of the failure of integration, the formation of parallel societies, and the existence of reverse discrimination, where ethnic Germans increasingly become the victims of mocking, discrimination, and violence by immigrants (*Die Zeit* 2006). Furthermore, for the German public, Neukölln became a general showcase for the true meaning of the failed integration of immigrants in Germany.

However, the Rütli disaster also opened a political window of opportunity for a new way of administering integration policy at the local level. If Neukölln's problems could be solved politically, so could the problems in similar problem areas all across the nation. The concentrated media attention around Rütli as an immigrant problem school provided the district administration under Neukölln's mayor, Heinz Buschkowsky, with an opportunity to create a strong political profile for Neukölln within the realm of integration policy. Given the media prominence, Neukölln's response to the Rütli issue would receive nationwide attention.

Neukölln's government officials subsequently developed a top-down approach to integration policy, which primarily focuses on control of the immigrants' cultural and religious conduct, as well their assimilation to German values. It is framed as a response to the image of violent immigrant youth, who do not have a proper command of German, exhibit aggressive behavior and conservative Muslim religious beliefs, and are dependent on the extensive German social welfare system. Given the apparent urgency of the Rütli issue, a political response focused on security, control, and top-down enforcement appears to be the strategically logical political response.

Buschkowsky and Integration

Neukölln's district mayor Heinz Buschkowsky is the strong personality and mastermind behind Neukölln's approaches to immigrant integration. His administration developed an extensive integration program (see www.ber lin.de/ba-neukoelln/migrationsbeauftragten/integrationspolitik.html and

Appendix C) which has received nationwide acclaim and has served as a model approach for many other cities and communities throughout the country. The official website of the district of Neukölln (as cited above) features a lengthy essay reflecting on the meaning of integration. Integration is defined by the Buschkowsky administration as a lifelong process, which in order to be successful requires the cooperation of Germans and of immigrants living in the district. As does Kreuzberg, the district of Neukölln employs an integration officer, whose office is an integral part of the overall administration. Not all twelve municipal districts of the city of Berlin have a local integration officer, though the current Berlin government, led by Social Democrats, is lobbying to make the creation of a district- or community-based integration office a requirement in every district of the city.

The Buschkowsky administration has worked out a ten-point agenda for integration, which is presented on the district's official website. Overall, on the basis of these ten points, immigrants are largely defined as the problem, with the receiving society and local government presented as problem solvers (Appendix C). Despite its strong emphasis on the importance of cooperation between immigrants, administration, and "German" neighborhood residents, the ten points imply that immigrants themselves present the main obstacle to the integration process. According to Buschkowsky's integration agenda, immigrants need to be (re-)educated and encouraged to participate in German life, but they also need to be policed.

The ten points include the rather strong suggestion that Muslim immigrants need to be reminded of and educated about the "free democratic basic order" outlined by the German constitution. This statement appears to rest on two central assumptions. First, it presupposes that most immigrants are, in fact, practicing Muslims, and, second, it suggests that Muslim religious beliefs generally and fundamentally clash with German or Western democratic principles. These assumptions are particularly relevant when it comes to women: female immigrants are said to be in need of special support because they are generally assumed to experience male oppression in their communities, an assumption based on the interpretation of Islam as fundamentally undemocratic and misogynist. Islam and the cultural identity of Turkish and Arabic immigrants are framed as the central obstacle to integration in Neukölln. The ten points leave unanswered the question whether mere cultural assimilation of immigrants into German society can actually improve their social status, or whether some of their problems may also be rooted in prejudice against or rejection of immigrants, as has been suggested by many of my interviewees in chapter 3. In general, Neukölln's integration agenda voices significant generalizations about an immigrant group and its religious faith, when in fact the group is highly heterogeneous in terms of cultural background and religious observance. The Turkish community in Berlin is deeply split along the lines of religion and secularism. According to a survey funded by a Christian Democrat nonprofit organization, the Konrad Adenauer Foundation, 43 percent of Turkish immigrants in Germany overall organize their lives completely or mostly according to the rules of Islam. Another 27 percent follow the rules of Islam only partially, while slightly more than a quarter of all German Turks do not identify with religion at all and describe their lives as more or less secular (Von Wilamowitz-Moellendorff 2001).

However, even if we accept the fact that some cultural adjustments—religious or otherwise—are necessary for immigrants from different cultures to live in Germany, the ten points on immigration by the district of Neukölln illustrate only one side of the integration process. Although it focuses on the practice of undemocratic variants of Islam among immigrants, Neukölln's ten-point integration policy does not address the problems Turkish immigrants experience as a result of their different names and their different skin and hair color. By ignoring the reality of the immigrant experience, Neukölln's integration policy can be seen as a halfway measure that is open to severe criticism. Several professional social workers of Turkish immigrant background interviewed for this book were highly critical of the high-visibility integration programs of the Neukölln administration. They noted, for instance, that although the idea of creating support programs as well as child care and education initiatives represents a positive development, it is questionable how effective these programs are in their current state. Some of them accused the district administration of being more interested in staging a high-profile media campaign rather than trying to implement fundamental changes and long-term improvements to integration policy. Several social workers of immigrant background were especially critical of the fact that the district's employment initiatives hire immigrant women with no professional education as social workers to support other immigrant women in the integration process.[15] They argued that these women have no formal education in the field and themselves require the support of professional social workers. They are therefore not adequately qualified to provide professional psychological support to other immigrant women in order to aid the integration process. According to my interviewees trained in social work, the *Stadtteilmütter* program in Neukölln is merely a self-promotion campaign for the district's mayor, Buschkowsky.

Their critical perspective has not prevailed. According to the district of Neukölln's official website, the program has received glowing reviews in the local and national media in Germany, as well as nine German awards and one international one. It has also served as a model program for other inner-city districts in Berlin, as well as several other cities throughout Germany; the city of Cologne has already implemented a similar program, and the *Stadtteilmütter* initiative is now part of the official integration program of the Christian Democrat administration in the German state of North Rhine Westphalia.

The rather negative attitude regarding Neukölln's social integration programs among highly educated Turkish immigrant women conveys a feeling of frustration with high-profile, top-down integration policies. It reflects their desire to be more actively involved in creating and shaping those programs—not merely as participants, but as directors in charge. They imply that lived integration approaches may be less visible but are often more effective than top-down policy approaches, which are pregnant with political symbolism and often embrace their media success more than they implement actual changes on the ground. Nevertheless, the more blue-color interviewees from Neukölln all expressed their enthusiasm about Buschkowsky's program, from which they benefit directly.

Buschkowsky did not only implement a strong integration agenda in Neukölln. He also symbolically transformed the very school that had driven teachers to desperation and the city of Berlin to sending in police protection. Starting during the 2009–10 school year, the former Rütli school was merged with several other schools in order to create a new comprehensive school, in which an ethnically and intellectually diverse student body studies as a community, with the possibility for students to obtain any of the three degrees (*Hauptschule* degree, *Realschule* degree, or the *Abitur*). This is a model project, called Campus Rütli—"Education through Integration"—funded by the city of Berlin, creating what has been called the First Community School (*erste Gemeinschaftsschule*), emphasizing the aspect of community over segregation of students on the basis of educational attainment or ethnicity.

Although the improvements of educational facilities and the special investment of government money into expanding and improving schools in problem areas is laudable and goes beyond any previous government initiatives toward integration, the jury is still out on the effect that Campus Rütli can have on Neukölln as a whole. So far, the program has been received positively in policy circles, as well as among the German and German Turkish publics. Campus Rütli may present a chance for politicians and immigrants to collaborate in finding new strategies for combining political and lived integration approaches. Its approach is unique in that it incorporates the neighborhood and the students' families into the education experience. This means that Campus Rütli's educational concept is built on the official recognition that social and residential segregation exists in Neukölln and creates disadvantages—especially for immigrant children—with regard to educational attainment and upward social mobility. In acknowledging the social context in which its students operate, Rütli is able to design an educational experience specifically targeted at its student population. For instance, it actively embraces multilingual education as a chance for children and educators to utilize and improve the linguistic potential of immigrant and German youths (*Focus* 2008b). It remains to be seen how well Campus Rütli will have performed once it produces the first graduates. Currently, media attention is exclusively positive, and Campus Rütli is being advertised as a model project for integration nationwide.

Apart from Campus Rütli, the underlying assumptions of Neukölln's integration agenda seem to be symptomatic of an integration policy that polices immigrants instead of investigating the root causes of their issues. It is important to note that the Buschkowsky administration's policy approach was bolstered by the famous Häussermann study. Hartmut Häussermann was a prominent German urban sociologist at Humboldt University Berlin, whose working group commissioned a study about the social development of different areas in the district of Neukölln between 2001 and 2006.[16] The study relied on a number of social indices that were used to measure the social decline or improvement of individual local cells within the district of Neukölln. The indicators included the number of residents, from which the group measured in- and outmigration of Germans and individuals of immigrant background, divided by age groups, in order to capture processes of ethnic segregation. In addition, the indicators measured the level of unemployment among Germans and immigrants, as well as long-term unemployment, unemployment by age group, and recipients of different categories of social welfare, in order to capture processes of social segmentation. Häussermann concluded that particularly those cells with high numbers of immigrants, located in the northern, more densely populated urban areas of Neukölln, could be identified as problem areas, which are declining in social status. These problem areas are also increasingly ethnically segregated, with people of immigrant background living in the poor northern parts of the district, and ethnic Germans living in the more affluent southern areas. He emphasized that the schools located within the increasingly segregated problem areas were in need of increased political attention. Häussermann, Kapphan, and Förste (2008) argued that educational opportunity in particular is of crucial importance for the improvement of opportunity for immigrants. This report provided social scientific support to Buschkowsky's approach, and it further improved his reputation as a local engine of integration.

Neukölln's high-profile approach to immigrant integration policy has had a twofold effect: its district mayor has gained German- and Europewide prominence, and Neukölln has become an example of district-level, government-administrated integration programs. Neukölln's top-down approach to integration represents a direct contrast, if not an antidote, to Kreuzberg's bottom-up, grassroots-dominated culture, in which the direct democracy initiatives of its citizens have been more prominent and influential than the policies of the local administration.

Excursus: A Local Machine? Neukölln's Local Politics Today

Neukölln's Social Democratic mayor, Heinz Buschkowsky, is somewhat controversial in the district and beyond for his latent public support for certain aspects of Sarrazin's controversial book, *Germany Does Away With Itself,* and his public statements that multiculturalism has failed in Germany. Yet he is clearly the central public persona behind integration policy in Neukölln and the nationwide face of Neukölln's integration program. His critical influence on Berlin's and Germany's integration policy discourse and his self-proclaimed identity as a street-level politician bear on this book's central thesis, which argues for a differentiation between top-down and lived integration discourses that converge in Buschkowsky's dual public persona. Therefore, before proceeding to the concluding remarks on this comparison of Kreuzberg and Neukölln, I provide a detailed introduction.

Buschkowsky has been district mayor since 2001. His prominence beyond Neukölln's and Berlin's borders is a consequence of one of his most famous—and most controversial—political statements: "*Multi-Kulti ist gescheitert*" (multiculturalism has failed) (*Der Tagesspiegel* 2008a). German chancellor Angela Merkel reiterated the same phrase in her famous speech on October 16, 2010, in Potsdam, Germany. Buschkowsky is the face of Neukölln's local government, ruling over the district with a strong hand, in some aspects similar to the classic Irish Democrat political machine bosses of Boston, New York, and Chicago. Buschkowsky certainly does not support any of the corruption these regimes were characterized by. However, he uses similar tactics of street politics.[17]

Classic political machines were prevalent in urban areas of the United States of the mid- to late 1800s. They were dominated by Irish immigrant communities, and their power was dependent on a strong presence in neighborhoods and precincts—literally on street corners. Members of the machines had one foot on the street and the other in city hall. The precinct captains represented the foothold in the neighborhood. They would answer to the aldermen, who were representing the entire ward in city hall and who were in turn headed by the machine boss, who in most cases was the city mayor (Judd and Swanstrom 2011). The boss was generally from a poor or working-class background and had a loud, energetic personality and rough manners. Machine politicians did not strive to be intellectuals, and they did not practice white-collar mannerisms or attend afternoon teas.

Buschkowsky's inner-party political career is based on some of the same elements that gave the Daleys in Chicago (or the early Kennedys) so much political clout. His most important political asset is his engagement with the neighborhood. Buschkowsky does not rely on precinct captains. He walks the streets himself and engages in conversations with the local residents. He describes his real office to be located on the street corner, not in an office building. He was born in Neukölln; his mother came from Silesia (now Poland) to Berlin. His father was a locksmith, his mother a secretary. They were seen as a traditional working-class family, and Buschkowsky grew up in a small one-room apartment in southern Neukölln. His father permanently ruined his health working to realize the family's dream by building a small family home on the outskirts of southern Neukölln (Der Tagesspiegel 2008a).

Buschkowsky's upbringing and family history are said to have had a strong effect on his political career. He became a Social Democrat—a Neukölln-style Social Democrat—who never left his neighborhood. Buschkowsky studied public administration in Berlin and then quickly worked his way up the hierarchy of administrative offices in the small world of the political enclave that was West Berlin in the 1970s and 1980s. According to Der Tagesspiegel (2008a), in Neukölln, Buschkowsky moved up through the party ranks thanks to his good connections within the infamous Britzer Kreis (Britz circle).[18] Even in working-class Neukölln, which would be expected to vote unanimously Social Democrat, the Christian Democrats were dominating the political scene in the 1980s. Thus, to be successful, aspiring Social Democrats had to be "robust and down-to-earth" (Der Tagesspiegel 2008a)—attributes that helped Buschkowsky become district mayor for the first time in 1989, then again in 2001. Buschkowsky can hardly be described as an elitist intellectual; he is a heart-and-soul politician, a homebody who enjoys his presence in and personal connections to the neighborhood. He would rather attend a local street fair than spend his time in meeting rooms and offices. He prefers politics at the party base and on the street corner to the ivory towers of state and federal policy makers in order to understand how policies affect daily life (*Der Tagesspiegel* 2008a).

Buschkowsky is also a controversial character. His criticism of his own district's increasing poverty and the formation of parallel societies has been met with disapproval by his party colleagues, who note that Buschkowsky himself has significantly contributed to local policy in Neukölln for more than twenty years, and therefore he should be seen as at least partly responsible for the outcomes. His complaints, they argue, are therefore directed at what they understand to be the effects of his own policies.

Buschkowsky has also commented publicly on the controversial book published by his party comrade, Thilo Sarrazin, *Germany Does Away With Itself*. According to the German weekly *Der Spiegel* (September 6, 2010), Buschkowsky noted that Sarrazin ignored a number of details that Buschkowsky claims to have given him specific advice on, such as the specific differentiations in religious practice and doctrine among different groups within the Muslim faith: "He didn't include in his book many of the things that I had explained to him in detail. . . . Among the Alawites [Alevis], gender equality, the condemnation of violence and education are important principles of life" (quoted in *Der Spiegel,* September 6, 2010). However, Buschkowsky has also noted that he agrees with Sarrazin on several crucial points, such as the formation of parallel societies among Muslim immigrants and the supposedly counterproductive political correctness among some multiculturalists, which, according to Buschkowsky, leads to an ignorance of social reality: "It is the usual refusal to acknowledge reality, the whitewashing, that I find [problematic] even among integration officials. The biggest enemy of a reasonable integration policy is ignorance" (*Der Spiegel* 2010).

What is particularly interesting about Buschkowsky as the driving force behind integration policy in Neukölln's vastly popular integration campaign is the fact that Buschkowsky, who identifies himself as an explicitly local politician conducting politics for and from the streets of Neukölln, drives such a strong top-down approach to integration policy. With the exception of Campus Rütli, Buschkowksy's street experience and intimate familiarity with the neighborhood—which presumably includes the immigrant areas— have not found expression in Neukölln's integration program. In fact, integration policy in Neukölln appears to be based on preconceived notions about immigrant identity rather than active engagements with immigrants themselves. In that context, Buschkowsky's rejection of the ivory tower of high politics appears strikingly ironic. His partial support for Sarrazin's theses on immigrants in Germany seems to be further evidence that at best, Buschkowsky's interactions with immigrants in his own district have been superficial. At worst, his statements raise the specter of a street-level politician for ethnic Germans only. This apparent lack of active engagement with the immigrant citizens in his district has not affected his image as a street-level politician, which has lent him and his integration program tremendous credibility as a model program for tackling integration issues across the nation.

In sum, the credibility of Buschkowsky's strong top-down integration approach relies heavily on his image as a street-savvy politician. Through the power of well-thought-out campaigns and media images, Buschkowsky has been able to embed his political persona in the lived space of the community and utilize this advantage to advance his top-down integration policy.

Bottom-Up versus Top-Down Policy Making

In Neukölln, we encounter a strong official discourse on integration, where the local government as central authority defines the main tenets of integration, as well as the problems that integration policy is supposed to address. On the other hand, Kreuzberg's integration approach, insofar as it even exists in the first place, is much weaker. These different policy approaches are partly contingent on the way policy makers frame the presence and on the clustering of immigrant minorities in certain areas of the city. In the cases of Kreuzberg and Neukölln, it is therefore not merely the political approaches and outcomes that differ, but their very approaches of policy makers to immigration and the way they frame immigrant clustering in the public discourse. In other words, in Neukölln, immigrant clustering emerged as a persistent problem with the Rütli crisis and continues to be framed as such by Buschkowsky and his administration. This framing has led to a strong top-down integration policy program as the solution to an apparent immigrant problem. In Kreuzberg, on the other hand, no dominant policy discourse exists that frames immigrant integration as an explicit issue that needs to be addressed. As a consequence, no strong solution in the shape of a policy program is needed.

John Kingdon (1995) differentiates between conditions and problems. Conditions, he notes, do not turn into problems until the moment someone decides that something should be done about them. Identifying problems is a complex process. Problem definition is not simply the decision of policy makers or public figures. In fact, Kingdon (1995, 93) argues that "demonstrating that there is indeed a problem to which one's solution can be attached is a very real preoccupation of participants in the policy process." Policy makers usually use indicators to demonstrate that a condition is in fact a serious problem. As Kingdon points out, even data supportive of the seriousness of one problem or another do not speak for themselves but have to be interpreted or framed in a certain way by those who present them. Immigration, unlike many other issues, is actually one of the few problems whose existence the public rarely needs to be sold on. In general, for a large variety of different reasons, (European) general publics tend to hold relatively strong attachments to the issue of immigration (Lahav 2004). European publics appear to be reluctant at best about immigration— though scholars tend to agree that the number of indicators and reasons for negative views on immigration vary greatly (Citrin and Sides 2007). Therefore, policy makers in Germany tend to have an easier time justifying their definition of immigration as an actual problem rather than merely a condition.

However, policy makers' frames about immigrants and integration may not only be the consequence of public opinion on immigration, but also the cause for it. A 2011 study on integration in Berlin, entitled "Wie tolerant ist Berlin?" (How tolerant is Berlin?) (Liljeberg and Krambeer 2011), presents a sociodemographic analysis of Berlin's immigrant population, as well as the perceptions of ethnic Germans toward immigrants. Overall, the study finds that with regard to immigrants, Berlin is a rather tolerant city: 74 percent of Berliners without an immigrant background have generally positive perceptions of immigrants. Broken down by district, however, the picture is more complicated. The study finds that it is generally older ethnic Germans, with little formal education and who live in districts among few to no immigrants, who exhibit the most negative opinions on immigration. For instance, almost half (48 percent) of respondents from the former East Berlin district of Hellersdorf, a largely ethnic German district located at the edge of the city, see immigration as mainly negative.[19] On the contrary, ethnic Germans who live in districts with larger immigrant populations exhibit more positive perceptions of immigrants. In this context, Neukölln appears to be the exception. In Neukölln, 25 percent of respondents showed negative perceptions of Turkish immigrants, in comparison to much lower rates in other districts with comparably large immigrant populations, such as Friedrichshain-Kreuzberg (18 percent), Tempelhof-Schöneberg (16 percent), and Mitte (15 percent).

Liljeberg and Krambeer's 2011 study provides food for thought. Why is Neukölln such an outlier with regard to public opinion of ethnic Germans regarding immigrants? It is possible that Neukölln's exceptionally top-down, hands-on, high-profile integration approach is moving its ethnic German public toward a more negative perception of the immigrant population. In fact, Jacobs and Shapiro (2000) argue that policy makers generally ignore public opinion outside of election years and largely follow their own political convictions. Jacobs and Shapiro make the case that policy makers are invested in tracking public opinion mainly because they are interested in changing it. Their research indicates that policy makers have the potential to lead public opinion instead of accommodating it. If this is in the case of Neukölln's integration policy, and its framing of integration is largely a means of control and assimilation, then Buschkowsky's integration approach is far more consequential for the coexistence of ethnic Germans and immigrants than just providing employment opportunities.

In any case, integration policy provides an avenue for policy makers to emphasize certain problems and solutions, thereby also affecting public opinion. Because of the diversity of issues associated with immigration, problem definition can vary from value statements about national identity and culture (such as immigrants—particularly those of a different religion—presenting a challenge to persistent norms and values, as well as the dominant language), as well as about economic (competition for jobs) and welfare (immigrants are accused of being a drain on the welfare state) issues.

Problems, once they have been convincingly defined, then become attached to proposed solutions; they are, according to Kingdon (1995), coupled. Kingdon argues that in the policy process, it is rarely the case that solutions are created once problems have been identified—quite the contrary: "Solutions float around in and near government, searching for problems to which to become attached or political events that increase their likelihood of adoption" (172). The political advocates of certain solutions attach them to a problem once the problem has been defined and framed accordingly.

According to Baumgartner and Jones (1993), policy makers who are in favor of more attaching certain solutions to problems also

> take advantage ... of public or media concern with the issue and push for new legislation. Generally speaking, this new legislation commits funds and creates new institutions. These new institutions and the people who work for them do not disappear even if public or media concern fades away. In fact, they can easily perpetuate themselves, because for the first time they may be able to generate statistics or reports that substantiate what they have suspected all along: that their issue is of alarming proportions, and increased government vigilance is called for. (169)

In addition, Baumgartner and Jones note that as government activity and the expansion of institutions around a certain issue increase media coverage, research, and public opinion are also affected by this. In other words, the amount of public attention given to a specific issue is self-perpetuating: once it has been defined as a problem and a proposed solution is on the road to implementation, there is also a good chance that the issue will receive increased and continuous attention.

In Neukölln, the process described by Baumgartner and Jones (1993) can clearly be observed. Problem definition of immigrant integration as a crucial local issue with nationwide implications for Germany as a whole had been coupled with the opening of a window of opportunity for policy implementation. The incremental growth in inclusiveness in German citizenship policy and the high-profile Rütli incident spurred the creation of new institutions and policies in Neukölln around the issue of integration. Whether it is effective or not, Buschkowsky's integration policy is the result of his administration's successful problem definition of immigrant integration as a serious issue. Media attention, which reached a climax with the emergence of the Rütli school as a powerful symbol of failed Germanywide Turkish integration elevated Buschkowsky and his high-profile integration campaign to become a Germanywide example for integration. If the problems in Neukölln could be tackled, they could be tackled anywhere else in Germany. Campus Rütli and Neukölln's integration program continue to attract media attention across the nation.

Whether Neukölln's integration program is in fact successful remains to be seen. The 2006 Häussermann study, conducted two years after the Rütli incident, at the same time when many of the high-profile integration programs in Neukölln were starting to take shape, does not indicate that social segmentation and ethnic segregation in northern Neukölln are letting up. Or perhaps it may take much longer to see the effects of these programs.

Given its working-class history, one might be inclined to conclude that Neukölln—especially its older, more urban northern parts—has always been at the social margins of Berlin. However, it is striking that women of Turkish immigrant background in Neukölln feel much less at home in Neukölln than they feel in Kreuzberg, despite the fact that Neukölln has been making an active effort to provide them with a number of well-funded, permanent employment opportunities, such as the *Stadtteilmütter.*

One of the reasons for this could lie in the very nature of Neukölln's integration programs: problem definition and coupling—the attachment of a policy solution to the previously defined problem—as well as the final policy implementation happen from the top down. Here, the dominant political understanding of integration as control and assimilation of immigrants to the local culture and society is strongly reflected in the integration policy program formulated by Buschkowsky and his administration. Buschkowsky himself, though a heart-and-soul street-level politician, reiterates and endorses some of the stereotypes about (Turkish) immigrants brought forth by Sarrazin in *Germany Does Away With Itself.* It is fair to say that the jury is still out when it comes to evaluating the success of Buschkowsky's integration programs. Their implementation is likely too recent for them make any measurable difference. For the time being, it is safe to say that Neukölln's integration programs have actually produced some positive outcomes for immigrants: the Turkish immigrant women from Neukölln are highly appreciative of the opportunity to find potentially permanent employment in the district's programs, such as the *Stadtteilmütter.* Thus, blue-collar Turkish immigrant women tend to benefit from some aspects of Neukölln's Secondspace integration programs. However, as some of the white-collar immigrant women from Kreuzberg argued in the interviews I conducted, Neukölln's approach to integration is not sufficient. Immigrants are not encouraged to create their own avenues to integration but are instead artificially supported by employment initiatives, which are not sustainable or efficient, and which are described by the women as mere media campaigns.

The collaborative and integrative structure of Campus Rütli presents a notable exception from the rule of top-down integration policy in Neukölln. It remains to be seen what kind of effect the first generation of Campus Rütli graduates and the long-term inclusion of the highly diverse student body as well as their families, cultural backgrounds, and neighborhoods in this promising educational project will have on integration in Neukölln as a whole. It seems possible that Campus Rütli might present an opportunity to merge the lived integration strategies of the immigrants with policy approaches to integration.

The roots of the differences between Kreuzberg's and Neukölln's integration strategies, it appears, can in part be found in the two districts' different histories, especially with regard to social activism. Kreuzberg's strong social movements and its historical inclination toward direct democracy appear to have shaped a social culture that binds its residents together. Bottom-up approaches to politics in general are deeply historically embedded in Kreuzberg's social fabric. From my analysis, Kreuzberg emerges, at least for the time being, as a true Thirdspace of lived experience that, time and time again, has managed to actively influence spatial policy from below. Thus, a strongly formalized local government policy on integration (or any other social issue, for that matter) is neither necessary nor appreciated in

Kreuzberg. The question remains, however, how long Kreuzberg can resist gentrification, and how its local culture will be affected by the arrival of new gentrifiers. It emerges from the research in this book that it is, as always, the immigrants who get displaced first. Without an established social culture of resistance and strong social networks, it is unlikely that displaced individuals of Turkish immigrant background will be able to recreate their Kreuzberg elsewhere—not even in neighboring Neukölln.

Overall, this chapter has demonstrated that location and space matter in many ways. The neighborhood perspective unveils an additional layer of political, sociocultural, and historical information that can significantly affect integration policy as well as lived integration from neighborhood to neighborhood. A micro-level perspective and an exploration of the social context is therefore vital for understanding social processes and interactions. Social interactions are deeply embedded in the local culture in both Neukölln and Kreuzberg, which actively shapes the political approaches to and public receptions of integration programs in both localities. However, politics and social relations in Kreuzberg and Neukölln are not only historically contingent, but can also be actively influenced by present-day policy making. If a control-focused approach to integration policy, like the one in Neukölln, can potentially affect public opinion on immigration negatively, it is not just the past but also the future that will shape the process of immigrant incorporation in Berlin and elsewhere.

CONCLUSION

Learning from Immigrant Neighborhoods

> We learn at the last to look at our brothers as aliens. Alien men with whom we share a city, but not a community. . . . But we can perhaps remember, that those who live with us are our brothers, that they share with us the same short moment of life, that they seek as do we, nothing but the chance to live out their lives in purpose and in happiness, surely this bond of common fate, this bond of common roles can begin to teach us something, that we can begin to work a little harder, to become in our hearts brothers and countrymen once again.
>
> —Robert F. Kennedy (1968)

THE POLITICAL DEBATE about integration and integration policy continues at all levels of German politics and society. This book has explored the dominant framing of this discourse in the public arena (for example, by policy makers and the media) and has juxtaposed that framing to the hitherto unexplored perceptions of the immigrant themselves and the lives they live in their neighborhood communities. The analysis has presented the same issue—integration in Berlin—from two completely different perspectives: the policy debate on integration, and immigrants' lives in the neighborhood. Bringing these two perspectives together provides an understanding of how Turkish immigrants in particular have become the focus of integration policies, but their underrepresentation in the political arena has provided them with little agency in the debate so far.

There can be no question that the topic of integration is extraordinarily complex. Integration policy approaches and ideas regarding integration differ at the national, state, and local governmental levels, as well as within political parties. For example, within one governmental entity, the city of Berlin, twelve self-governing districts are entitled to develop their own local policy approaches to integration. This complexity can be linked to the fact that the content of integration policy remains contested. The majority population and the country's immigrant citizens have not yet agreed on a definition of the term *integration*. There are also signs of change in Berlin's integration discourse. The increasing presence of a still small number of policy makers of immigrant background in local government, such as Eren Ünsal or Bilkay Öney, is making a crucial contribution to transforming the discourse. Immigrants have begun to make their voices heard as political actors and decision makers; they are helping to address and shape the Berlin integration debate. Politically involved Turkish community organizations, such as the Turkish Union Berlin-Brandenburg (TBB), are another important political actor in the integration debate. Their role in the process is manifold and complex. The number of Turkish community organizations with sufficient credibility to influence mainstream politics in Germany overall is limited. Therefore, organizations such as the TBB are expected to fulfill a dual role in the public debate. They have to speak with one voice when they represent the Turkish immigrant community as a whole, particularly in interactions with German policy makers and the media, while taking care to also accommodate the myriad and diverse perspectives that characterize their ethnic community. The findings indicate that the TBB has indeed managed to perform this dual function successfully. By overcoming the divisions within the Turkish immigrant community along the lines of religion and ethnicity, the TBB has been able to become a political force in Berlin's integration debate on behalf of the whole Turkish community.

This research contributes a new perspective to the complex debates by examining immigrants' experiences, life practices, and views on integration. The immigrants' lived reality reveals that integration also includes a spatial dimension: the urban immigrant neighborhood. Immigrant neighborhoods are powerful sites of identity formation that stand apart from the dominant discourse. Neighborhoods reflect the differences in German and Turkish cultural experiences but are also the sites where individuals from both cultural backgrounds find strategies to live next to and with each other. In exploring integration as a neighborhood practice, this book adds an additional layer of analysis: the neighborhood context. This additional layer unveils local differences in integration policy, the immigrants' lived integration, and the way in which they are partially embedded in the social context of the neighborhood itself. The protest culture in Kreuzberg's past has ultimately led to a different sociopolitical environment in comparison to Neukölln, which has also affected how Turkish immigrant women have integrated themselves into these neighborhoods and how they experience them.

Recap

How Are Immigrants Talked About?

Party platforms and official party programs put different emphases on the importance of integration as a political goal. Although some parties (Green Party, Social Democrats, Christian Democrats) emphasize integration as a main policy goal, other parties (Left Party, Libertarians) lack specific statements on integration or provide only a general, national-level approach to integration without the formulation of a specific strategy in context of Berlin, or more specifically the city's immigrant neighborhoods. Furthermore, the central emphases in integration strategies focus on protecting women's rights in the face of those different cultural practices that the German majority population feels alienated by. In addition, integration policies seek first to ensure the immigrants' internalization of the main tenets of German basic democratic order, and second to provide better educational attainment, in turn leading to better access to the labor market. The left-of-center parties define integration as a mutual and interactive process between host population and immigrants. The Christian Democrats emphasize the centrality of immigrant cooperation, including the need for them to conform to German culture and language, for the potential success of the integration process. In other words, the center-left parties tend to define integration as a bidirectional process between immigrants and the host population, whereas the center-right parties view integration as one-directional and tend to demand cultural and linguistic conformity from immigrants.

Aside from the differences between political parties in their approach to integration and their general emphasis on integration as a policy goal, there are also important individual differences among those involved in the integration debate. In other words, party identification is not always a predictor of individual stances on integration, despite the strict party discipline in Germany. This means that two individuals from the same party can have quite different opinions on integration policy. These individual differences indicate that there is a strong emotional dimension to integration policy, which for many policy makers and bureaucrats has a personal dimension as well.

In personal conversations with policy makers, parliamentarians, and government bureaucrats, a new group of culturally competent voices in the integration discourse stands out. The group includes two identifiable sets of members: first, young, highly educated individuals with immigrant backgrounds, who are able to integrate their own experiences as immigrants into the discourse; and second, Germans who have been active in the formulation of integration strategies at the neighborhood level and who have gained crucial real-life experience through their numerous interactions with different immigrants. Many of these individuals recognize the real problems of immigrants, which are related to aspects of visibility and consist of (predominantly Muslim) religious symbolism, but which are also connected to markers of ethnicity such as accents, non-German names, or appearance. Although many of the decision makers involved in integration policy recognize these problems, the political parties show a persistent, notable resistance to addressing the issues of immigrants. A mostly German perspective remains dominant in the policy arena.

The contribution of the representatives of the Turkish immigrant community has emerged as another important factor in the political debate on integration in Berlin. The TBB is the largest and most politically involved Turkish community organization in Berlin; it is closely associated with the Social Democrats. Instead of formulating its own political agenda on integration policy, the TBB helped to create the integration agenda of the Social Democratic Party in Berlin, and the organization adheres to this agenda. The close association between the TBB and the governing political party raises questions about the political agenda of the TBB and its ability to represent an immigrant population as diverse (with regard to ethnicity, religion, and culture) as the Turkish community in Berlin. However, the close affiliation with the Social Democrats benefits the TBB and its members because the organization gains inside access to Berlin's local government, which can have important positive effects for the representation of Turkish immigrants in the city. It is important to reiterate that the Turkish community is highly diverse and strongly divided along the lines of religion, culture, and ethnicity, so that the TBB representatives' efforts to speak for the Turkish immigrant community as a whole can be judged remarkably successful. The TBB is aware of its responsibility for overcoming the internal differences among Turkish immigrants in order to establish a better position in Berlin politics for the Turkish community as a whole. Perhaps the strenuous efforts to bridge internal differences are due to the fact that, as several TBB representatives expressed during the interviews, German Turks share a common immigrant history. That history often includes similar experiences of rejection, even among those with high levels of education and higher ranks within the social fabric of German society. Apparently, common life experiences, coupled with an immigrant identity, have evolved as a uniting element when it comes to policy formulations within the community. This finding is highly significant for the future of the integration debate in Germany overall. Currently, German policy makers seem to address integration issues broadly through generalized approaches that are intended to solve the immigrant integration issue nationwide. In stark contrast, the immigrants' lived experiences are strongly localized and take place at the neighborhood level. The gap between the highly general discourse on integration and the reality of the immigrants' local experiences can be bridged at least partially by the intercultural competence of the policy makers of second-generation immigrant background, who are entering the political discourse in Berlin. Their personal, localized experiences with integration are turning out to be critical motivators for their political engagement and may become drivers for changing the integration debate from the bottom up. In conceptual terms, there is reason to expect that the life experiences of policy makers will eventually transform the policy-level debate on integration as intercultural competence among Germans and Turkish immigrants increases. Such an outcome has the potential for bridging the gap between the abstract ways of imagining what integration should be at the policy level and the immigrants' practices and daily lives at the neighborhood level.

The current policy discourse on integration attempts to appeal to the general voting public by formulating facile frames (Edelman 1988; Stone 2002) for addressing the situation of immigrants and integration policy that favor negative images of Turkish immigrant citizens. At the district level, however, a different dynamic can be observed, at least in the case of Neukölln. As noted in chapter 4, Buschkowsky's heavy-handed, controlling approach to integration policy may actually have a negative impact on public opinion toward immigrants among the district's ethnic German residents. This finding indicates that integration policy is a powerful tool for fostering a constructive discourse on immigration, and policy makers must be aware of their tremendous responsibility.

Regardless of their origin, simple policy frames about immigrants can be successfully challenged through confrontations with social reality via interaction or personal experience. Intercultural competence gained through personal or professional experience broadens any individual's perspective and opens the door to a conceived integration policy approach, which is influenced by the lived experiences of integration. Perhaps the most hopeful finding in this research is the recognition that the places of intersection and interaction between the policy level and level of the immigrants' lived experience can lead to alternative policy conceptions. Whether these alternative conceptions can at some point become the dominant policy remains to be seen.

How Do Immigrants Talk about Themselves?

The neighborhood is central in the identity formation of Turkish immigrant women. It provides a feeling of belonging that the women cannot obtain in broader German or Turkish society. Nevertheless, the new home of the neighborhood is often lost in the political debate about where home is. The local immigrant neighborhood substitutes for a lack of clear national attachments for individual immigrants. The established immigrant neighborhood, where unique social networks have formed among immigrants as well as between German Turkish and ethnic German residents, becomes a special place of self-identification for second-generation Turkish immigrant women. Unlike ethnic Germans, German Turks are not able to attach themselves fully to a larger national identity. Most immigrant women, no matter their age, social class, religious views, or profession, feel that they exist somewhere in between what is considered mainstream German or Turkish national identity. They exhibit a feeling that has been said to be typical for immigrants of the second generation: a "neither here nor there" identity (Soysal 2002). This split or hybrid identity affects their personal integration process. They struggle between loyalty and belonging to two different identities: German and Turkish. Kasinitz et al. (2008) suggest that second-generation immigrants identify so strongly with the local context because it becomes an intermediary between their conflicting identities. Second-generation immigrants' neighborhood affiliation is also strongly tied to aspects of visibility in the broadest sense. This means that Turkish immigrant women feel that they become visible as a result of certain markers of difference in both Turkey and Germany. These markers of difference are related to a cultural or religious practice that differs from what is considered the German mainstream, most notably the head scarf. They are also ethnic in nature, such as a Turkish accent or appearance. Many women noted that it is specifically their Turkish identity, and not necessarily their immigrant identity, that results in rejection from the German majority. The specific markers of Turkish identity, not necessarily visible markers of difference in general, possess negative connotations in German society.

A 2010 study led by the Kriminologisches Forschungsinstitut Nieder-sachsen (Criminological Research Institute) of the German state of Lower Saxony found that Turks are by far the least popular immigrant minority in Germany. Brader, Valentino, and Suhay (2008) observe a similar phenom-enon in the reactions of mainstream Americans to Latinos, noting that it is often the largest immigrant group that sparks the most negative reactions among the general public, as these groups are perceived as specific threats to their ways of life on the basis of mere numbers. The findings lead to an important conclusion: Turkish immigrant women link their exclusion from the German mainstream largely to ethnic markers of difference that cannot be overcome through integration policy. Yet no official integration policy addresses these specific elements that prevent the women's complete equal-ity in German society. Their experience confirms the criticality of ethnic markers. Women like Deniz and Bilge, who carry markers of difference that are not necessarily associated with Turkish immigrant identity (Bilge's fair skin and eye color leads people to believe that her accent is French or Polish; Deniz's dark complexion and curly hair has people identify her as Latina) report that they do not experience the same kind of rejection based on those (non-Turkish) markers of difference until they reveal their Turkish identity.

A return to Turkey is not a solution either. In Turkey, German Turkish women are perceived as Germans, or *almancı*. They dress differently from the mainstream, and they have a specific *almancı* accent, which is often a combination of a less-than-native command of Turkish mixed with a rural Anatolian accent. In both urban and rural areas of Turkey, this accent is looked down on, partly because emigrants or expatriates are said to have turned away from or given up their loyalty to Turkey in favor of socioeco-nomic opportunity, and partly because of the negative working-class con-notations of rural Anatolia compared to Turkey's urban centers.

Turkish immigrant women are painfully aware of the visibility created by their ethnocultural markers of difference and of their symbolic role in the policy discourse on integration in Berlin. Their neighborhood, where they have developed long-term social networks, is a place where they can escape their individual visibility, where their individual difference to main-stream society becomes invisible as they blend into the neighborhood as a "place of hybridity and *mestizaje*" (Soja 1999, 272). The process reduces the women's individual visibility and increases that of the immigrant neigh-borhood as a whole.

In the perceptions of some Germans, such as Christian Democratic par-liamentarian Kurt Wansner, these immigrant neighborhoods are making the host country, Germany, invisible. Wansner is perhaps the most outspoken critic of immigrant neighborhoods, but he is the not only center-right policy maker and politician who is hostile to the idea of integration conceived as a Thirdspace home for Berlin's Turkish immigrants. The Turkish immigrant women interviewed all perceive the immigrant neighborhood as an entry point into the new society (Kasinitz et al. 2008 report similar findings on a variety of immigrant groups in New York City). They do so regardless of their various religious and ethnic backgrounds, and their different socioeconomic positions within the Turkish immigrant community. The immigrant neighborhood provides them with a place that truly feels like home. It is a place where they can integrate themselves and feel integrated in return.

At this point, the immigrants' integration practice diverges from political notions of how integration should be conceived and measured. Conceptually, the immigrant neighborhood represents a true lived-space integration practice, where integration is lived apart from mainstream norms and politically conceived measurements. This space is special because it provides a lived negotiation of two identities, which stand apart from political prescriptions of what integration should be. The immigrant neighborhood becomes an example for the approximation of two identities, German and Turkish, that are often framed as incompatible in public discourse. These identities clash most strongly in immigrants' lives: immigrants have to negotiate their dual identities and navigate through a new social and political culture that remains unwelcoming toward their visible differences. The lived space of the immigrant neighborhood represents a place where immigrants are at home in spite of the challenges presented by the larger environment.

The neighborhood as the basic social unit of belonging in urbanized human life takes on special meaning for immigrants in shaping their lives in a challenging environment and negotiating their hybrid identities (Orum 1998). Yet neighborhoods, even those in the same city, are not all alike. The neighborhoods of Neukölln and Kreuzberg take on different forms of lived space. Although they have in common their high share of immigrants, their low per capita income, and their history as working-class neighborhoods, the composition of immigrants in those neighborhoods differs, as do the immigrants' histories of living inside the neighborhood. Turkish immigrants living in Kreuzberg have better-established networks than in Neukölln. In addition, a majority of the established, highly educated white-collar Turkish immigrants live in Kreuzberg, whereas Neukölln remains more strictly blue collar and low income. Kreuzberg residents have established tighter kinship, personal, and business networks. Coupled with Kreuzberg's tradition of social activism and direct democracy, the district has created a tolerant space for Thirdspace practice among immigrants. In addition, Kreuzberg's nationwide reputation as an exemplary multicultural enclave has attracted not merely the German intelligentsia, but in recent years also increasingly middle-class Germans. The parts of Kreuzberg that exhibit the highest density of immigrants are not necessarily all low-income areas, as they are in Neukölln. Middle-class Germans embracing Kreuzberg's multicultural identity move to the ethnically diverse areas of Kreuzberg, and immigrants who have made it socioeconomically remain inside Kreuzberg's immigrant neighborhoods instead of moving away to more explicitly middle-class areas or to Berlin's outer districts, which have a more suburban character—that is, Kreuzberg's immigrant areas are gentrifying. This phenomenon has been a double-edged sword for the immigrants: it has given Kreuzberg a much better reputation than Neukölln, but it has also increasingly displaced lower-income immigrant families, who cannot afford the rising rents in Kreuzberg.

In sum, Kreuzberg's openness toward hybrid-identity neighborhoods goes hand in hand with its residents' general suspicion of policy approaches from above and their support for alternative solutions. Thirdspace (or lived space) presents such an alternative. It blends well with Kreuzberg's image as a nationwide model for multicultural coexistence and has made the need for a strong integration policy platform seem less urgent than in Neukölln.

The high-density immigrant communities of Neukölln, meanwhile, have a generally more low-income, working-class profile than their counterparts in Kreuzberg. Immigrants who make it socioeconomically do not remain in Neukölln. Their loyalties to their immigrant neighborhood are relatively weak, particularly if they have moved fairly recently—for example, as a result of finding employment or being displaced by gentrification—and have not formed strong personal ties to the neighborhood. However, the fact that many of the women moved to Neukölln for the employment opportunities that the district offers minorities and the long-term unemployed may turn out to be an avenue for change, and might eventually create new communities with stronger common attachments to the neighborhood. The Neukölln women I interviewed for this book have met and become friends through their work on the *Stadtteilmütter* project mentioned in chapter 3. The investments the district of Neukölln has made in the program may eventually result not only in employment for less well educated Turkish women, but may also help create the social networking opportunities they crave and regret having lost by moving. Therefore, lived integration may actually set in through the implementation of policy programs for integration. Political approaches to integration on the one hand and lived integration on the other do not have to be mutually exclusive.

The highly educated, more politically active women of Kreuzberg, however, suspect political motives behind Neukölln's integration programs. Many of them consider the project a media hoax meant to distract attention from the district's persistent social problems and convey the impression that immigrants are well taken care of.

In general, the differences between Neukölln and Kreuzberg appear to have paradoxical effects. Neukölln's symbolic image as an area of failed multiculturalism with increasing rates of social and ethnic segregation, as well as pockets of poverty, has placed the district under more pressure than Kreuzberg to implement an effective integration program. In response, Neukölln offers lower-class immigrant women better employment opportunities that rely on the strong social aspect of its integration programs. Although the lower-class immigrant women in Neukölln appreciate these opportunities, the higher-class immigrant women in Kreuzberg condemn the programs as promotional political strategies without long-term social effects.

It is too early to draw serious conclusions about the effectiveness of Neukölln's integration programs. However, a few findings from this research are telling. Although the women interviewed were well aware of the advantages to living in Neukölln, they nevertheless do not feel as at home in Neukölln as the Kreuzberg women do in Kreuzberg. Neukölln's strong top-down policy approaches to integration, which have led to a less positive way of framing immigrants in the neighborhood, can be perceived as making it more difficult for the immigrant women to make a home there. The absence of Neukölln's tradition of direct democracy and bottom-up policy solutions are resulting in a dramatically smaller niche for and existence of immigrant activism in Neukölln than in Kreuzberg. Clearly, the policy discourse dominates integration practice in Neukölln. It provides economic benefits to immigrants while making them subject to top-down integration programs that center on control and assimilation rather than nurture grassroots Thirdspace practice as in Kreuzberg. Campus Rütli represents a notable exception, but only time will tell of its actual successes within the neighborhood.

Conceptual Implications

The book traces a new, empirical perspective on the integration process, represented by the gap between the integration discourse and lived integration in Berlin's immigrant neighborhoods. Observations on how this gap could potentially be bridged generate several theoretical insights. Beyond the empirical findings gained by analyzing social and political processes, the book also expands on the conceptual idea of lived spaces, hybrid spaces, or Thirdspace. This research looks at the immigrant experience in a new way, a way to understand the experienced or lived place at a micro level: the neighborhood. There, it explores a new perspective—space—for understanding the immigrant experience.

The study's empirical findings have significant conceptual effects on the continued theoretical development of hybrid identity and its interaction and potential convergence with the policy discourse. One of them is the designation of intercultural competence, for example, which is applicable to a small group of policy makers, government administrators, and parliamentarians who have become engaged in changing the formulation of Berlin's local integration policy. The group's intercultural competence is derived from either their personal experiences as individuals of immigrant background in Berlin, and the challenges that come along with that, or their professional interactions with the real-world legal, political, and social issues that immigrants or individuals of immigrant background face in German society. Intercultural competence creates a bridge between the policy discourse and hybrid identity: once they become an accepted presence in the political realm, these individuals have the ability to shape mainstream conceptions of integration at the local and citywide level, informed by and familiar with the lived ways of integration and the real-world obstacles to integration they have observed or faced themselves.

The intersections between conceived and lived approaches to policy problems are meaningful in the sense that they have the potential to dissolve the inherent power differential between the two, infusing the dominant policy discourse with the lived experiences of those at the margins at whom the policies are directed. It is likely, however, that the gap between policy discourse and lived space can never be fully dissolved because it lies in the nature of social processes that once a marginalized group becomes empowered, another group will take its place at the margins. Additionally, the power of co-optation should also not be underestimated. Political parties seek to attract certain marginalized groups—not because they have an actual interest in improving their situation, but rather to appeal to a new group of voters. This can easily lead to a co-optation of lived space by the policy discourse without actually implementing policies that lead to sustainable outcomes.

The comparative analysis of immigrant neighborhoods in Berlin has expanded the conceptual potential of lived space and added to its conceptual properties and scope by applying it to a new setting and a specific political and social issue. In doing so, this research has highlighted the role space plays in social processes not merely as an abstract concept, but as a real phenomenon. The cultural and historical identity of Kreuzberg and Neukölln affects both the way policy is developed and the way that German and Turkish residents construct and practice their own identities. Space as place and as social context provides an important background to policy and identity formation. As such, it is also constantly in flux. The identity of space is malleable and changes over time. Historical circumstance has transformed Kreuzberg into an enclave of popular resistance and grassroots democracy, while Neukölln has moved in a different direction.

Similarly, historical circumstance, such as the Rütli crisis, which made nationwide headlines, has opened a window of opportunity for policy intervention and the creation of a strong top-down integration program in Neukölln, a district that is similar to Kreuzberg in socioeconomic terms but that is different in terms of its historical interpretation of democracy. This in turn has affected how policy approaches are publicly received. In conclusion, this research suggests that the neighborhood not only affects immigrant identity in general, but also that different sociohistorical characteristics of each neighborhood space can have different effects on the way immigrants integrate themselves into the neighborhood and how they perceive their participatory role.

Policy Implications

Intercultural Competence

Intercultural competence and the possible convergence of Secondspace and Thirdspace hold a real opportunity for the improvement of integration policy and the situation of immigrants. At the same time, intercultural competence itself represents a conceptual hybrid, which dissolves the ethnic and political boundaries that previously dominated the debate on immigration in Germany. When interculturally competent individuals with culturally hybrid backgrounds enter the policy discourse as important political actors, they shatter the ethnic boundary that has separated immigrants as subjects of policy making on the one hand, and Germans as policy makers on the other hand. The influx of culturally competent immigrants into the realm of integration policy in particular topples the monopoly German policy makers have historically had on framing the local and national integration debate. In this way, it may also have the potential to further dissolve the boundaries between the policy discourse and lived integration.

The participation of interculturally competent individuals in policy and decision making is likely to have positive effects on integration policy, such as fostering more hybrid policy approaches. For instance, Bilkay Öney, the German Turkish integration officer, explicitly remarked that she understands both the Turkish immigrant perspective and that of the German majority. She can switch positions between representing one or the other side, thereby implicitly representing both sides at the same time. However, the presence of hybridity in any society may receive a positive reception. Hybridity as a phenomenon is difficult to convey politically in simple, understandable terms. Typically, black-and-white categorizations and oversimplifications govern public debates. Real-life politics, and especially the framing of political issues, notoriously ignore categorical complications. If they are not ignored, the potential dissolution of racial and ethnic boundaries often sparks fear and resistance among the general public. Sarrazin's polarizing book, *Germany Does Away With Itself*, is a powerful example of these strict categorizations. The high numbers of Turkish immigrants in Germany lead him to believe that the country is going to be "conquered" by Muslims. Sarrazin's misperception is only one of the many misperceptions of Turkish immigrants caused by overgeneralization and black-and-white policy frames.

In the political discourse, Turkish immigrants continue to be framed as Muslims whose religious principles are diametrically opposed to a liberal democratic society. In a demographic study conducted for the Konrad Adenauer Foundation, a Christian Democratic think tank in Germany, Von Wilamowitz-Moellendorff (2001) found only a minority of German Turks strictly follow the rules of Islam. The study indicates that a majority of German Turks are either secular, nonpracticing Muslims or only loosely affiliated with the Muslim religion. The data clash with the political discourse, which frames Turkish immigrants as devout Muslims who are poorly integrated and poorly educated. The Turkish community is characterized as strongly affected by domestic violence against women and honor killings, which in turn are linked to their religion, Islam. Religiously motivated violence must be addressed and prosecuted, but it should not be used as the defining characteristic of the Turkish immigrant community per se.

Discrimination and Quotas

The Berlin government has taken steps to address the issues of Muslim immigrant women on the job market by publishing brochures that educate them about their rights and encourage them to report cases of discrimination. However, the government has largely ignored the less manageable causes of immigrant marginalization and stereotyping, such as ethnic markers of difference in appearance or accent. The implementation of minority quotas, at least in the realm of public service, would help remedy this difficult problem by allocating a certain portion of jobs to immigrant minorities. That way, the public sector could set an example, and others might follow suit. Such a quota system was added to the local political Social Democrat agenda in Berlin in September 2009, notably by Kenan Kolat, head of the TBB and its Germanywide umbrella organization, the Türkische Gemeinde Deutschland (Turkish Community of Germany). As of December 2012, the provision had not been implemented. The state of Berlin's new integration law, *Integrationsgesetz,* which was enacted in September 2010, explicitly underlines the importance of such quotas in civil service jobs. However, it curiously abstains from determining any such quotas in paragraph 4, where it says, "The [Berlin] Senate underlines its goal of increasing the quota of employees of immigrant background in the public service corresponding with their proportion in the general population. To this end, there will not be a legally enforced quota" (www.berlin.de/imperia/md/content/lb-integration-migration/publikationen/recht/partintg_bf.pdf). Thus, the law explicitly notes the need for a quota, but then states that the law itself will neither determine what that quota should be nor enforce it. The discussion of quotas documents some hopeful beginnings, but without a legally binding provision, it will remain largely ineffective.

Integration and the Mainstream

The largest immigrant group in any country is likely to experience higher rates of rejection as a result of its strong numerical and thus more visible presence (Brader, Valentino, and Suhay 2008). The majority population perceives it as a specific challenge to mainstream culture. That perception rests on a mistaken understanding of how a national mainstream culture evolves. It is important for policy makers and the general public to realize that the very definition of mainstream culture is always in flux. Even before the arrival of guest workers in the 1960s, the German national mainstream was (and continues to be to this day) challenged by a broad variety of cultural changes, such as the expansion of the global media, and through it the arrival of American pop culture in Germany. Mainstream German national identity, as most other national identities, has never been static and will continue to incrementally change and evolve—but, as the research presented in this book indicates, not without conflict and resistance.

The resistance by the general public to challenges to national mainstream culture needs to be taken into consideration by policy makers in creating integration policy and measuring the success of immigrant groups at becoming integrated. Yet demands for integration should not only focus on the responsibilities of the immigrants but also acknowledge the crucial role of the host population. The process of integration must be mutually constitutive between host and immigrant populations in order to be effective. Some local political parties in Berlin on the center left of the political spectrum have already come to this realization, and their political platforms and main tenets of integration policy emphasize the importance of mutuality. More can be done. Policy makers should take the initiative and strengthen public awareness within the population—specifically that of teachers and employers—of the steps they can take to ensure successful immigrant integration.

In conclusion, in order for the integration of Turkish immigrants in Germany to be successful, the dominant conceptions of integration policy need to fundamentally change. Turks in Germany are said to be the country's largest but most poorly integrated immigrant group, according to a number of studies, most notably the 2009 integration study by the Berlin Institut für Bevölkerung und Entwicklung (Berlin Institute for Population and Development), which used the immigrants' socioeconomic status, educational and professional attainment, and interactions with the majority population as indicators for successful integration (Institut für Bevölkerung und Entwicklung 2009) This result implies that integration policy directed at ameliorating exactly the factors the study measured (and not the immigrants) has failed. It further suggests that those who implemented the policy should be held responsible for its failure, and not the policy's subjects, the immigrants.

In fact, rather than indicating a total failure of integration, the results of this study demonstrate that the indicators of successful integration conceived by policy makers are simply an insufficient way of measuring integration. Immigrants do incorporate themselves into their new environment and create a home for themselves. However, their integration cannot be easily measured by broad indicators, such as socioeconomic status or educational attainment. Integration is a much more complicated process that involves making a home and feeling at home in a new locale. It is also a dual process, in which the immigrants not only accept the new country as their home, but are also accepted as worthy members by the new society. The stories told by Turkish immigrant women I interviewed indicate that Turkish immigrants in Germany tend to encounter obstacles in attaining educational and socioeconomic equality as a result of the rejection they experience from the general public. It appears that only when they are accepted by the new society will they be able to succeed socioeconomically.

Future Avenues of Research:
Learning from the Neighborhood

The integration debate in Germany, which centers on the contestation of German national identity by the permanent presence of newcomers in the country, obscures the existence of all the places of home that immigrants have created for themselves in the neighborhood. Their experiences and practices of making a home for themselves in their neighborhood need to be taken into consideration by the political integration debate. The neighborhood perspective teases out the immigrants' alternative, micro-level, lived approaches to integration. In general, the neighborhood—and its importance as a place where social problems arise and are addressed by those affected by them—is underresearched in the political science literature. From the data presented in this book, the urban neighborhood arises as a powerful conceptual and empirical tool for understanding the issues in outlining sustainable avenues to integration and creating sensible political solutions. At the same time, the neighborhood as unit of analysis opens up new avenues for future work, particularly in comparative urban politics and sociological assessments dealing with processes of identity formation and minority struggles.

Turkish immigrants in Berlin are not exceptional in their reliance on the neighborhood as a lived space of alternative life practices. Different immigrant and minority groups in different cities around the world may have similarly relevant neighborhood-based experiences that should play a role in the receiving country's debate on immigrant incorporation. Expanding the analysis of the neighborhood as a lived space of minority life practices can provide important comparative insights into other countries' immigration debates and other cities' strategies for approaching diversity. In addition, the inclusion of a different urban setting in the exploration of immigrant and minority neighborhoods places the neighborhoods in a comparative context, allowing for a better understanding of the dynamic between immigration debates and immigrants' strategies of making a home for themselves in the neighborhood.

Comparing the findings from this research to a different local and national context with other minority groups facing different kinds of struggles will enrich the picture. More established groups, for instance, who are better represented in the local administration, could also provide important insights into the long-term, direct effects of intercultural competence on integration and/or minority policy: Are immigrant and minority groups, once they reach a tipping point of numerical representation in the local administration, able to fundamentally change the dominant discourse and policy? Or are they eventually co-opted by the political agendas of certain political parties? For how many generations do allegiances with a certain ethnicity or immigrant group last? At what point do ethnic markers of difference become absorbed into the national mainstream?

There are also different points of entry for using space as a conceptual tool for research. The political framing and self-perception of immigrant women provide an important avenue for exploring approaches to integration and difference. However, immigrant and minority men represent a different, equally interesting point of entry for this kind of research. Because they take different positions in a society than women, immigrant men also tend to face different challenges. Their performance in the realms of education and professional success in many cases is worse than that of immigrant women, as was emphasized by almost all policy makers, government bureaucrats, and parliamentarians I interviewed for this book. Like women, immigrant men tend to be turned into mere subjects in policy debates. Neighborhood-based research can help move toward creating a genuine understanding of their lives.

In sum, as this research has shown, the urban neighborhood provides a powerful tool for understanding social processes, hybrid identities, and alternative conceptions of life and identity of minority groups. For city-based social science research, it represents an irreplaceable micro-level analytical tool, and it points to many fascinating avenues of research that remain to be explored.

APPENDIX A

Zeynep's and Bilge's Kreuzkölln

THESE MAPS SERVE as a visual illustration of the women's attachment to the neighborhood. Their spacial references to the parts of their neighborhood they frequent are visualized here. This is to underline how strongly the women's lives revolve around the neighborhood. Zeynep, for instance, refers to a number of streets that she has lived on, all of which are located in close vicinity to the Möckernbrücke subway stop. She has spent all her life in this small part of the neighborhood and intimately identifies with it. Similarly, Bilge's descriptions of home are full of references of Kreuzkölln, the area where Kreuzberg and Neukölln meet and melt into one another. Her work and her leisure areas (mainly along the Hasenheide) all lie within the small triangle on the map.

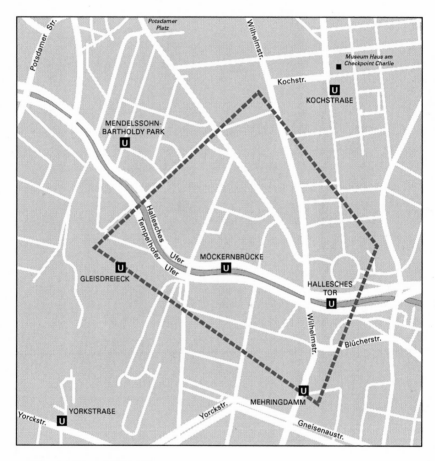

Map A.1. Zeynep's Kreuzköllm.

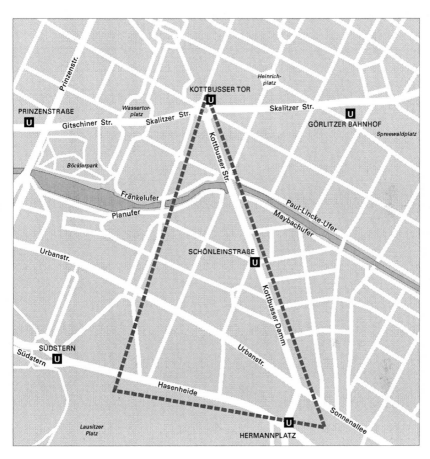

Map A.2. Bilge's Kreuzkölln.

APPENDIX B

Berlin Senate

THE TABLES ILLUSTRATE THE STRUCTURE of the governmental executive in Berlin as it was staffed in 2009 and visualizes the position of my interviewees within it. The senate administrations and topical concentrations, which are highlighted in boldface type, are the foci of my investigation. The names and offices represent the individuals I interviewed. It is important to note that since 2009, the administrative offices within the Berlin executive have been reorganized and redistributed. The latest version of the organizational chart (which is updated regularly) can be found online (www.berlin.de/).

The Governing Mayor of Berlin, Klaus Wowereit

The Berlin Mayor's Office: Harald Wolf, Ingeborg Junge-Reyer

- The Head of the Senate Chancelory, State Secretary Barbara Kissler
- State Secretary for Cultural Matters, André Schmitz
- The Federal Representative and E.U. Representative for Citizenship Engagement, State Secretary Monika Helbig
- Speaker of the Senate, State Secretary Dr. Richard Meng

Senate Administration	Education, Science, and Research	Finances	Health, Environment, and Consumer Protection	Interior Issues and Sport
Senator	Prof. Dr. E. Jürgen Zöllner	Dr. Ulrich Nußbaum	Katrin Lompscher	**Dr. Erhart Körting**
State Secretaries	Claudia Zinke	Dr. Christian Sundermann	Dr. Benjamin-Immanuel Hoff	Ulrich Freise
	Dr. Hans-Gerhard Husung	Iris Spranger		Thomas Härtel
Central Services/State Representatives	Schools	Wealth	Health	**State, Administration, and Labor Law**
	Secondary Education	Finances	Environmental Protection	**Constitutional Law**
	Youth and Family	Budget, Credit	Environmental Policies	Public Safety and Order
	Universities	Tax Matters	Consumer and Health Protection	Sport
	Research	Central Data Archive of the Finance Minister		
	Quality Ensurance Teachers' Education Operative Oversight for General Education			

Senate Administration	Integration, Labor, and Social Issues	Justice	Urban Development	Economy, Technology, and Women
Senator	Dr. Heidi Knacke-Werner	Gisela von der Aue	Ingeborg Junge-Reyer	Harald Wolf
State Secretaries	Dr. Petra Leuschner Kerstin Liebich	Hasso Lieber	Helga Dunger-Löper Maria Krautzberger Regula Lüscher	Dr. Jens-Peter Heuer **Almuth Nehring-Venus**
Central Services/State Representatives	Social Issues Labor and Professional Education State Representative for Disabled People **State Representative for Equality against Discrimination** **State Representative for Integration and Migration**	Personnel, Organization, and Budget Law Justice Executive Common Law Office for the States of Berlin and Brandenburg	City and Recreational Space Planning City Development and Projects Geological Information, Measurement Housing, Urban Renewal, Social City Construction Ministerial Matters of Construction Traffic	Economic- and Technology Policy, Economic Order Economic Development **Women and Equality**

APPENDIX C

The Buschkowsky Administration's Ten-Point Integration
Agenda for the District of Neukölln[1]

*1. "All people must live in according to the criteria of a 'free democratic
basic order.'[2] We live [in Neukölln] according to the principle of 'sociospatial
mixing.'"*
Interestingly, further elaboration on point 1 on the district's website indicates that the emphasis on "free democratic basic order" is specifically
directed at immigrants. Apparently the administration is seeking to appeal
to immigrants, urging them to apply these democratic principles to their
way of life despite the fact that they may be Muslims. Similarly, the term
sociospatial mixing mainly refers to immigrants; the administration defines
it as its own attempt to prevent the creation of parallel societies.

2. "We take immigrants seriously as equal partners."
Here, the administration wants to encourage immigrants to integrate their
abilities into its workforce. It proposes the introduction of an unofficial
quota, according to which the district of Neukölln seeks to educate and
hire between 30 percent and 45 percent of its workforce among immigrants.

3. "Everybody gets a chance for designing his or her own life independently."
This again is directed specifically at immigrants and implies that immigrants
should not perceive themselves as victims of discrimination, but should
instead take their lives into their own hands. Furthermore, the administration notes that female immigrants need special support, as they often experience gender-based oppression and lack equal opportunity for work and
education at home, within their family structure, and within immigrant
communities.

4. "A tolerant Neukölln accepts everyone and has clear rules. Those who break the rules will have to expect an intervention of the community."

This implies that the district will intervene if families do not comply with German law—for example, by sending their children to school.[3] This statement is again specifically directed at immigrants. In addition, the website introduces the idea of policing crime-ridden areas in the neighborhood, emphasizing the problem of petty crime among immigrant youths. As a remedy, the local administration in Neukölln proposes more rigor in the persecution of young criminals while at the same time increasing psychological support.

5. "The openness to be creative and innovative and everyone's individual abilities and competencies can serve as an engine for upward mobility in society."

This statement is supposed to encourage immigrants to take the initiative for their own upward mobility, such as pursuing a good education to increase their chances for a successful career. It also suggests, however, that if immigrants make an effort, they will be rewarded. This implies that immigrants generally lack the motivation to pursue an education or a career, and it assumes that German society will generally be receptive of any effort by immigrants to be successful. However, it ignores the fact that immigrants often encounter larger obstacles in social upward mobility than a mere lack of motivation.

6. "Education is key for integration."

This point is to emphasize and reinforce the previous point. It suggests that in order to be successful, immigrants need to pursue an education. Furthermore, the website underlines the importance of learning and knowing German, and of adopting "German" qualities such as reliability and punctuality. It is also suggested that families are key in encouraging children to learn and be successful, but it is noted that "unfortunately, traditional immigrant families adhere to the principle of submission of their children, which often involves violence as well." The website also lists several initiatives by Neukölln administration to encourage and support children's creativity and their participation in activities outside the home.

7. "Integration cannot be successful through projects alone."

To emphasize this point, the website also highlights the importance of long-term support as opposed to merely implementing short-lived projects to support integration. Such long-term support, according to the Neukölln administration, includes "soft support" jobs, child care, and education initiatives, but also more rigorous enforcement of integration by police and the justice system.

8. *"Rules have to be adapted to population change."*
This point essentially suggests that the district's schools and social initiatives for children have to be adapted to the presence of many immigrant families. This implies that, according to the Neukölln administration, immigrant families present new challenges to the social and education systems, which should be met with stricter regulations.

9. *"Out integration policy is based on the concrete problems of the people."*
Here, the local administration's specific integration programs and initiatives are listed in order to stress the strong policy support integration receives in the district of Neukölln. The administration emphasizes the importance of community building and the creation of relationships of trust and cooperation among individual citizens and residents of different ethnic groups.

10. *"We define and solve problems together."*
This point highlights what can really be seen as the biggest achievement of the district: it has created an advisory immigrant council, where immigrant citizens can participate and provide feedback in defining and approaching integration. This advisory council has no legislative powers and fulfills merely an advisory function. However, it provides a platform for immigrants to voice their issues and concerns—an important step in integrating immigrants themselves in contemplating integration.

NOTES

Introduction

1. Until the late 1990s, former German chancellor Helmut Kohl still proclaimed that Germany was not a country of immigration.

2. Unless otherwise noted, the translations from German into English throughout this book are my own.

3. The term *guest worker*—in German, *Gastarbeiter*—was used in reference to the originally intended temporary status of immigrants in the country. In the guest worker agreements that the West German government struck with several southern European nations, the stay of the workers in Germany was always meant to be temporary (as guests) instead of permanent.

4. The idea of *Ausländerklassen* and the separation of German and immigrant children in school was based on the authorities' intention to ensure that guest worker children were taught in their parents' mother tongue, so as to increase their job opportunities in their countries of origin. This policy therefore emphasizes the temporary nature of the guest worker status.

5. As such, the *Rückkehrförderungsgesetz* was a national government measure to support guest workers' return to their country of origin, legally and financially. For a more detailed explanation, see chapter 1.

6. In referring to representatives, civil servants or bureaucrats from city- and district-level executives and/or legislatures, I will use the general term *policy makers* throughout this book. It is used as a general term in reference to anyone in the public realm who is involved in shaping, framing, and discussing integration policy. Even though I differentiate in the initial introduction of my interviewees between executive and legislative policy makers, this is not necessarily relevant for my analysis, which is primarily concerned with capturing the views on integration of public figures in Berlin's political realm involved in integration policy. In addition to policy makers, my elite interviews include Turkish community representatives from the Turkish Union Berlin-Brandenburg (TBB), the largest Turkish community organization in Berlin. They will be referred to as Turkish community representatives throughout the book.

7. My usage of the verb *integrate* in connection with immigrants' self-perceptions is not to conflate what immigrants do with what they may in fact be imagined to do in the political discourse. Thus, by using the word *integrate,* I do not mean to presume that immigrants in fact have a vested interest in integration as do policy makers in Germany. I merely seek to allude to integration here in order to propose that immigrants' ways of living in their neighborhoods and local communities may present alternative ways of incorporation into their surroundings that could, at the same time, be seen as alternative definitions for the controversial and contested term *integration.*

8. In Kreuzberg, the per capita income in 2005 was approximately 775 euros per month; in Neukölln, it was approximately 750 euros. Both districts are among those districts with the lowest per capita income in the city of Berlin (*Berliner Mietmagazin* 2005).

9. *Kiez* is a German term referring to a local scene of small neighborhood bars and restaurants, as well as tight-knit neighborhood networks on the block, where people know each other.

1. Integration or Exclusion?

1. *Ius soli* means literally "law of soil," indicating that those born within a national territory may acquire citizenship on the basis of being born on a nation's soil. *Ius sanguinis* means literally "law of blood," indicating that national citizenship is acquired through bloodlines and ancestry only. This indicates that the national community defines itself not necessarily by territory but by ancestry.

2. The term *Volk* literally means "the people." This, however, does not always translate perfectly. Because most people are familiar with the term *Volk,* I will refrain from translating it for the remainder of this work.

3. *Aussiedler* means "repatriated ethnic Germans," and it commonly refers to the descendants of ethnic Germans from Eastern Europe and the former Soviet Union. As long as German citizenship was based on descent, these groups had the right to naturalize as German citizens. The revisions of the citizenship law passed in 2000 amended that rule. Since 2000, only those *Aussiedler* who have sufficient knowledge of the German language are eligible for citizenship. Their language skills must be family based; if they are acquired through a language class, the *Aussiedler* is ineligible for repatriation. The situation of *Aussiedler* or "those belonging to the German *Volk*" falls under the regulation of the *Bundesvertriebenengesetz* (federal expellee law). Paragraph 6 defines those belonging to the German *Volk* as someone not living in Germany who has "acknowledged her-/himself as a part of the German *Volk,* in so far as this acknowledgment is confirmed in certain markers such as heritage, language, education, and culture." This category, however, is to be distinguished from "people of German heritage," or *Deutschstämmige,* who left Germany voluntarily to immigrate to another country. If, for instance, a Canadian, an Australian, or an American citizen of German heritage lets his or her German citizenship lapse voluntarily, then he or she is considered a regular non-E.U. foreigner according to German law. The reason for special treatment of ethnic Germans in Eastern Europe has been justified in post–World War II Germany by the fact that

those ethnic Germans often experienced discrimination by communist regimes because of their German heritage.

4. In this book, the term *guest worker* refers to immigrants who arrived before the expansion of German citizenship law in 2000, as these foreigners were still largely perceived as temporary guest workers in a general political and legal sense. Since the expansion of the law in 2000, they are referred to as guest worker immigrants to mark the fact that they were now increasingly perceived as permanent immigrants in a political and legal sense. This, as this chapter illustrates, also profoundly changed the definition of the national community and underlined the importance of the existence of an integration policy.

5. The Third Wave feminist movement in Germany was closely connected to and intellectually inspired by the one in the United States. Among other things, the movement in Germany sought a revision of the position of women in the country's overall family and social structure, and accordingly a revision of the legal provisions that this structure was based on.

6. The Social Democratic Party (SPD) in Germany, Germany's oldest party, which was founded by the country's first worker movement during Bismarck's time at the end of the 19th century, is seen as the traditional political supporter of Turkish immigrants in Germany, as their immigration history is inextricably connected with their working-class identity.

7. The 2005 round of amendments to Germany's citizenship law includes a provision that allows for dual citizenship under certain circumstances. If German citizens move to a foreign country and can prove that their quality of life would be significantly improved by naturalizing in their new country of residence but that they, at the same time, still have strong personal and family ties to Germany and thus want to keep their German citizenship, they may be entitled to dual citizenship provided they file a *Beibehaltungsantrag* (a special request to keep German citizenship while taking on a second citizenship) before they naturalize in the new country.

8. For this purpose, the German government granted specific family reunification visas for spouses and children of guest workers.

9. The term *immigrant citizen* refers to the presence of citizens with different ethnic and cultural backgrounds within the national community. Their presence as legal citizens changes the commonly accepted definition of the content of national identity and membership within the national community.

10. Mesut Özil is a world-class German soccer player who played on the national team during the 2010 Soccer World Cup. He is the grandchild of Turkish guest worker immigrants, holds dual German and Turkish citizenship, and is a practicing Muslim.

11. Özdemir, born in 1965 in the German state of Baden-Württemberg, is the son of a Turkish guest worker family. He acquired German citizenship in 1983 and is currently one of the leading members of the German Green Party. Özdemir also represented the Green Party in the E.U. parliament from 2004 through 2009. He has been outspoken on issues of immigration and integration in Germany and the European Union, and he has gained popularity especially among young Germans because of his easygoing liberal

political style and his looks. After the 2008 U.S. presidential elections, Özdemir has sometimes been called the German Obama. His way of speaking—he has a local Baden-Württemberg accent, thus implicitly representing a local German identity—has also led some to call him a model integrated German Turk.

12. Throughout the book, I use *diversity* to refer to ethnic diversity—that is, the increasing presence of other ethnic groups in Germany—a fact that policy makers have attempted to remedy by using integration or assimilation policies.

13. Throughout the book, I refer to assimilation and integration as political approaches. Thus, when I use these terms in the context of Germany, I simultaneously acknowledge its inherent contestedness. To distance myself from these loaded political concepts, I sometimes use the more neutral phrase "incorporation of immigrants."

14. In Germany, students who want to obtain a practical or professional degree graduate high school after grade 10; students seeking higher education at the university level must attend high school until grade 13 and obtain a university entry certificate *(Allgemeine Hochschulreife)*.

15. In the case of Berlin, a district *(Bezirk)* is a self-governing administrative unit of the city similar to a ward, but it is comparatively bigger and thus more comparable to a borough.

16. *Interculturally competent* denotes people who are familiar with another culture or language besides the German ones and can thus help bridge communication gaps between immigrants and receiving population.

17. A related and compelling question in this context is the threshold at which we actively experience difference, and thus the degree to which an accent matters. Although this question cannot be explored in full in this book, it may be worth noting that the empirical findings presented in chapter 2 show that a slight accent often becomes conflated with the inability to speak proper German. Hence, in the public eye, there often appears to be no differentiation between a mere accent and a lack of language skills (see chapter 2, interview with Reinke).

18. In a different line of argument, ethnic enclaves (as in the case of Nazi Germany) were deliberately created by the state to exert social control and spatially stress group differences. Although compelling, this is hardly the case in most industrially advanced democracies, where ethnic enclaves are often framed as disturbing the sociocultural fabric of the urban environment in the political discourse. However, the fact remains that certain policies in industrially advanced democracies can implicitly perpetuate the formation of ethnic enclaves, through ethnic, racial, religious, or social discrimination.

19. Lefebvre (1984) has termed this *l'espace vecu;* Soja (1996) calls it lived space.

20. It could be argued that the notion of hybridity takes for granted a rather static notion of cultures. Although it is most certainly the case that cultures themselves are inadequately described as static and stable constructs of identity, it has been established that they always rely on a certain (possibly inadequate) definition of identity (Anderson 1991; Benhabib 2002; Brubaker 1992). The notion of hybridity can be seen as a means of dissolving the hard concepts that define cultural identity, and thus provide an avenue of thought that moves beyond static definitions on culture, while at the same time taking them into consideration.

2. Talk of the Town

1. In referring to representatives or bureaucrats from city- and district-level executives and/or legislatures, I use the general term *policy makers*. It is used as a general term in reference to anyone in the public realm who is involved in shaping, framing, and discussing integration policy. Even though I differentiate in the initial introduction of my interviewees between executive and legislative policy makers, this is not necessarily relevant for my analysis, which is primarily concerned with capturing the views on integration of public figures in Berlin's political realm involved in integration policy.

2. Of course, people are not just passive in receiving elite frames; they are also active processors of information. Elites have a great degree of influence over the public debate, but people still bring their own biases, preferences, and ideas to information processing and public debates. Elites often cater to biases by framing issues in a way that appeals to the public.

3. This included the speakers for integration policy of all parties represented in the Berlin parliament: Raed Saleh for the SPD, Udo Wolf for the Left Party, Bilkay Öney for the Green Party, Kurt Wansner for the CDU, and Rainer-Michael Lehmann for the Libertarians (see Figure 6).

4. For instance, the head scarf debate was redirected to the state level after a 2005 federal constitutional court decision, which ruled that although there were no legal provisions in place to prohibit individuals in public office from displaying religious symbols at work, states should introduce such legislation to regulate these issues. Thus, in essence, this court decision had two aspects: first, there was no legislation in place to regulate such issues, but it should be developed. Second, developing this very legislation lies not in the powers of the federal government but rather with the state. Berlin subsequently introduced a neutrality law *(Neutralitätsgesetz)*, according to which no religious symbols may be displayed by public employees in jobs related to law enforcement, K through 12 education, and justice. This includes the Muslim head scarf, the Christian cross, and the Jewish yarmulke.

5. This selection of interviewees is based on the 2008–9 speakers for integration policy represented in the Berlin parliament.

6. As the traditional workers' party, the SPD has been a long-standing ally of the Turkish immigrant population. As former guest workers, their status in Germany was determined by their identity as workers. After recognizing this as an opportunity to tap into a new electorate in the late 1970s and early 1980s, the SPD became a strong advocate of immigrant rights, dual citizenship, and municipal voting rights for non-E.U. citizens.

7. The BVV votes on the district budget, but the Berlin parliament makes the final decision. Beyond that, it may make recommendations to the district administration, but it does not have any decision-making power.

8. The Socialists, Die Linke, which splintered off the SPD in 2005, is a coalition party of former left-wing Social Democrats and former members of the postunification East German Socialist Party. Their appeal has been less broad than that of the SPD, even though the Socialists has successfully challenged the SPD in several former East German states. So far, they have not made a broad effort to appeal to the immigrant population.

9. Yurdakul (2009) documents the history of the TBB's relationship with the SPD in Germany, which has been strongly shaped by the history of Turkish guest workers and their self-identification as workers. The guest workers' working-class identity drew them to the traditional workers' party, the SPD, which in turn took on the guest workers as a growing electorate.

10. Görlitzer Strasse and Oranienstrasse are prominent streets in Kreuzberg.

11. This was confirmed in my interviews with women of Turkish immigrant background (see chapter 3). The interviews were conducted in German, and the women were often apologetic about their "bad German." It turned out that all women were perfectly fluent in German but often had Turkish accents. From their previous experience with native German speakers, they interpreted their accents as "bad German."

12. In August 2009, Kolat sparked a controversy in Germany by suggesting to the Turkish newspaper *Hürriyet* that German schools should abandon the word *genocide* in connection with the Ottoman massacre of Armenians between 1915 and 1918 because it would put too much psychological pressure on students of Turkish immigrant background and "endanger their inner peace" (*Frankfurter Allgemeine Zeitung*, August 7, 2009).

13. This sparked a wave of urbanization, with rural migrants flocking in large numbers to Turkey's urban centers, resulting in the development of large shantytowns, or *gecekondu* (literally "built overnight"), creating a new urban underclass but also increasing the importance and centrality of cities in Turkish society.

14. Although Turkish immigrants, as former guest workers, identified with the working-class aspect of the SPD, the descendents of the guest worker generation may no longer self-identify as homogeneously working class. Thus, the SPD may become increasingly controversial as a political affiliation for the Turkish immigrant community as a whole.

3. *Mein Block*

1. I do not claim that immigrants in fact consciously seek to integrate themselves into German society or have any interest in formulating an integration strategy. By framing their way of life, their own ways of integration and identity, however, I try to underline that immigrants' life practices in the neighborhood can in fact be seen as alternative practices to a top-down recipe for integration.

2. This way of accounting for immigrants' roots in Germany is specific to the German policy discourse on immigration. Although most traditional immigration countries would call someone born in the country of immigration, for example, first-generation American or first-generation Canadian-born, in Germany, the first generation of immigrants born in Germany are referred to as the second generation or as a second-generation Turkish immigrant. This is as opposed to those who were born in Turkey and came to Germany as adults, who are referred to as the first generation of Turkish immigrants. This way of perceiving German-born immigrants is left over from the traditional ethnic German perception of national identity. The expression "one-and-a-half-generation

Turkish immigrant" refers to immigrants who were born in Turkey but immigrated to Germany before the age of eighteen. This way of describing immigrants implies one of the main issues in immigrant integration in Germany: immigrants still pose a challenge to the traditional perception of German ethnonational identity and are not simply perceived as Germans, even if they were born in Germany.

3. *Currywurst* is a regular sausage, fried, doused in ketchup, and topped with curry powder. The *Döner Kebap* consists of Turkish bread containing salad, spicy garlic sauce, and sliced lamb meat.

4. Among Turkish immigrants, long summer visits to family in Turkey are a notorious and popular custom. For second-generation immigrants, spending long summers with family and relatives in Turkey is the only way they have experienced Turkey in reality. Special Turkish travel agencies in Germany have made it their main business to help Turkish families with their air travel to and from Turkey every summer.

5. The term *almancı* is a derogatory term used by Turks in Turkey for those who immigrated to Germany and remained there in large numbers even after the guest worker recruitment ended. The Turkish suffix *-cı* attached to the word stem *alman*, "German," signifies profession. Thus the term may be roughly translated as "those whose business is German/in Germany." It has strongly opportunist implications, indicating that the *almancı* turned away from their homeland for personal socioeconomic gains in Germany. Besides dress and behavior, *almancı* are identified in Turkey mainly by their specific way of speaking Turkish. *Almancı* Turkish is characterized by a rural dialect (many former Turkish guest workers to Germany came from rural areas in eastern Anatolia) and poor grammar (partly because most of the children of former Turkish guest workers in Germany never formally learned Turkish in school but rather adopted the spoken language of their parents).

6. *Heimat* is a specific German term that refers to the homeland as more than merely a place of residence of citizenship. The term *Heimat* is often used by German expellees from the formerly biethnic territories in the Czech Republic or Poland and implies a nostalgic longing for the lost home. This term cannot be adequately translated into English, but it is comparable to the longing for the lost homeland expressed by Turkish immigrants in Germany.

7. The German education system is complicated and differs by state *(Land)*. In Berlin, after grade 6, a recommendation is issued by two teachers on the basis of a student's academic merit, recommending whether he or she should go on to a college-track high school *(Gymnasium)*, which ends after thirteenth grade and provides students with the academic credentials to go on to university, or whether the student should go on to a practical high school *(Realschule)*, which ends after 10th grade and channels students into a more practical career path. However, parents can override the teacher recommendation. By law, parents make the final decision, a fact that many Turkish families are unaware of. There also existed a lower-level version of the *Realschule*, called *Hauptschule*, abolished for the 2010–11 school year, which ended after 10th grade as well, and provided students with a basic level of general education. Students can apply to schools different from the ones they were recommended for, but it is up to the individual school to decide whether

the student should be admitted. This system has come under scrutiny in Germany because of the early selection process, which is formally based on students' academic performance but is in reality not very transparent.

8. Bilingual and bicultural schools are common throughout Europe. At the German school in Istanbul, courses are taught in German and Turkish, and students are required to take courses in both languages. They can obtain both a German and a Turkish high school diploma, which enables them to enroll at a university.

9. However, according to the same study, every fifth Berliner of non-immigrant background reports to have no relationships with immigrants at all (Hertie Stiftung 2009).

10. Most Germans reported that these regular contacts with individuals of immigrant background had been initiated through common circles of friends. Most individuals of immigrant background reported that their friendships with Germans were the result of neighborhood relations (Hertie Stiftung 2009).

11. Berliners, even those from former West Berlin, still refer to former West Germany as West Germany, as much as they refer to the former GDR as the East. Typically, because of the different legal status of former West Berlin under Allied control, as well as the privileged status of former East Berlin as the capital of the former GDR, Berliners see themselves as an exception—different from either West Germany or the East.

12. These are the names of Kreuzberg's most notorious subway stations on Berlin's famous underground line U-1; see also maps.

13. Zehlendorf is a district in the southwest of Berlin, which also notoriously includes the city's richest area.

14. The *Stadtteilmütter* (city district mothers), the project that Sibel, Mutlu, Latife, Gülen, Binnaz, Fadik, Zeynep, and Melike work under, is financed as a local, district-related social project. Although most districts have introduced this project locally, the working conditions and contracts differ by district, with Neukölln offering the best contract. If the women move away from their district, they lose their job.

15. Perhaps the most compelling example of this is Mary Pattillo's (2007) breathtaking account of her experience as an African American gentrifier in Chicago's Bronzeville neighborhood.

4. Location as Destiny

1. These representatives are appointed by the district mayors. They are bureaucrats (mostly without party affiliation) and have no political autonomy of their own.

2. The term *immigrant background* in the German context is applied liberally. The Federal Statistical Office, Statistisches Bundesamt, defined individuals with immigrant background for the German microcensus from 2005 through 2012 as follows: "Everyone who immigrated after 1949 into the territory of today's Federal Republic of Germany, as well as all foreigners born in Germany, and all Germans born in Germany who have at least one parent who immigrated after 1949 or was born as a foreigner in Germany" (Statistisches Bundesamt 2011, 6).

3. In 2004, according to Berlin's statistical office, the per capita monthly income in Neukölln was 750 euros per month; in Kreuzberg, it was 775 euros per month (Statistisches Landesamt Berlin 2004, cited in *Berliner MieterMagazin* 2005).

4. Short for *Gesetz über die Bildung einer neuen Stadtgemeinde Berlin* (law on the formation of a new urban community Berlin). It was ratified by the Prussian parliament on April 27, 1920, and went into effect on October 1 of the same year.

5. After this great expansion, Berlin only experienced four more occasions of territorial growth, all of which were insignificant in comparison to the great expansion in 1920. The district of Zehlendorf in the south was incorporated in 1942, and the three districts to the east, Marzahn, Hohenschönhausen, and Hellersdorf, were added in 1979, 1985, and 1986, respectively (Wernicke 1998).

6. Throughout the Cold War, West Berlin received significant financial subsidies from the federal government. The *Berlin-Hilfe-Gesetz* (Berlin support act), which passed the German Bundestag in 1962, was supposed to provide financial aid to West Berlin to ensure that the standard of living for its citizens was commensurate with that throughout the rest of the Federal Republic.

7. Many of the old downtown blocks in the eastern inner city districts had not been significantly renovated since the end of World War II. For example, they feature coal stoves, which were difficult to use but made for incredibly low heating and warm-water bills.

8. The territory of Kreuzberg was, as opposed to Neukölln, already a part of the city of Berlin in 1920 with the ratification of the *Gross-Berlin-Gesetz*. However, it had not acquired district status until that point.

9. The postwar postal codes included a four-digit number before the city name. The eight largest urban areas in (West) Germany had numbers in 1000 intervals: 1000 for Berlin, 2000 for Hamburg, 3000 for Hannover, 4000 for Düsseldorf, 5000 for Cologne, 6000 for Frankfurt am Main, 7000 for Stuttgart, and 8000 for Munich. In addition, each postal code included a number for the postal district. These two-digit numbers would signify which local post office a letter would be sent to in order to be delivered. Berlin had nine postal districts, which came to signify certain areas of the city. A letter sent to Kreuzberg would thus either go to "1000 Berlin 61" or "1000 Berlin 36."

10. Rudi Dutschke was a German sociologist and Marxist student activist. He was an integral part and leading figure of the 1968 student movement. Dutschke was shot in the head several times in April 1968 by a young man with right-wing political tendencies. Even though Dutschke initially survived his severe brain injuries, finished his degree in the United Kingdom and Denmark, and eventually returned to the movement in the 1970s, he died of an epileptic seizure in 1979. The seizure was a late consequence of his injuries. The student movement held Axel Springer Press, a conservative publishing house, which still dominates the landscape of German print media, directly responsible for the assassination attempt on Dutschke. Several Springer newspapers had rallied against the student movement in an aggressive fashion in the months leading up to the assassination attempt in April 1968.

11. West Berlin was officially Allied territory, occupied by the three Western Allied powers: the United States, Great Britain, and France. In that position, it also remained under de facto sovereignty of these three powers. Residents of West Berlin were technically West German citizens, but they held provisional passports of the Federal Republic because they did not technically reside on the soil of the Federal Republic of Germany. In addition, West Berlin was officially not represented in the West German parliament. It was

also a demilitarized zone, in which no German military existed, which meant that male German residents of West Berlin were exempt from the otherwise mandatory military service.

12. Düspohl (2009, 147) notes that, for example, 67 percent of the Turkish guest workers recruited by Siemens Berlin were women. However, this was only true for those women who came as guest workers. Many of the women who arrived on family unification visas were from a far different background.

13. This is based on Germany's election system, which is a hybrid between a winner-take-all system and a proportional representation system. Though the majority of parliamentarians are elected according to the proportional majority of their party, party representatives can also move into the federal parliament via a *Direktmandat* (direct mandate)—a relative majority of votes for a local representative. Ströbele is a founding member of the (West) German Green Party, originally called Alternative Liste (alternative list), based on its antiestablishment roots in the 1968 student movement. Ströbele also actively took part in the student movement.

14. The *Hauptschule* has since been abolished in Germany. See chapter 3, note 7, for a detailed explanation of the German school system.

15. This is in reference to one of Buschkowsky's most popular employment and integration initiatives: the *Stadtteilmütter* (city district mothers). The idea behind this program is that after six months of training, long-term unemployed immigrant women are employed by the local government to support fellow immigrant women in the integration process. This involves simple tasks, such as making house visits, showing other women where to receive child care, and how to pay their bills and mail letters. The initiative is supposed to fulfill two key goals: to get immigrant women involved and provide them with temporary employment, and to help new immigrants through social workers of the same gender and ethnic group. The program was originally intended as a short-term employment measure for long-term unemployed immigrant women. However, in 2009, the district of Neukölln approved additional funding, creating permanent positions, as well as further expanding the program throughout the district.

16. Häussermann died in October 2011.

17. The 2003 documentary by Marshall Curry entitled *Streetfight,* which describes the 2002 mayoral election campaign in Newark, New Jersey, makes a similar argument: that urban politics is literally lost and won in the streets. In this way, urban politics differs remarkably from state- or national-level politics.

18. Britz is a community within the district of Neukölln, a stronghold of the right wing of the Social Democrats, which was particularly powerful in the 1980s. According to the *Tagesspiegel* report (2008a) Frank Bialka, an important inner-party power broker, was a good friend of Buschkowsky's.

19. "Negative perception of immigrants" in this study was defined as ethnic Germans identifying with the following statements: (1) "I would prefer it if all foreigners in Germany were forced to return to their countries of origin"; (2) "The Germans have to do anything in their power to defend their own culture against immigrants, even through the use of force, if necessary"; (3) "The many foreigners in Germany are decisively responsible for the high unemployment rates" (Liljeberg and Krambeer 2011).

Appendix C

1. Data are taken from the District of Neukölln's website (www.berlin.de/ba-neukoel ln/migrationsbeauftragten/integrationspolitik.html).

2. This same term is used in the German constitution; it is translated literally here because it has no equivalent in English.

3. According to German law, every child is entitled to receive at least a basic (K through 10) education. Parents are thus required to send their children to German public school. They can opt out of this requirement by sending their children to a private school recognized by the German state. If parents fail to comply with this requirement, police will enforce it by collecting the children every morning and accompanying them to school. Buschkowsky has also stated publically that the district's administration will immediately cut the publicly funded child allowances for those families who refuse to send their children to school.

BIBLIOGRAPHY

Abbott, Andrew. 1997. "Of Time and Space: The Contemporary Relevance of the Chicago School." *Social Forces* 75, no. 4: 1149–82.

Abu-Lughod, Lila. 1991. "Writing against Culture." In *Recapturing Anthropology: Working in the Present*, ed. R. Fox, 137–62. Santa Fe, N.M.: School of American Research.

Agamben, Giorgio. 2005. *State of Exception*. Chicago: University of Chicago Press.

Alba, Richard, and Victor Nee. 2005. *Remaking the American Mainstream: Assimilation and Contemporary Immigration*. Cambridge, Mass.: Harvard University Press.

Anderson, Benedict. 1991. *Imagined Communities: Reflections on the Origins and Spread of Nationalism*. 2nd ed. London: Verso.

Angelos, James. 2012. "There's Nothing More German Than a Big, Fat Juicy *Döner Kebab*." *Wall Street Journal*. April 18. wallstreetjournal.com.

Anzaldúa, Gloria. 1999. *Borderlands—La Frontera: The New Mestiza*. 2nd ed. San Francisco: Aunt Lute Books.

Argun, Betigül Ercan. 2003. *Turkey in Germany: The Transnational Sphere of Deutschkei*. New York: Routledge.

Baier, Dirk, Christian Pfeiffer, Susann Rabold, Julia Simonson, and Cathleen Kappes. 2010. *Kinder und Jugendliche in Deutschland: Gewalterfahrungen, Integration, Medienkonsum*. Hanover: Kriminologisches Forschungsinstitut Niedersachsen e.V.

Baum, Matthew A., and Philip B. K. Potter. 2008. "The Relationships between Mass Media, Public Opinion, and Foreign Policy: Toward a Theoretical Synthesis." *Annual Review of Political Science* 11:39–65.

Bauman, Zygmunt. 1995. "Making and Unmaking Strangers." *Thesis Eleven* 43:1–16.

Baumgartner, Frank R., and Bryan D. Jones. 1993. *Agendas and Instability in American Politics*. Chicago: University of Chicago Press.

Benhabib, Seyla. 2002. *The Claims of Culture: Equality and Diversity in the Global Era*. Princeton, N.J.: Princeton University Press.

Berkowitz, Dan. 1994. "Who Sets the Media Agenda? The Ability of Policymakers to Determine New Decisions." In *Public Opinion, the Press, and Public Policy*, ed. David J. Kenhammer, 81–102. Santa Barbara, Calif.: Greenwood Press.

Berliner MieterMagazin. 2005. Dossiers: "Berliner Einkommensentwicklung: Die Schere geht weiter auf." April 2005. www.berliner-mieterverein.de.

Berliner Morgenpost. 2010. "Mittes Bürgermeister lehnt Integrationsgesetz ab." September 5.

Berlin Institut für Bevölkerung und Entwicklung. 2009. *Ungenutzte Potentiale: Zur Lage der Integration in Deutschland* (Unused potentials: about the state of integration in Germany). Berlin: Berlin Institut für Bevölkerung und Entwicklung.

Berlin kann mehr: Wahlprogramm zu den Berlin-Wahlen am 17. September 2006. www .cduberlin.de.

Bertaux, Daniel. 1981. *Biography and Society: The Life-History Approach in the Social Sciences.* Beverly Hills, Calif.: Sage.

Bertaux, Daniel, and Martin Kohli. 1984. "The Life Story Approach: A Continental View." *Annual Review of Sociology* 10:215–37.

Bissoondath, Neil. 2002. *Selling Illusions: The Myth of Multiculturalism.* Toronto: Penguin.

Bollens, Scott A. 1999. *Urban Peacebuilding in Divided Societies: Belfast and Johannesburg.* Boulder, Colo.: Westview Press.

Bömermann, Hartmut, Klaus Rehkämper, and Ulrike Rockmann. 2008. "Neue Daten zur Bevölkerung mit Migrationshintergrund in Berlin zum Stand 31.12.2007." *Zeitschrift für amtliche Statistik Berlin-Brandenburg* 3:20–28.

Bowlby, Chris. 1986. "Blutmai 1929: Police, Parties and Proletarians in a Berlin Confrontation. *Historical Journal* 29:137–58.

Brader, Ted, Nicholas A. Valentino, and Elizabeth Suhay. 2008. "What Triggers Public Opposition to Immigration? Anxiety, Group Cues, and Immigration Threat." *American Journal of Political Science* 52, no. 4: 959–78.

Brewer, Paul R. 2003. "Values, Political Knowledge, and Public Opinion about Gay Rights: A Framing-Based Account." *Public Opinion Quarterly* 67, no. 2: 173–201.

Brubaker, Rogers. 1992. *Citizenship and Nationhood in France and Germany.* Cambridge, Mass.: Harvard University Press.

———. 2001. "The Return of Assimilation? Changing Perspectives on Immigration and Its Sequels in France, Germany, and the United States." *Ethnic and Racial Studies* 24:531–48.

Bundesverfassungsgericht. 1990. "Entscheidung vom 30.10.1990. Ausländerwahlrecht in Schleswig-Holstein. (German Constitutional Court decision regarding the foreigner voting law in the German state of Schleswig-Holstein.)

Bundeszentrale für politische Bildung. 1999. "Deutschland: Reform des deutschen Staatsangehörigkeitsrechts umstritten." *Migration und Bevölkerung,* Ausgabe February 1999 (accessed online).

———. 2007. "Bergiffe rund um Ausgrenzung, Integration und Migration." *Glossar* (accessed online).

Çağlar, Ayse. 2001. "Constrainig Metaphors and the Transnationalisation of Spaces in Berlin." *Journal of Ethnic and Migration Studies* 27, no. 4: 601–13.

Castells, Manuel. 1997. *The Power of Identity.* Malden, Mass.: Wiley-Blackwell.

Castles, Stephen. 1995. "How Nation-States Respond to Immigration and Ethnic Diversity." *Journal of Ethnic and Migration Studies* 21, no. 3: 293–308.

Chong, Dennis. 1993. "How People Think, Reason, and Feel about Rights and Liberties." *American Journal of Political Science* 37, no. 3: 867–99.

Citrin, Jack, and John Sides. 2007. "Immigration and the Imagined Community in Europe and the United States." *Political Studies* 56:33–56.

Cole, Phillip. 2000. *Philosophies of Exclusion: Liberal Political Theory and Immigration.* Edinburgh: Edinburgh University Press.

Commissioner for Integration and Migration of the Senate of Berlin, ed. 2007. "Encouraging Diversity—Strengthening Cohesion. Integration Policy in Berlin, 2007–2011." Integration concept of the Berlin government.

Community Relations, Directorate of Social and Economic Affairs. 1998. *Measurement and Indicators of Integration.* Council of Europe. Strasbourg: Council of Europe Publishing.

Constant, Amelie F., and Douglas S. Massey. 2003. "Self-Selection, Earnings, and Out-Migration: A Longitudinal Study of Immigrants to Germany." *Journal of Population Economics* 16, no. 4: 631–53.

Damelang, Andreas, and Max Steinhardt. 2008. "Integrationspolitik auf regionaler Ebene in Deutschland." *Focus Migration.* Kurzdossier (short dossier) 10. May.

Davison, Andrew. 1998. *Secularism and Revivalism in Turkey: A Hermeneutic Reconsideration.* New Haven, Conn.: Yale University Press.

De Certeau, Michel. 1984. *The Practice of Everyday Life.* Berkeley: University of California Press.

Deutsche Welle. 2010. "Kontroverse zu Wulff-Äusserung über Islam." October 7. www.dw-world.de.

Dörr, Silvia, and Thomas Faist. 1997. "Institutional Conditions for the Integration of Immigrants in Welfare States: A Comparison of the Literature on Germany, France, Great Britain, and the Netherlands." *European Journal of Political Research,* 31, no. 4: 401–26.

Dumper, Michael. 1997. *The Politics of Jerusalem since 1967.* New York: Columbia University Press.

Düspohl, Martin. 2005. "Mythos Kreuzberg—ein historischer Streifzug." In *Texte zum Kongress Mythos-Kreuzberg der Heinrich-Böll-Stiftung.* Berlin: Heinrich-Böll-Stiftung. www.diversity-boell.de/downloads/integration/MythosKreuzbergStreifzug.pdf.

———. 2009. *Kleine Kreuzberg Geschichte.* Berlin: Kreuzberg-Museum.

Edelman, Murray. 1988. *Constructing the Political Spectacle.* Chicago: University of Chicago Press.

Ehrkamp, Patricia. 2005. "Placing Identities: Transnational Practices and Local Attachments of Turkish Immigrants in Germany." *Journal of Ethnic and Migration Studies* 31, no. 2: 345–64.

———. 2006. "'We Turks are no Germans': Assimilation Discourses and the Dialectical Construction of Identities in Germany." *Environment and Planning A,* 38, no. 9: 1673–92.

Ehrkamp, Patricia, and Helga Leitner. 2003. "Beyond National Citizenship: Turkish Immigrants and the (Re)construction of National Citizenship in Germany." *Urban Geography* 24, no. 2: 127–46.

Elster, Jon. 1983. *Sour Grapes: Studies in the Subversion of Rationality.* Cambridge: Cambridge University Press.

England, Kim V. L. 1994. "Getting Personal: Reflexivity, Positionality, and Feminist Research." *Professional Geographer* 46, no. 1: 80–89.

Erdoğan, Recep Tayyip. 2008. "Speech in Cologne." Dokumentation: "Das sagte Ministerpräsident Erdoğan in Köln." *Die Welt.* February 11.

Erman, Tahire. 2001. "The Politics of Squatter *(Gecekondu)* Studies in Turkey: The Changing Representations of Rural Migrants in the Academic Discourse." *Urban Studies* 38, no. 7: 983–1002.

Eurobarometer. 2005. "Social Values, Science and Technology." *Special Eurobarometer* 225, Wave 63.1—TNS Opinion and Social.

Faas, Daniel. 2007. "The Europeanization of German Ethnic Identities: The Case of German and Turkish Students in Two Stuttgart Secondary Schools." *International Studies in Sociology of Education* 17, no. 1–2: 45–62.

Faist, Thomas. 1994. "How to Define a Foreigner? The Symbolic Politics of Immigration in German Partisan Discourse, 1978–1993." *West European Politics* 17, no. 2: 50–71.

Favell, Adrian. 2001. "Integration Policy and Integration Research in Europe: A Review and Critique." In *Citizenship Today: Global Perspectives and Practices,* ed. Alexander Aleinikoff and Doug Klusmeyer, 349–99. Washington, D.C.: Brookings Institute/Carnegie Endowment for International Peace.

FDP Berlin Press Release. 2008. Im Gespräch mit DITIB. October 29. www.fdp-berlin.de.

Findlay, A. M., and F. L. N. Li. 1997. "An Auto-biographical Approach to Understanding Migration: The Case of Hong Kong Emigrants." *Royal Geographical Society* 29, no. 1: 34–44.

Florida, Richard. 2002. *The Rise of the Creative Class and How It's Transforming Work, Leisure, Community, and Everyday Life.* New York: Basic Books.

Focus. 2008a. "Streit um Kopftuch-Heft." *Focus Magazine* 37. www.focus.de.

———. 2008b. "Rütli wird zur Gemeinschaftsschule." *Focus Online,* January 30. www.focus.de.

Frankfurter Allgemeine Zeitung. 2009. "Völkermord im Lehrplan. Die armen Schüler." August 7, 2009. www.faz.de.

———. 2010. "Sarrazin verlässt freiwillig Bundesbank: 'Das halt auf Dauer keiner durch.'" September 10.

French, John Mark, and Annika Marlen Hinze. 2010. "From the Inside Out: Citizenship and the Constitution of National Identity." *Studies in Ethnicity and Nationalism* 10, no. 2: 255–70.

Gaffikin, Frank, David C. Perry, and Ratoola Kundu. 2010. "The City and Its Politics: Informal and Contested." In *The City, Revisited: Urban Theory from Chicago, Los Angeles, and New York,* ed. Dennis R. Judd and Dick Simpson, 305–31. Minneapolis: University of Minnesota Press.

Gesemann, Frank. 2006. "Grundlinien und aktuelle Herausforderungen der Berliner Integrationspolitik." *Politische Steuerung von Integrationsprozessen* 3:195–213.

Das Gesetz zur Regelung von Partizipation und Integration in Berlin (PartIntG). (Law for the regulation of participation and integration in Berlin.) Berlin: Gesetz- und Verordnungsblatt für Berlin. December 28, 2010.

Goodenow, Carol, and Olivia M. Espin. 1993. "Identity Choices in Immigrant Adolescent Females." *Adolescence* 28, no. 109: 173–84.

Gottdiener, Mark. 1995. *Postmodern Semiotics*. Malden, Mass.: Blackwell.

Nilüfer Göle. 1996. *The Forbidden Modern: Civilization and Veiling*. Ann Arbor: University of Michigan Press.

Grimm, Jacob. 1890. *Kleine Schriften von Jacob Grimm*. Vol. 8. Gütersloh: C. Bertelsmann Verlag.

Gutiérrez, Kris D., Patricia Baquedano-Lopez, and Carlos Tejeda. 1999. "Rethinking Diversity: Hybridity and Hybrid Language Practices in the Third Space." *Mind, Culture, and Activity* 6, no. 4: 286–303.

Habermas, Jürgen. 1995. "Address: Multiculturalism and the Liberal State." *Stanford Law Review* 47, no. 5: 849–53.

Hall, Stuart. 1991. "Old and New Identities, Old and New Ethnicities." In *Culture, Globalization, and the World System*, ed. Anthony D. King, 41–68. London: Macmillan.

Hannerz, Ulf. 1987. "The World in Creolization." *Africa* 57, no. 4: 546–59.

Hartmann, Rainer, Barbara Hörsch, and Joachim Neujahr. 1998. "Neukölln—Ein Bezirk ohne Ausländer?" In *Alltag und Politik in einem Berliner Arbeiterbezirk. Neukölln von 1945 bis 1989*, ed. Detlef Schmiechen-Ackermann, Ute Stiepani, and Claudia Toelle, 329–56. Bielefeld: Verlag für Regionalgeschichte.

Häussermann, Hartmut, Andreas Kapphan, and Daniel Förste. 2008. "Die Entwickung der Verkehrszellen im Bezirk Neukölln, 2001–2006." *Bericht für das Bezirksamt Neukölln von Berlin*. Berlin. June 28.

Heckmann, Friedrich. 2003. "From Ethnic Nation to Universalistic Immigrant Integration: Germany." In *The Integration of Immigrants in European Societies: National Differences and Trends of Convergence*, ed. Friedrich Heckmann and Dominique Schnapper, 45–78. Stuttgart: Lucius & Lucius.

Hertie Stiftung, Gemeinnützige. 2009. *Hertie Berlin Studie*. Hamburg: Hoffmann und Campe.

Hesse, Hermann. 1943. *Das Glasperlenspiel. Versuch einer Lebensbeschreibung des Magister Ludi Josef Knecht samt Knechts hinterlassenen Schriften*. Zurich: Fretz & Wasmuth Verlag.

Hobsbawm, Eric, and Terence Ranger, eds. 1983. *The Invention of Tradition*. Cambridge: Cambridge University Press.

Huntington, Samuel. 2004. "The Hispanic Challenge." *Foreign Policy* (March/April): 30–45.

Integration Verlangt Taten Statt Worte. www.die-linke-berlin.de.

Isin, Engin. 2000. *Democracy, Citizenship, and the Global City*. London: Routledge.

Jacobs, Lawrence R., and Robert Y. Shapiro. 2000. *Politicians Don't Pander: Political Manipulation and the Loss of Democratic Responsiveness*. Chicago: University of Chicago Press.

Joppke, Christian. 2005. "Exclusion in the Liberal State: The Case of Immigration and Citizenship Policy." *European Journal of Social Theory* 8, no. 1: 43–61.

———. 2007. "Beyond National Models: Civic Integration Policies for Immigrants in Western Europe." *Western European Politics* 30, no. 1: 1–22.

Jurgens, Jeffrey. 2005. "Plotting Immigration: Diasporic Identity Formation among Immigrants from Turkey in Berlin." Ph.D. diss., University of Michigan, Ann Arbor.

Judd, Dennis R., and Todd Swanstrom. 2011. *City Politics: The Political Economy of Urban America.* 8th ed. New York: Pearson Longman.

Kappert, Petra, Ruth Haerkötter, and Ingeborg Böer. 2002. *Türken in Berlin, 1871–1945.* Berlin: De Gruyter.

Kartal, Bilhan. 2009. "Der Türkische Migrationsprozess in der BRD. Deutschland, die Türkei und EU-Beitritt." Paper presented at Berlin Humboldt Kolleg Beitrittsprozess der Türkei zur EU und ihre Widerspiegelung auf die deutsch-türkischen Beziehungen, May 7–10, 2009.

Kasinitz, Philip, John H. Mollenkopf, Mary C. Waters, and Jennifer Holdaway. 2008. *Inheriting the City: The Children of Immigrants Come of Age.* New York: Russell Sage Foundation.

Katz, Elihu, Jay G. Blumler, and Michael Gurevitch. 1973. "Uses and Gratifications Research." *Public Opinion Quarterly* 37, no. 4: 509–23.

Kaya, Ayhan. 2001. *Sicher in Kreuzberg: Constructing Diasporas: Turkish Hip Hop Youth in Berlin.* Bielefeld: Transcript Verlag.

Kaya, Ayhan, and Ferhat Kentel. 2005. *Euro-Turks: A Bridge or a Breach between Turkey and the European Union? A Comparative Study of German Turks and French Turks.* Brussels: Centre for European Policy Studies.

Kennedy, Robert F. 1968. "Remarks of Senator Robert F. Kennedy to the Cleveland City Club, Cleveland, Ohio, April 5, 1968." John F. Kennedy Library and Museum. www .jfklibrary.org.

Kingdon, John. 1995. *Agendas, Alternatives, and Public Policies.* 2nd ed. New York: Longman.

Klemek, Christopher. 2011. *The Transatlantic Collapse of Urban Renewal: Postwar Urbanism from New York to Berlin.* Chicago: University of Chicago Press.

Klitscher, Jörg. 2001. "Der Häuserkampf in Kreuzberg." *Geschichte und Geschichten,* Berlinische Monatsschrift 6:150–54.

Koopmans, Ruud. 2003. "Good Intentions Sometimes Make Bad Policy: A Comparison of Dutch and German Integration Policies." In *The Challenge of Diversity: European Social Democracy Facing Migration, Integration, and Multiculturalism,* ed. René Cuperus, Karl A. Duffek, and Johannes Kandel, 163–68. Innsbruck: Studien Verlag.

Kraidy, Marwan M. 1999. "The Global, the Local, and the Hybrid: A Native Ethnography of Globalization." *Critical Studies in Media Communication* 16, no. 4: 456–76.

Lahav, Gallya. 2004. "Public Opinion toward Immigration in the European Union: Does It Matter?" *Comparative Political Studies* 37, no. 10: 1151–83.

Lefebvre, Henri. 1984. *The Production of Space.* Malden, Mass.: Blackwell.

Liggett, Helen, and David C. Perry, eds. 1995. *Spatial Practices.* Thousand Oaks, Calif.: Sage.

Liljeberg, Holger, and Sindy Krambeer. 2011. *Wie tolerant ist Berlin? Ergebnisbericht zu einer repräsentativen Bevölkerungsbefragung zu Integrationsthemen in Berlin.* Berlin: INFO Research Group. Unabhängiges Meinungsforschungsinstitut INFO GmbH.

Lutz, Helga, Ann Phoenix, and Nira Yuval-Davis. 1999. "Introduction: Nationalism, Racism and Gender—European Crossfires." In *Crossfires: Nationalism, Racism, and*

Gender in Europe, ed. Helga Lutz, Ann Phoenix, and Nira Yuval-Davis, 1–25. London: Pluto Press.

Machiavelli, Niccolò. (1513) 1989. *The Prince*. Chicago: University of Chicago Press.

Malik, Kenan. 2010. "Multiculturalism Undermines Diversity." *Guardian*. March 17.

Martín-Barbero, J. 1993. *Communication, Culture, and Hegemony: From Media to Mediations*. Newbury Park, Calif.: Sage.

Merkel, Angela. 2010. "Rede zum Deutschlandtag der Jungen Union in Potsdam." October 16. Available as "Merkel Gegen Seehofer: Der Islam ist Teil Deutschlands," October 16, www.n-tv.de.

Mills, Amy. 2010. *Streets of Memory: Landscape, Tolerance, and National Identity*. Athens: University of Georgia Press.

Modan, Gabriella Ghalia. 2007. *Turf Wars: Discourse, Diversity, and the Politics of Place*. Malden, Mass.: Blackwell.

Neue Zürcher Zeitung. 2010. "Deutschlands Ghetto. Augenschein im Berliner Bezirk Neukölln. September 19, 2010. www.nzz.ch.

Offe, Claus. 1998. " 'Homogeneity' and Constitutional Democracy." *Journal of Political Philosophy* 6, no. 2: 113–41.

Ohlinger, Rainer, and Ulrich Raiser. 2005. *Integration und Migration in Berlin: Zahlen—Daten—Fakten*. Berlin. Available via the Berlin government website: www.berlin.de/imperia/md/content/lb-integration-migration/statistik/zahlen_daten_fakten.pdf.

Orum, Anthony M. 1998. "The Urban Imagination of Sociologists: The Centrality of Place." *Sociological Quarterly* 39, no. 1: 1–10.

Özcan, Veysel. 2004. "Germany: Immigration in Transition." In *Migration Information Source: Country Profiles*. Washington, D.C.: Migration Policy Institute. www.migrationinformation.org/feature/display.cfm?ID=235.

Pattillo, Mary. 2007. *Black on the Block: The Politics of Race and Class in the City*. Chicago: University of Chicago Press.

Plaza, Dwaine. 2006. "The Construction of a Segmented Hybrid Identity among One-and-a-Half-Generation Indo-Caribbean and African Caribbean Canadians." *Identity: An International Journal of Theory and Research* 6, no. 3: 207–29.

Program grün. 2006. "Grün wählen, bevor Sie rot sehen!" Wahlprogramm der Grünen für die Kommunalwahlen 2006 in Berlin. September. gruene-berlin.de.

Rein, Martin, and Donald Schön. 1993. "Reframing Policy Discourse." In *The Argumentative Turn in Policy Analysis and Planning*, ed. Frank Fischer and John Forrester, 145–66. Durham, N.C.: Duke University Press.

Reissland, Carolin. 2005. "Migration in Deutschland, 1955–2004. Von der 'Gastarbeiter'-Anwerbung zum Zunwanderungsgesetz." In *Normalfall Migration*, ed. Klaus J. Bade and Jochen Oltmer Zeit-Bilder, 15:127–32. Bonn: Bundeszentrale für Politische Bildung.

Richardson, Tim, and Ole B. Jensen. 2003. "Linking Discourse and Space: Towards a Cultural Sociology in Analysing Spatial Policy Discourses." *Urban Studies* 40, no. 1: 7–22.

Roy, Ananya. 2005. "Urban Informality: Toward an Epistemology of Planning." *Journal of the American Planning Association* 71, no. 2: 147–56.

————. 2009. "The 21st Century Metropolis: New Geographies of Theory." *Regional Studies* 43, no. 6: 819–30.

Sandercock, Leonie. 1998. *Towards Cosmopolis: Planning for Multicultural Cities.* New York: Wiley.

Sarrazin, Thilo. 2010. *Deutschland Schafft Sich Ab: Wie wir unser Land aufs Spiel setzen.* Munich: Deutsche Verlags Anstalt.

Sartori, Giovanni. 1970. "Concept Misformation in Comparative Politics." *American Political Science Review* 64, no. 4: 1033–53.

Sassen, Saskia. 1996. "Whose City Is It? Globalization and the Formation of New Claims." *Public Culture* 8:205–23.

Schiffauer, Werner. 1997. "Zur Logik von kulturellen Strömungen in Großstädten." In *Fremde in der Stadt. Zehn Essays zu Kultur und Differenz,* ed. Werner Schiffauer, 92–127. Frankfurt am Main: Suhrkamp.

Senatsverwaltung für Integration, Arbeit und Soziales. 2008. "Mit Kopftuch auβen vor?" Schriften der Landesstelle für Gleichbehandlung—gegen Diskriminierung, no. 2. Berlin: Senatsverwaltung für Integration, Arbeit und Soziales.

Sido. 2004. "Mein Block." *Maske.* CD. Berlin: Aggro Berlin.

Sjoberg, Gideon, Norma Williams, Ted R. Vaughan, and Andrée Sjoberg. 1991. "The Case Study Approach in Social Research: Basic Methodological Issues. In *A Case for the Case Study,* ed. Joe R. Feagin, Anthony M. Orum, and Gideon Sjoberg, 27–79. Charlotte: University of North Carolina Press.

Soja, Edward W. 1996. *Thirdspace: Journeys to Los Angeles and Other Real-and-Imagined Places.* Cambridge, Mass.: Blackwell.

————. 1999. "Thirdspace: Expanding the Scope of the Geographical Imagination." In *Human Geography Today,* ed. Doreen Massey, John Allen, and Philip Sarre, 260–78. Cambridge: Polity Press.

————. 2000. *Postmetropolis: Critical Studies of Cities and Regions.* Oxford: Blackwell.

Soysal, Yasemin N. 2001. Changing Citizenship in Europe: Remarks on Postnational Membership and the Nation State." In *Rethinking European Welfare: Transformations of Europe and Social Policy,* ed. Janet Fink, Gail Lewis, and John Clarke, 65–76. London: Sage.

————. 2002. "Locating Europe." *European Societies* 4, no. 3: 265–84.

Der Spiegel. 1977. "Städtebau: SOS für SO 36." 13:218–20.

Der Spiegel. 2010. "Es gibt viele Sarrazins." 36: September 6.

Stanley, L. and S. Wise. 1993. *Breaking Out Again: Feminist Ontology and Epistemology.* London: Routledge.

Statistisches Bundesamt. 2011. *Bevölkerung und Erwerbstätigkeit. Bevölkerung mit Migrationshintergrund—Ergebnisse des Mikrozensus 2010.* Wiesbaden: Statistisches Bundesamt.

Stolcke, Verena. 1995. "Talking Culture: New Boundaries, New Rhetorics of Exclusion in Europe." Ethnographic Authority and Cultural Explanation, special issue, *Current Anthropology* 36, no. 1: 1–24.

Stomporowski, Stephan. 2004. "Die misslungene berufliche Integration Jugendlicher mit Migrationshintergrund." *bwp@ Berufs- und Wirtschaftspädagogik* 6:1–20.

Stone, Deborah. 2002. *Policy Paradox: The Art of Political Decision Making.* Rev. ed. New York: Norton.

Strohmeier, Klaus Peter. 2006. *Segregation in den Städten.* Gesprächskreis Migration und Integration, Abteilung Wirtschafts- und Sozialpolitik. Berlin: Friedrich Ebert Stiftung. library.fes.de/pdf-files/asfo/04168.pdf.

Der Tagesspiegel. 2008a. "Porträt: Wer ist Heinz Buschkowsky?" July 13.

Der Tagesspiegel. 2008b. "Streit um Kopftuch-Broschüre des Senats." September 8.

Der Tagesspiegel. 2009. "Kreuzberg: Immer Gleich auf den Barrikaden." January 5.

taz. 2009. "Mesut Özil ist ein Eisbrecher." March 27. www.taz.de.

TBB Berlin. 2007–9. Tätigkeitsbericht des Vorstandes 04.03.2007–24.05.2009. www.tbb-berlin.de.

Thränhardt, Dietrich. 2008. "Kommunales Wahlrecht für Ausländer." *Anhörung des Innenausschusses des Deutschen Bundestages.* Innenausschuss A-Drs 16(4)459 D. September 22.

Triandafyllidou, Anna. 2001. *Immigrants and National Identity in Europe.* London: Routledge.

Voigt-Graf, Carmen. 2004. "Towards a Geography of Transnational Spaces: Indian Transnational Communities in Australia." *Global Networks* 4, no. 1: 25–49.

Von Wilamowitz-Moellendorff, Ulrich. 2001. "Projekt Zuwanderung und Integration: Türken in Deutschland—Einstellungen zu Staat und Gesellschaft." Working Paper 53. Herausgeber: Konrad-Adenauer-Stiftung, e.V. Sankt Augustin.

Walzer, Michael. 1983. *Spheres of Justice.* New York: Basic Books.

Die Welt. 2009: "Migration: Warum die Türken bei der Integration nicht mitspielen." January 25. www.welt.de.

Weiss, Karin, and Dietrich Thränhardt. 2005. "Selbsthilfe, Netzwerke, und soziales Kapital in der pluralistischen Gesellschaft." In *SelbstHilfe: Wie Migranten Netzwerke knüpfen und soziales Kapital schaffen,* ed. Karin Weiss and Dietrich Thränhardt, 8–44. Freiburg: Lambertus.

Wernicke, Kurt. 1998. "Von der Bildung Gross-Berlins 1920 bis zur Gegenwart." In *Berlin von A bis Z. 26,566 Stichwörter zur Geschichte und Gegenwart der deutschen Haupstadt.* Berlin: Luisenstädtischer Bildungsverein e.V. www.luise-berlin.de/histo rie/wernicke/kapitel/siebenteskapitel.htm.

White, Jenny B. 1997. "Turks in the New Germany." *American Anthropologist* 99, no. 4: 754–69.

Winter, Bronwyn. 2008. *Hijab and the Republic: Uncovering the French Headscarf Debate.* Syracuse, N.Y.: Syracuse University Press.

Wimmer, Andreas. 2002. *Nationalist Exclusion and Ethnic Conflict: Shadows of Modernity.* Cambridge: Cambridge University Press.

Worbs, Susanne. 2010. "Integration in klaren Zahlen? Ansätze des Integrationsmonitorings in Deutschland." *Focus Migration.* Kurzdossier (short dossier)16. May.

Wulff, Christian. 2010. "Rede von Bundespräsident Christian Wulff beim Festakt zum 20. Jahrestag der Deutschen Einheit am 3. Oktober 2010 in Bremen." *Nachrichten des Deutschen Bundestages.* www.bundesregierung.de/Content/DE/Bulletin/2010 /10/98-1-bpr-einheit.html.

Yurdakul, Gökçe. 2006. "State, Political Parties, and Immigrant Elites: Turkish Immigrant Associations in Berlin." *Journal of Ethnic and Migration Studies* 32, no. 3: 435–53.

—— 2009. *From Guest Workers into Muslims: The Transformation of Turkish Immigrant Associations in Germany.* Newcastle: Cambridge Scholars Press.

Yuval-Davis, Nira. 1997. *Gender and Nation.* Thousand Oaks, Calif.: Sage.

—— 2000. "Citizenship, Territoriality and the Gendered Construction of Difference." In *Democracy, Citizenship, and the Global City,* ed. Engin F. Isin, 171–88. London: Routledge.

Yuval-Davis, Nira, and Floya Anthias, eds. 1989. Introduction to *Woman, Nation, State,* i–ix. London: Macmillan.

Die Zeit. 2006. "Rütli-Hauptschule. Unter Polizeischutz. Ein Einwanderungsland ist entsetzt wegen seiner Probleme: Berlin-Neukölln ist kein Einzelfall. Eine Nachrichtenanalyse." Vol. 14. April 5.

Zille, Heinrich. (1924) 1975. *Berlin aus meiner Bildermappe.* Rudolstadt: Greifenverlag.

INDEX

acceptance of differences, 54–55; ethnic visibility, 62–63; internal group differences, 64–65; religious symbols, 62; visibility of differences and, 59

American immigrant experience, xv

assimilation, xviii; *versus* integration, 35

Berlin: administration structure, 111–12; district reform (map), 125; German identity, xxiv; incorporation of suburbs, 113; map after district reform, 83; neighborhood identification, 113–14; neighborhood identities, 112; Senate charts, 167–69

Buschkowsky, Heinz, 130–31, 133, 135–38; 10-Point Integration Agenda, 171–73

CDU (Christian Democrats): dual citizenship, 6–7; voting rights for guest workers, 4

citizenship law in Germany, 2–3; 2000 amendment, 6; *Die Welt*, 34–35; dual citizenship, 6–7; history, 3–7; immigrant citizens, 10; *ius soli*, 6

citizenship versus emotional identity, 92

cultural diversity: equal opportunity and, 48; intercultural competence, 67–71

culturation, 20

Currywurst, 87

Deniz interview, 84–85

Die Welt, 34–35

difference: acceptance of, 54–55; ethnic visibility, 62–63; internal group differences, 64–65; religious symbols, 62; visibility, 58–59

discrimination: quotas and, 158; women, 60–61

district reform, Friedrichshain-Kreuzberg, 124–28

divided loyalties, 91

Döner Kebap, xiv, 87

dual citizenship, 6–7

dual identity for children, 94

dual rejection of immigrants, 89–90

education issues: college-track versus non-college-track, 93–94

emotional identity versus citizenship, 92

empirical findings of study, 155–56

enclaves, 24–25; hybrid identity, 25–26; transnationalism, 25

equal opportunity: cultural diversity and, 48

Erdogan, Recep Tayyip: speech to Turkish immigrants, 23–24

ethnic enclaves. *See* enclaves

ethnic visibility, 62. *See also* visibility of differences

European identity, 12
European Union: citizenship law and, 2–3
exclusion: integration policy and, 2, 19–25

family law, Third Wave feminist movement, 4
food: *Döner Kebap*, xiv; ethnic, immigrants and, xi
foreigner policy *versus* integration policy, 6
framing, 36–38; center-right *versus* center-left parties, 48–49; opinion leaders, 37–38; policy discourse and perception of immigrants, 38
France, assimilation, 22–23
Friedrichshain, 116; district reform and, 124–28
Friedrichshain-Kreuzberg: Franz Schulz (mayor), 125–26

gentrification of Kreuzberg, 109, 115–16
German Turks, integration, xx
Germany: assimilation of immigrants, xviii; immigration, xv; immigration denials, 59–60; integration discourse, xv, xvii–xix
Green Party: neighborhoods, 48–49; women immigrants, 49
guest workers: bilateral agreements, 7; Kreuzberg, 114–16; Neukölln, 114–16; permanent status, 122–23; program termination, 8; return migration, 7; Turkish families, 4; Turkish worker immigration, 7–8; voting rights, 4
Gymnasium, difficulties entering, 93–94

head scarves, women and, 60–62; Kreuzberger women interviewed, 85; Neukölln women interviewed, 86–87
homogenity argument, 23–24
hybrid belonging of neighborhoods, 106; Kreuzberg, 153
hybrid identity, 25–26; space and, 76; spatialized hybridity, 27
hybridity, 25–26; spatialized, 27

identification: hybrid identity, 25–26; integration policy and, 20; neighborhood, 75–76. *See also* immigrant identity
identity: versus citizenship, 92; dual for children, 94; minority groups devaluation, 89; neighborhoods and, 105, 107. *See also* specific types of identity
identity formation: dialogue and interaction, 78; experiences and, 93; as individual process, 88; neighborhoods, 101–2; women and, 78–79
identity negotiation, personal nature, 88
immigrant citizens, 10
immigrant identity: hybrid identity, 76; space and, 76
immigrants: assimilation, xviii; Berlin distribution, xx–xxi; dual rejection, 89–90; ethnic food and, xiv; hybrid identity, 25–26; integration discourse (Germany), xv, xvii–xix; lived perspective, 29–30; practices, micro-level, xvi; second-generation, xxvi; stereotypes, xiv; women as symbolic figures, xxvi–xxvii. *See also* guest workers; Turkish immigrants
immigration: to America, xiv–xv; author's, xiii, xiv; Berlin's identity, xiv; Germany, xv; Germany's denials, 59–60
immigration policy, labor market and, 8
individual stances on integration, 53–54
integration: versus assimilation, 35; assimilation in France, 22–23; contested term, 22; current state of debate, 14–18; definitions by policy makers, 56–57; differences and, 54–64; exclusion and, 19–25; German Turks, xix–xx; immigrant neighborhood and, 76; individual stances, 53–54; interviews, 41–47; linguistic, 63; mainstream and,

158–60; monitoring, 20–21; multiculturalism and, 15–18; national mainstream and, 11–14; neighborhoods and, 108–9, 152–53; personal experiences with receiving society, 78; policy makers and, 33–36; as process, 68; responsibility, 68–69; spatial approach, xxi–xxiii; term definition, 14; Turkish community representatives, 64–67; visibility and, 76; women as symbols, 40–41, 77–78

integration discourse: changes in, 146; complexities, 145–46; contributors, 147–49; future of, 149–50; German, xvi–xix; Islam prominence in, 38–39; neighborhoods and, 150–54; TBB and, 146

integration law, 70–71

integration policy: Buschkowsky 10-Point Integration Agenda, 171–73; culturation, 20; exclusion and, 2; versus foreigner policy, 6; framing, 48–49; identification, 20; interaction, 20; Kreuzberg, 126–27; national identity and, 1; neighborhoods and, 52–53; Neukölln, 129–35; placement, 20; platforms, 47–52; success measurements, 19–20

interaction: integration policy and, 20

intercultural competence, 67–71, 156–58

internal group differences, 64–65

interviews: barriers to researcher, 79–80; contacting subjects, 80; divided loyalties, 91; dual identity for children, 94; dual pressures of women, 89–90; dual rejection, 89–90; emotional identity *versus* citizenship, 92; identity formation, experiences and, 93; Kreuzberger women, 84–85; meetings, 80–81; mythical connection to Turkey, 90–92; Neukölln women, 85–87; power relationship, 82; representation, 81–82; researcher becoming part

of the story, 79–80; settings, 80–81; Turkish women immigrants, 78; white-collar informants versus blue-collar, 81

Islam: integration discourse, 38–39; Muslim perception, 99; visibility and, 98

Kreuzberg, xxi–xxiii; demographics, 113; district reform, 124–28; Friedrichshain and, 116; gentrification wave, 109, 115–16; German residents, 107–8; guest workers, 114–16; Harlem worries, 120–22; historical background, 116, 119; hybrid-identity neighborhoods, 153; integration policy, 126–27; Kreuzberg 36, 123–24; little Istanbul, 99; map, 117; Neukölln integration policy comparison, 138–43; protest culture, 126; reunification and, 123–24; student movement, 119–20; urban renewal, 120–22

Kreuzberger women's interviews: Ayse, 85; Aysegül, 85; Betigül, 85; Bilge, 85; Ceyda, 85; Deniz, 84–85; Elif, 85; Esin, 85; Melike, 85; Özge, 85; Senem, 85; Zeynep, 85

Kreuzkölln, 163–65

Kurdish ethnic identity and language, 87–88

labor market: ethnic visibility, 62–63; immigration policy and, 8

law: integration law, 70–71

linguistic integration, 63

little Istanbul (Kreuzberg), 99

lived perspective of immigrants, 29–30

lived space of neighborhoods, 82–83

loyalty, divided, 91

Maastricht treaty: voting rights and, 5

mainstream: integration and, 11–14, 158–60

maps: district reform, 118, 125; Kreuzberg, 117; neighborhoods, women's attachment to, 163–65

media: elite frames, 37; policy makers and, 34; spatialized identity and, 36; symbolic meaning and, 36

"Mein Block" (Sido), 75–76

Merkel, Angela, multiculturalism, 16–17

minority group identity, devaluation, 89

multiculturalism, xviii–xix; integration and, 15–18

Muslim identity. See Islam

national identity: European identity, 12; integration policy and, 1

National Socialists, Rassengesetze, 4

neighborhoods, 73–74; Berlin, identities, 112; future research avenues, 160–61; Germans' attachment similarities, 107–8; hybrid belonging, 106, 153; identification with, 75–76; identity and, 105, 107; integration and, 108–9, 152–53; integration policy and, 52–53; integration practices and, 76; little Istanbul (Kreuzberg), 99; lived space, 82–83; Neukölln compared to Kreuzberg, 103–4; policy making and, 48; political debate and, 150–54; social history, 112; social structures tied to, 123; as third identity, 77; Turkish immigrant women, 100–1; visibility in, 95–99, 151–52; women's attachment, maps, 163–65

Neukölln, xxi–xxiii; Buschkowsky, Heinz, 130–31, 133, 135–38; compared to Kreuzberg, 103–4; demographics, 113; guest workers, 114–16; historical background, 128–29; integration policy, 129–35; Kreuzberg integration policy comparison, 138–43; Rütli school letter, 129–30

Neukölln women's interviews, 85–87; Binnaz, 86; Fadik, 86; Gülen, 86; Latife, 86; Mutlu, 86; Sibel, 86

opinion leaders: framing and, 38

Özdemir, Cem, 18

place as venue, 30–31

placement, 20

platforms, integration policy, 47–52

Pocahontas, 28–29

policy discourse: perception of Turkish immigrants, 38. See also integration discourse

policy implications of study, 156–60

policy makers: integration and, 33–36; integration definition, 56–57; media and, 34; neighborhoods and, 48

policy platforms, integration, 47–52

political discourse: framing and, 37–38; policy makers and integration, 33–36; spatialized hybridity and, 27–28; symbolic meaning, media and, 36. See also integration discourse

political involvement of immigrants, 127

protest culture of Kreuzberg, 126

quotas, 158

Rassengesetzen, 4

rejection, dual, 89–90

religious symbols, 62

researcher becoming part of the story, 79–80

reunification, 123–24

rural-urban divide in Turkish society, 66–67

Rütli school letter (Neukölln), 129–30

Sarrazin, Thilo, 15–16

Schulz, Franz, 125–26

second-generation immigrants, xxvi

Secondspace, 37

Senate charts (Berlin), 167–69

Sido, "Mein Block," 75–76

social history, neighborhoods, 112

social structures: neighborhoods and, 123

space: immigrant identity and, 76;
Secondspace, 37; spatial practice and,
26–28; as tool, 30–31
spatial approach to integration, xxi–xxiii,
28–30
spatial practice, 30–31; space and, 26–28
spatialized hybridity: political discourse
and, 27–28
spatialized identity: media and, 36
SPD (Social Democrats): neighborhoods
and, 48; voting rights for guest
workers, 4–5
stereotypes of immigrants, xiv, 99
symbolic meaning: media and, 36
symbols: interviews, 41–47; women as
for integration, 40–41

TBB (Turkish Union Berlin-Branden-
berg), integration discourse and, 146,
148–49
10-Point Integration Agenda
(Buschkowsky), 171–73
Third Wave feminist movement: family
law and, 4
Thirdspace, 27
transnationalism, enclaves, 25
Turkish community representatives:
integration and, 64–67
Turkish immigrants: *Die Welt*, 34–35;
distribution across Berlin's central
districts, 83–84; divided loyalties, 91;
dual pressures of women, 89–90; dual
rejection, 89–90; guest worker
immigration, 7–8; homogeneity,
87–88; identity subcategories, 88;
Kurdish ethnic identity and language,

87–88; mythical connection with
Turkey, 90–92; naturalizations, 10–11;
perception of and policy discourse,
38; phases, 9–10; political involvement, 127; prime minister Erdogan,
speech, 23–24; religion versus
secularism, 87–88; return-promoting
law (Rückkehrförderungsgesetz), 9;
settlement phase, 10; spatial exclusion,
24–25; status changes, 8–9; as
stereotypical immigrants, 99; women
and neighborhoods, 100–2; women's
interviews, 78

urban renewal, Kreuzberg, 120–22
urban space, xxiii–xxvii

visibility of differences, 58–59, 151;
ethnic visibility, 62–63; Muslim
identity and, 98; neighborhoods and,
95–99; religious symbols, 62
Volk, 3–4
Volksdeutscher, 4
Volksgemeinschaft, 3–4
voting rights: guest workers, 4;
Maastricht treaty, 5

women immigrants: discrimination, 60–
61; dual pressures, 89–90; Green Party,
49; head scarves, 60–62; identity
formation and, 78–79; interviews, 41–
47, 78; neighborhoods, 100–2; maps,
163–65; as symbols for integration,
xxvi–xvii, 40–41, 77–78; white-collar
versus blue-collar, 81
Wulff, Christian, multiculturalism, 16–17

(continued from page ii)

5 *Selling the Lower East Side: Culture, Real Estate, and Resistance in New York City*
CHRISTOPHER MELE

4 *Power and City Governance: Comparative Perspectives on Urban Development*
ALAN DIGAETANO AND JOHN S. KLEMANSKI

3 *Second Tier Cities: Rapid Growth beyond the Metropolis*
ANN R. MARKUSEN, YONG-SOOK LEE, AND SEAN DIGIOVANNA, EDITORS

2 *Reconstructing Chinatown: Ethnic Enclave, Global Change*
JAN LIN

1 *The Work of Cities*
SUSAN E. CLARKE AND GARY L. GAILE